W. Coleman

The Power of Television

The Power of Television: A Critical Appraisal

Conrad Lodziak

St. Martin's Press, New York

First Published in the United States of America in 1986

Printed in Great Britain

ISBN 0-312-63397-1

Library of Congress Cataloging in Publication Data

Lodziak, Conrad.
  The power of television.

  Includes bibliographies and index.
  1. Television broadcasting—Social aspects.
I. Title.
PN1992.6.L6   1986   302.2'345   86-17706
ISBN 0-312-63397-1

Contents

Introduction   1

1. Studying the Power of Television   5

2. Ideological Readings of Television   37

3. The Ideological Effectiveness of Television   68

4. The Maligned Audience   99

5. Television and Leisure-Time   128

6. Television and Social Fragmentation   159

7. Critical Social Theory and the Study of Television   190

Index   207

Introduction

Television has been blamed for escalating violence, for the erosion of traditional morality and the promotion of promiscuity, for the production of a mediocre and trivial popular culture, for steering people into consumerism, for directing the ideological climate toward conservatism, for encouraging terrorism and civil disturbances, for the disintegration of the family, for transforming electoral politics, for intellectual passivity among the viewing public, for laziness, obesity, and so on. The list is almost never-ending and not confined to television's alleged 'negative effects'. Thus television has been acclaimed for educating the public, broadening experience and changing attitudes in pro-social ways. It has been noted, for example, that an estimated one hundred million Americans watched the final episode of *Roots*, and that more people have seen a Shakespeare play on television than the sum total of all theatre audiences over the past three hundred years.

This all adds up to support the idea that television is sufficiently powerful to make a considerable difference in society. The assumption that television is powerful is widely shared by concerned members of the public and media researchers alike. One American professor is so convinced of television's power that he has entitled a recent book: *Television as an Instrument of Terror*.[1] There are those who would consider that such a title is fully justified. By the age of eighteen, the average young person in America, it has been calculated, will have witnessed fifteen thousand murders on television. A lawyer in Miami, in defending a fifteen-year-old boy charged with the murder of an old lady in June 1977, claimed that the boy had been driven temporarily insane by watching too many detective thrillers on television.

Unfortunately it is not possible to establish with any degree of certainty whether or not such claims are justified. No amount of scientific research or governmental commissions will ever be able to prove, one way or the other, what kinds of impact portrayals of violence on television have on the audience. It will be important to spell out some of the major reasons why this is so. This is a task taken up in Chapter 1. The impossibility of establishing with any certainty the power television exerts over the viewing public, however, is not confined to the problem of violence. It applies to *all* claims about television's power. It is partly because of the futility of particular kinds of scientific approaches in television research that researchers have attempted to arrive at conclusions about television's power through the development of theoretical arguments. In other words, many of the claims about television's power rest on attempts to draw up compelling reasons in support of particular claims.

The bulk of this book will be concerned with assessing the kinds of popular and theoretical argument which are made to convince us of television's crucial power. Since television's power, it is widely argued, is an ideological one, Chapters 2, 3 and 4 will be devoted to an examination of television's ideological role in contemporary Western societies. Indeed, critical media theory and research has been and still is preoccupied with the problem of ideology. However, the issue of television's ideological power is so broad that it has been necessary to restrict attention to those kinds of argument which have been marshalled to support claims that television effectively manipulates the audience ideologically, in ways which enable the prevailing social order, with all its inequalities and injustices, to be maintained. This claim, it will be recognised, is increasingly popular among the Left. Much of the reasoning in support of this claim, advanced by political activists and critical media theorists alike, is grossly deficient.

Media theorists have tended to view television and the mass media as primary agents in social reproduction, by virtue of the ideological service they undoubtedly provide for dominant groups. Insufficient attention has been given to examining ideological forces other than television and the mass media, and forces other than ideology in social reproduction. One major consequence of this is that critical media theory is permeated with a media-centredness and an ideology-centredness which exaggerates and misplaces the power of television. These deficiencies arise from an inadequate understanding of power in conjunction with a view which seriously misrepresents the motivations and intellect of subordinated individuals. Further, these deficiencies are not confined to critical media theory or to elements on the Left, but loom large in *all* media theory and research. Television's power is so strongly assumed that, rather than being the object of analysis, it tends to prescribe research practices and theoretical reasoning.

Fortunately, in spite of its media-centredness, some media theory and research has avoided the deficiencies noted above. There is, as we shall see in Chapter 2, a useful variety of approaches available for the ideological analysis of television programmes. Although not directly relevant to the specific focus of this book, there are many valid studies which attempt to shed light on the underlying play of power in television production. The ownership and control of television companies, the determining influence on programming exerted by advertisers, the interventions of government, the ideological servitude of broadcasters, and the implications of all these factors for the future of television, including public service broadcasting, are all relevant for a theory of television production and policy.

The powerful interests involved in determining the range, balance, and content of programmes is one thing, the actual impact of television programmes on the audience is another. Too often media-centred theory ignores and violates this distinction between, on the one hand, *the power to produce programmes*, and on the other, *the power-effectiveness of the programmes on the audience*. Further, the literature on television is too ready to identify television as a primary cause of certain effects which have already been produced by forces other than television. Media theory and research needs to be shaken out of its media-centredness, and it is the main task of this book to begin to do this.

Media-centredness and its attendant deficiencies has not only led to misleading conclusions about television's power, it has also provided a major stumbling block in other areas of research. Media-centred reasoning is unable either to explain why television has become the dominant leisure activity of a majority in Western societies or to grasp the social significance of this. Thus it will be argued in Chapter 5 that it is only by considering the full impact of non-media forces in determining the range of actions available to individuals that these problems can be adequately understood. This argument is extended in Chapter 6, in order to locate the significance of television viewing as an obstacle to social change. Finally a number of implications of the central arguments of the book for television research within critical social theory are presented in the concluding chapter.

Note

1. Arthur Asa Berger, *Television as an Instrument of Terror*, New Brunswick, NJ, Transaction, 1980.

1 Studying the Power of Television

In the introduction to this book, it was noted that television has been identified as the cause of a vast range of 'positive' and 'negative' effects. The lay person might expect research to provide evidence on, for example, whether or not television causes aggressive behaviour and violence, whether or not it makes people passive, the ways in which television helps or hinders the development of children, and so on. If answers to the various questions raised about its power can be provided, then presumably policy-makers will be able to take steps to eliminate the harmful effects of television. Such answers, too, might be useful to those parents who might seek guidance in supervising their children's viewing.

Over the past twenty-five years or so, there has been a considerable research effort in an attempt to establish 'the facts' about television's power. The results of this research effort have been far from clear-cut. Yet the research continues. As McQuail has noted of the mass media: 'if we did not fundamentally believe them to have important long term consequences, we could not devote so much time to their study'.[1]

One of the central tasks of this book is to examine the bases of the belief, shared both by some members of the public and researchers, in the power of television. This task necessarily involves looking at *how* researchers support this belief, and this is directly connected to *how* they go about studying the effects of television. At this stage two broad approaches to the study of television's power can be identified: behaviourist, on the one hand; and 'critical', on the other. The critical perspectives are more concerned with long-term ideological effects, and tend to be heavily theoretical. Much of this book will be concerned with the critical perspectives. First, however, it is necessary to consider the behaviourist approach, which, as Fejes notes, attempts 'to produce some science-like knowledge about the role of the media in human affairs'.[2] It is the dominant American approach to the study of television's power.

The behaviourist approach

Behaviourist approaches to the study of the effects of television have not only attempted to identify specific effects, in terms of the influences of television on behaviour, emotions, attitudes and knowledgeability, but they have also attempted to specify how these effects occur, on whom, and under what circumstances they are most likely to occur.

It is not my purpose here to summarise the major findings of this research tradition. To do so would be to produce an entirely different book. What is peculiar to behaviourist research on the effects of television is not so much the particular kinds of effects studied but the scientific methods used. Researchers employing these methods are convinced that they are producing 'hard evidence' about the effects of television. This conviction is based upon the belief that only studies employing scientific research methods are capable of discovering 'the facts' about television's power.

So it is necessary to examine how researchers have produced their findings, for whether or not we are able to count their findings as 'hard evidence' depends on how much confidence we have in their methods of investigation. But it is especially necessary to examine the research methods adopted because they are widely considered to be 'scientific'. The findings of 'scientific studies' are likely to carry more weight with the general public and policy-makers than studies devoid of scientific pretensions.

Until relatively recently there was a very lively debate in the social sciences about whether or not the social sciences could be sciences in the sense in which we speak of physics or biology as sciences. Much of this debate turned on the appropriateness or otherwise of traditional models of physical science for the study of human action.[3] An extensive literature critical of behaviourist approaches to research was produced.[4] In spite of this, however, the fruits of this debate seem to have had little impact on psychologists, members of the public, or many American television researchers.

In order to avoid the abstract tenor of much that has been written about research methodology, I shall illustrate my general comments on key aspects of the behaviourist approach by reference to the work of Eysenck and Nias in their book, *Sex, Violence and the Media*.[5] Eysenck is a prominent and influential advocate of scientific psychology, and one finds in his works a closer articulation between scientific psychology and the scientific study of the effects of television than is generally the case in media research. A brief summary of relevant aspects of *Sex, Violence and the Media* will be presented, followed by a consideration of the role of the psychological experiment, of psychological measurement, and of inference in behaviourist approaches to the effects of television.

Sex, Violence and the Media

There has been more research into the effects of the portrayal of violence on television than any other area of television research. The reasons typically given for this research interest include the high incidence of violent episodes during prime-time programming (Eysenck and Nias cite a figure of 7.5 violent episodes per hour during prime-time), the increasing amount of time given over to television viewing (to be discussed in detail in Chapter 5), the fact that children do regularly watch adult programmes scheduled during the late evening, and the actual number of crimes detected, which has increased substantially in recent years. The latter, of course, has not gone unnoticed. The public are regularly reminded of escalating crime rates by 'law and order' politicians. Eysenck and Nias cite a Gallup poll taken in Britain from a random sample of adults, in which 'crimes of violence' were considered to be 'a very serious social problem' by 85 per cent of those sampled.[6]

In the United States, public concern about escalating rates of violent crime led to a national commission, the National Commission on the Causes and Prevention of Violence, which reported in 1969. This was quickly followed by another commission, the Surgeon General's Scientific Advisory Committee on Television and Social Behavior, which reported on the links between television and violence in 1972.

Eysenck and Nias devote considerable attention to the Surgeon General's report. The findings of the commission actually indicated that there was a relationship, albeit a modest one, 'between the viewing of violence and aggressive behaviour'.[7] But Eysenck and Nias argue that the report was so poorly written that the impression was given 'that TV violence was perhaps after all of little consequence'.[8] The weaknesses in the writing-up of the report, they claim, were due to the 'fact' that this responsibility was placed in the hands of those unqualified to interpret research reports, and by the interference of television network representatives. Not only did the TV networks actually monitor the writing of the final report, but they played a decisive role in the selection of committee members for the commission. In their wisdom, for example, they rejected the nomination for committee membership of Albert Bandura, an internationally prominent psychologist. Bandura had conducted several experimental studies on the effects of viewing violence, repeatedly finding a positive relationship between viewing violence and aggressive behaviour. Commenting on his exclusion from the committee, Bandura made the pertinent comment that 'this sorry case further illustrates the need for procedures to ensure that in the future scientific advisory panels will not be controlled by the very industries whose practices they are supposed to evaluate'.[9] Eysenck and Nias go a step further by indicating that the commissions on violence (and one on pornography) 'involved lawyers, publishers and theologians rather than psychologists'.[10] Only the latter, it would seem, are qualified to evaluate the research evidence relevant to the commissions.

This, in fact, is closely tied to the major reasons why Eysenck and Nias wrote *Sex, Violence and the Media*. In their introduction and throughout the book, Eysenck and Nias produce statements to the effect that the evidence, particularly of experimental studies, consistently supports the view that there is a positive relationship between TV violence and aggressive behaviour. Further, 'only the most prejudiced could reject all this evidence and call the case "unproven"'.[11] The most prejudiced, we can gather, are those sociologists who, according to Eysenck and Nias, have been responsible for producing the bulk of the literature in this area, a literature which is insufficiently accurate in the reporting of research, and insufficiently critical 'in terms of known and agreed rules of investigative procedure in the psychological sciences'.[12] They go on to state that 'neglect of this critical appraisal is almost universal'.[13] We are left in no doubt that psychology is 'the only field of knowledge relevant to the issue in question'.[14]

Eysenck and Nias present a comprehensive review of all the important research on TV violence and pornography. Their critical comments are ostensibly guided by two major considerations: the extent to which research studies conform to 'established' methods of investigation, and the extent to which the designs of the research studies are informed by 'sound' psychological theory. By 'sound psychological theory', they mean psychological theory which is supported by evidence derived from 'properly conducted' laboratory experiments. We are led to believe that the basis for concluding that there is a causal link between TV violence and aggressive behaviour resides in the evidence of scientific studies, and furthermore, that this causal link can be explained by scientific theories.

If we accept the arguments presented by Eysenck and Nias, then we can be optimistic that it will be only a matter of time before we are in a position to make clear statements about other effects of viewing television. This kind of view can be a highly persuasive one. Excerpts from the various reviews of *Sex, Violence and the Media* suggest that Eysenck and Nias have been successful in their advocacy of a scientific approach to the study of TV violence. The accolades of reviewers from the liberal press sit compatibly alongside reviews from the Right.

The validity of *all* media-effects research of a behaviourist or scientific variety hinges on the value of the evidence generated through the psychological experiment, and/or some form of psychological measurement. There are, however, as we shall see, compelling reasons as to why this evidence cannot be accepted as valid.

The psychological experiment

A psychological experiment ideally involves the comparison of differences in behaviour exhibited by two 'equivalent' groups of people, who are placed in conditions which are identical except in one crucial respect. One group is provided with a 'stimulus', which is intended to account for any observed differences in the behaviour of the two groups. Eysenck and Nias refer to this ideal as the 'laboratory method' or 'laboratory experiment', as distinct from the 'field experiment', in which the attempt is made to approximate the experimental ideal in 'natural' rather than laboratory settings. It is rarely possible in experimental field studies to 'randomly assign' people to the two groups being compared. Usually the experimenter must use groups already formed. Indeed, Eysenck and Nias tell us that 'the main advantage of the *laboratory method* is that subjects can be randomly assigned to the conditions being compared. This effectively allows an interpretation of the results in terms of cause and effect'.[15]

The laboratory experiment has been used extensively to test the effects of viewing violence. Typically one group is exposed to a short film, usually $2\frac{1}{2}$ to 20 minutes long, in which the content is packed with violence. At the same time another group is shown a 'neutral' film of the same duration. The differences in the behaviour of the two groups are measured following exposure to the films. The measures selected are those which are intended, in some way, to measure aggression.

The experimental method is believed to be useful in other relevant ways, depending on what the stimulus is and how it is manipulated.

Thus it has been used to measure differences in responses to violence in cartoons, compared with violence in other fictional forms, or in television news or 'real life' situations. Comparisons, too, have been made between various types of group, in terms of their reactions to portrayals of violence. It has generally been found, for example, that young boys tend to react more aggressively following exposure to violence than girls and adults.

Advocates of the experimental method accept that, in principle, *any type of television programme* can be tested for its effects. There have been experiments, for example, which attempt to measure the persuasiveness of political campaigns and advertisements, and of the impact of particular programmes on attitude change, opinion formation, increasing knowledge, and so on.

Part of the potential appeal of *Sex, Violence and the Media* is that Eysenck and Nias, in presenting their case that TV violence has a causal role in promoting aggression, exhibit the ritual caution of the scientist. The authors do acknowledge that there is a difference between experiments using beans in jam jars and experiments involving human beings. 'Perfection', they state, 'is not to be found in human affairs'.[16] Eysenck and Nias also show some awareness that experiments have been heavily criticised for being 'unnatural', and thus for artificially manipulating behaviour which is unlikely to occur in everyday life beyond the laboratory. They cite Noble's pointed question on this issue:

Do we want to know with certainty what will happen in a highly specific set of circumstances, or do we want to know what is more or less likely to happen when media violence is seen 'in natural, everyday viewing situations'?[17]

The response provided by Eysenck and Nias to this question is 'that only by investigating the issue in a highly specific set of circumstances will we ever be in a position to understand what probably happens in everyday life'.[18]

But this 'highly specific set of circumstances', that is, the controlled experiment, does, as Douglas argues, pose 'the danger that we are studying research procedures, not the natural social world, the world of everyday life'.[19] Douglas's argument is the familiar one that the so-called evidence of experimental studies is the product of manipulation by the experimenter, and not a reflection of what 'naturally' happens. In trying to isolate the effects of viewing violence, for example, the experimenter must exaggerate the difference in what is presented to the two groups.

Fully conscious of this manipulation, which is fully intended, the researcher seeks to observe the differences between the experimental group (the viewers of violence) and the control group (the viewers of a neutral film), which reflect the manipulation. Observations of behaviour following the presentation of radically different films are thus observations which are prescribed by the content of the films. One might be surprised if no differences between the immediate post-viewing behaviour of experimental and control groups were recorded, since clearly the experiment has been designed to produce differences. Eysenck and Nias explicitly applaud this kind of manipulation, and are critical of experiments which are insufficiently manipulative.

If one were to characterise the majority of published studies, one would not go far wrong in saying that they seem to have been perversely designed, not to get the maximum effect of exposure on behaviour, but rather that the design completely ignores major rules deriving from experimental study and clinical experience.[20]

But violent scenes on television are usually located within a variety of contexts in which all sorts of other things are going on. The experimental manipulation abstracts the violence from such scenes and presents it in an isolated and concentrated form. The experiment thus does not remotely correspond to what actually goes on in normal viewing.

There are, however, far more serious objections to the experiment, which do undermine the validity of the kinds of conclusion drawn from experimental studies. These objections may be classed together and referred to as 'interactive effects'.

The interactive effects which take place in all social settings are quite simply the consequences of social interaction for the individuals involved, in terms of how the actions of others are perceived, how individuals respond to others, how individuals decide to act, and the variable consequences of all this for each of the others, and thus for the ensuing interaction. The shaping of social interaction, and its perception by each of the individuals involved, is susceptible to a vast range of changeable influences, which are dynamically interrelated.[21] It is not possible, at any given point in time, to describe precisely, and to predict precisely, what is going to happen next, and how each of the individuals involved will perceive and react to future events.

Manipulations in psychological experiments are thus embedded within a changing context of social interaction. The experiment itself, the actions and instructions of the experimenter, and the physical sur-roundings in which the experiment is conducted, all participate in, influence, and are influenced by the continuing and changing interactive effects. It is not possible to disentangle the influence of the experimental stimulus itself from all the other interactive influences occurring during an experiment. It is thus not possible to specify the extent to which the behaviour of research subjects is the result of the intended manipulations of the experimenter, or the result of unintended interactions generated during the experiment. Any experimental study which claims to have found *scientific* evidence in support of TV viewing as a cause of specified effects is misleading, to say the least.

How do experimenters respond to the criticism that 'experimental evidence cannot be treated as precise, scientific evidence'? One common response is to acknowledge the existence of one class of interactive effects, namely the 'demand characteristics' of experiments, and to argue that these effects operate 'equally' in experimental and control groups, and thus do not affect the validity of the comparisons made between these two groups. This is, however, a somewhat dated response. Adair notes that the notion of demand characteristics was 'originally intended to account for the subject's development of an awareness of the hypothesis that he would co-operatively confirm'.[22] But, as Adair points out, 'the concept of demand characteristics has been broadened to designate all cues in the experiment that may influence the subject'.[23] He goes on to indicate that research subjects may adopt co-operative, defen-sive, apprehensive or negative attitudes to any cue in the experiment, including the total experiment itself. There is an extensive literature detailing some of the major ways in which the experimenter unwittingly influences the interaction in an experiment.[24]

It is true, as Eysenck and Nias reason, that 'demand characteristics apply to the control subjects as well as to the experimental'.[25] But the broader conception of demand characteristics alerts us to the possibility that experiments may generate uncoordinated interactive consequences which may pull in different directions. Further, interactive effects by their very nature will differ from group to group. This suggests that we cannot assume that the interactive effects in the experimental and control groups will be the same. Yet experimenters must make this assumption when measuring differences between the two groups.

Whether we are seeking to establish that portrayals of violence on television cause aggressive behaviour, or whether we are attempting to identify particular television programmes as the cause of any type of effect, the evidence of psychological experiments is not particularly helpful.

A common response to the kinds of argument I have made is one which claims that I have placed impossibly stringent standards of precision on the experiment. Thus Eysenck and Nias state that: 'Experimental designs are complex and difficult to make foolproof; statistical analysis often has to take care of the many unwanted variables that sneak into the experiment and may confound our data. Conclusions are probabilistic, not certain.'[26] Later, they state with equal caution that: 'It is possible to find fault with most studies in psychology, and indeed in all science; this does not mean that a conclusion cannot be drawn even from imperfect evidence which is all that is usually available.'[27]

We can agree with Eysenck and Nias about 'imperfect evidence' and 'probabilistic conclusions'. But if this is all that we can expect to derive from experiments, then the value of the whole exercise is placed in doubt. Why bother to set up experiments if at the end of the day we can produce only 'rough and ready' conclusions? Are we not already in possession of 'rough and ready' conclusions, arrived at through theoretical and practical reasoning?[28] Eysenck and Nias might agree, for they argue that 'a good theory is often more reliable than empirical determinations'.[29] They go on to recall that Kurt Lewin, a principle figure in the history of psychology, 'used to say that a good theory is the most practical thing of all; with that we would entirely concur'.[30] But for Eysenck and Nias, and behaviourist psychologists in general, good theories 'usually emanate from laboratory studies'.[31] In the light of the above discussion this is an implausible view.

Psychological measurement in TV effects research

If, for some, experiments are deemed to be a necessary characteristic of a scientific approach to the study of the effects of viewing television, for others, non-experimental studies can be considered to be scientific if they are based on the use of 'observational instruments' designed to yield precise measures of, for example, attitudes, personality, knowledge acquisition, intelligence, aggression, emotional stability, and so on. In principle, advocates of scientific measurement in the social sciences believe that it is possible to obtain fairly precise data about the individual, including data which may be of relevance to specifying the impact of television viewing. But whereas the purpose of an experiment is to identify the *cause* of particular behaviours, observational instruments are used to *measure* these behaviours. As Eysenck and Nias correctly point out, if we find a strong relationship between compulsive TV viewing, high aggression scores, and particular personality types, as measured by a test of personality, we are in no position to suggest that television viewing is a cause of aggression. It could be that certain personality types are more aggressive than others, and more attracted to viewing violence. Alternatively, they may have been aggressive to start off with, or their personalities may have predisposed them to compulsive viewing.

Nevertheless, if measurements of behaviour alone cannot tell us anything about the power of television to influence what people do and think, they are involved in describing that alleged power. Further, they are used extensively in studies which attempt to relate high television viewing to the characteristics of individuals.

The most common line of argument which is used to defend the continuing use of the psychological experiment in television research is that which stresses that in spite of all the difficulties attending pschological experiments, the better designed experiments, at least, have provided consistent evidence. This implies a strong faith in the actual measurements used in experiments. In a sense, the measurements are considered to be sufficiently reliable to validate the experiments. But what of the validity of the measurements themselves? If there are sound reasons to suppose that the measurements are invalid, how can they validate the experiment? It is just this question which is raised by the severest critics of psychological measurements.

The validity of a measurement refers to the extent to which a test, rating scale, questionnaire, or some other similar measure, represents what it is intended to measure. If during an athletic season, a 100 metres runner consistently runs 100 metres in the 10.0 to 10.2 seconds range, electronically timed, then we can confidently say that he is faster over 100 metres, in that season, than another 100 metres runner who runs the 100 metres consistently in the 10.4 to 10.6 seconds range, electronically timed. In psychological measurements, however, we *cannot* claim that a twelve-year-old boy who consistently scores 130 points on an intelligence test is more intelligent than another twelve-year-old boy who consistently scores 110 points on the same test. The reason for this is that we cannot assume that an intelligence test measures intelligence. We can say that in response to *these* questions on *this* particular test, one boy consistently scores 20 points more than the other, but it is quite another matter to refer to the test as a test of intelligence.

Whether or not a psychological test is a valid measure of the psychological variable in question ultimately depends on our assessment of the degree of correspondence between the items on a test and what we consider to be an appropriate definition of the particular variable. Within psychology itself, there are a wide range of theoretical perspectives and a wide range of differences concerning the meaning of particular psychological qualities. Many definitions of 'intelligence', for example, do not lend themselves to being represented in the form of items on a test. All this suggests that we cannot take it for granted that the validity of psychological tests is a non-controversial matter, even amongst psychologists.

Yet television research of the behaviourist variety continues to use psychological tests as if the latter were unproblematic, or as if they accept the kinds of argument advanced by advocates in their use of tests. Thus, with the example of intelligence tests, some advocates will argue that whether or not a test is to be considered a valid measure of intelligence usually depends, in practice, on how well the scores on the test for the same people correspond to their scores on existing tests of intelligence. Of course, the existing tests may not measure intelligence. One intended solution to this dilemma is that if the test scores of the same group of people correspond to their achievement in school, and/or to how teachers rate their intelligence, then the test is considered to be an intelligence test. This, however, is not a satisfactory solution, since the same kinds of bias and prejudice may enter into test construction, teachers' ratings, and scholastic standards.[32] Thus Henderson notes that 'the behaviour patterns characteristic of the middle-class life situation came to be defined as "intelligent", and were used as the basis for our assessment, both formal and informal, of intelligence'.[33] He concludes that

differences in the distribution of intelligence are related less to the advantageous position of the middle-class in terms of the *acquisition* of intelligence and more to the *power* of the middle-class in *establishing the actual definitions* of intelligence.[34]

Observational instruments, then, represent a *definition* of whatever it is that they are supposed to measure. The controversy surrounding 'definition' applies to *all* psychological measurements, whether of intelligence, personality, attitudes or aggression. One source of consistent bias, and thus invalidity, resides in the fact that a measurement is by definition an attempt to 'operationalise' or 'instrumentalise' aspects of human psychology. The measures themselves represent *instrumental or operational definitions* of psychological qualities, and as such embody a cluster of biases compatible with instrumental values. Little wonder then that item analyses of various measures reveal that intelligence tests are directed at superficial manifestations of intelligence, a 'crossword puzzle' mentality, rather than profound reflective qualities.[35] In personality tests we find that the 'balanced, well-rounded, healthy' personality tends to approximate the 'automaton' qualities associated with the successful business man capable of eliminating the intrusion of emotions and sentiment in his daily conduct. In aggression tests there is a strong tendency towards a definition of aggression which reflects that view which casts women as non-aggressive, and the working class as having 'relatively weak inhibitions about hurting other people'.[36]

Questions concerning what psychological tests mean, and thus how best to interpret test scores, have been hotly debated by psychologists. There are those who believe that test scores reflect relatively stable psychological attributes, and thus are prone to interpreting consistent findings as a product of the individual's inherited psychological characteristics.[37] Psychologists who are less convinced about the existence of enduring psychological properties within the individual are more likely to interpret consistent findings in a way which privileges consistent environmental influences. Both groups, however (as is the case in the traditional 'heredity versus environment' debate on the sources of intelligence), assume the validity of the data derived from psychological tests. But the discussion above suggests that one probable source of consistent findings in studies using psychological measurements is the consistent bias contained within the actual tests. This suggests that an adequate appraisal of the findings of research which uses psychological tests involves a closer look at the actual measurements employed.

Television researchers tend to use psychological measures because they provide a convenient means of gathering data. In so doing, however, they run the risk of collecting data on variables which are defined in problematic ways. With respect to TV violence research, the measure of aggression adopted by the researcher may be convenient, but it may not be particularly useful in assessing aggressive behaviour. Where does 'determination' or 'will power' shade off into 'aggression'? Is there a distinction to be made between a 'self-confident assertiveness' and 'aggression'?

In responding to items on any test, one's response is prestructured by the item, in such a way that the inadequacies of definition inherent in the test may prevent the individual from responding truthfully. A hypothetical example can be used to illustrate this point. If on a questionnaire used to survey preferences for breakfast, people are asked: 'Would you prefer cat food on toast or ice cream?', the response of the vast majority would very likely show a preference for ice cream. Yet it is very unlikely that many people would freely list 'ice cream' as a favourite breakfast food. Extreme examples of this kind are rarely found in psychological measures, but there are many examples which do come close to matching this level of absurdity. Heim produces several examples of such items drawn from widely used intelligence and personality tests.[38] Of an item on the *Eysenck Personality Inventory* (EPI): 'Generally, do you prefer reading to meeting people?—Yes/No', Heim comments, 'it is not only the intellectual who mutters in his beard, "Depends on the book—depends on the people"'.[39]

It must be said that ambiguous and 'unsound' items on psychological tests are the rule rather than the exception. The example above typifies the ambiguity of all the items on the *EPI*. Similarly the *Junior Eysenck Personality Inventory* (JEPI) includes sixty items to which the respondent must answer 'Yes' or 'No'. The 'Yes/No' alternative prestructures responses to ambiguous items such as 'Do you like plenty of excitement going on around you?' and 'Do you often need kind friends to cheer you up?'. It is difficult to see how such items can be promoted in the name of science. On any test a variable percentage of the items will be ambiguous and/or irrelevant. Yet the total score for each individual is computed as if all items were of equal relevance. Further, responses which are based on 'considered reflection' sit alongside those which are 'off the top of the head'. It is difficult to resist the conclusion that psychological tests generate meaningless evidence, and that the precise statistical procedures to which test scores are subjected is quite inappropriate.

Eysenck and Nias quite rightly note that 'it is well known that the observational instruments we are using, and the experimental designs on which we rely, are extremely primitive'.[40] With this being the case, it has occurred to many critics that there is a fundamental contradiction in dressing up observations in the precise language of statistics. Research on the impact of television which uses psychological measurements promotes the impression of scientific rigour, and disguises the unscientific aspects of such research.

There is a further relevant and most important consideration with respect to what it is that responses to items on psychological tests actually mean. The problems generated for the validity of experiments by interactive effects (see pp. 11–13) also attend the administration of psychological tests. Since interactive effects cannot be measured, their influence on responses to psychological tests cannot be specified, and this in turn casts doubt on the wisdom of performing precise statistical operations on test data.[41]

Many experimenters are critical of the reliability and validity of psychological measures, and prefer, instead, to use 'behavioural measures'. These involve making recorded observations of individuals' behaviour on a task deemed to be a valid index of a psychological variable, relevant to the particular experiment in question. An example of such a behavioural measure is the Arnold Buss 'aggression machine'. Here, aggression is measured by the willingness of research subjects to apply electric shocks of varying intensity and duration in order to punish the mistakes of other individuals on some kind of simple learning task. These 'other' individuals are confederates of the researcher; they do not actually experience real shocks, but this knowledge is withheld from the research subjects.[42] Such a test does not, of course, get around the problem of avoiding interactive effects. While research subjects may not guess the purpose of the exercise, they are very likely to be curious about the task set, and this curiosity may affect their behaviour in different ways. In the case of the Arnold Buss aggression machine and its variants, there is a massive inference on the part of the researcher that the machine does in fact measure aggression. There is an extensive critical literature on such a use of 'electric shock' in psychological experiments.[43] What is clear from this literature is that the individual's response to a task demanding the administration of electric shocks is dependent on so many uncontrollable factors that it is doubtful that an observer is ever able to say precisely what the response means, and thus what the task measures.

Behavioural measures, as I have suggested, pose rather sharply the problematic nature of the inferences made in behaviourist approaches to research. This is widely recognised among psychologists, but it is far from clear that this is the case amongst television researchers adopting the methods of behaviourism.

The problem of inference

Joynson states that both experiments and psychological measures

are attempting to identify inner conditions of response on the basis of observation of outer conditions and responses alone, whether the responses are to mental tests or to experimental situations. In neither case is the inner condition directly observed, and the inference depends upon an altogether too tenuous and indirect link.[44]

Whether or not we accept the findings of behaviourist research on television's power depends on how much faith we have in 'the evidence' generated in this research. The 'evidence', as we have seen, comes in a 'scientific' mantle which belies the unscientific manner in which it has been produced. At each stage in the production of 'scientific knowledge', via the methods of behaviourist psychology, the researcher makes inferences. In the laboratory experiment the researcher infers that the observed differences between experimental and control groups are attributable to an 'isolated cause', such as a film packed with violent episodes. This inference is enabled by ignoring the multitudinous ways in which research subjects may experience the experiment. It is also enabled by a somewhat superficial psychology which allows the researcher to assume that the influence of the prior histories of research subjects can be wiped out by randomly assigning them to experimental and control groups. Finally, the observed differences between experimental and control groups are made by means of psychological and behavioural measures based on the inference that these measures actually measure the relevant psychological variable in question.

The inferences which are routinely structured into behaviouristic research methods, and which are intended to produce scientific evidence, are the product of an underlying theory—behaviourism itself. Although behaviourism is no longer the dominant theoretical perspective in Western psychology, it continues to exercise a dominance in that psychologists of a variety of theoretical perspectives continue to submit their theoretical claims to the test of behaviourism's methods. The pursuit of scientific evidence invariably draws the researcher into behaviourism, and the evidence obtained is used to give scientific credibility to the researcher's theoretical ideas and thus to raise the status of these ideas from mere 'speculation'.[45]

Critics of behaviourism have not only argued that behaviourism's research methods are unscientific, but that the very use of these methods imposes an overly simplistic and narrow way of thinking about the relation between the environment and the individual. On the one hand, television's effects are formulated in psycho-behavioural terms in ways which belie the complexity of human experience, and on the other hand, television, as part of the environment, is treated in isolation and in terms of stimulus properties, which again distorts its complexity. The dynamic interpenetrations of need, motivation, intent, values, interests, and so on, relevant to the interpretation of experience, must figure in any attempt to understand the power television exercises over the viewer. This understanding, too, needs to extricate itself from behaviourism's media-centredness which enables, for example, the verdict that watching violence on TV is a cause of violence. This conclusion is drawn without any consideration being given to social conditions, or to forms of violence other than interpersonal violence, such as the structural violence many associate with the family or the police, for example.

The methods of behaviourism are unable to grasp the more complex 'television–audience–society' interrelationships, and it is primarily for this reason that students of television turn towards theory for a more adequate understanding of television's power. Below, I shall outline the major theoretical approaches involved in the study of television's power. Following Curran *et al.*[46] and Fejes,[47] the main theoretical perspectives in media theory can be identified as pluralist, culturalist, structuralist and political economy.

Pluralism

In the words of Blumler and Gurevitch, pluralists see society as 'a plurality of potential concentrations of power (albeit not necessarily equal to each other) which are engaged in a contest for ascendancy and dominance'.[48] The mass media, within this view, can be seen as a stage on which 'this contest is conducted and public support for one or another grouping or point of view is mobilized'.[49] To say this much is to say very little, since it is difficult to see how this basic view provides direction for how we are to approach television's power. Blumler himself has pointed out that as a theoretical perspective and research approach there appears to be little shape to the range of pluralist studies of the mass media.[50]

McQuail has attempted to identify some of the key features of the pluralist approach to the mass media by contrasting, in an admittedly exaggerated form, pluralism with critical or 'dominance' approaches.[51] In his view, pluralism tends to see television production as 'creative, free and original' whereas critical theorists emphasise the way in which television production is 'standardized, routinized and controlled'. This contrast is clearly connected to radically different appraisals of television programme content. For critical theorists, programmes tend to reflect a dominant ideology, but pluralists are more likely to stress the representation of 'diverse and competing views' and the attempts of programmers to be 'responsive to audience demand'. This is compatible with what McQuail, along with most pluralists, sees as perhaps the most significant differences between critical and pluralist approaches, namely their views about the television audience, and the effects of television viewing. The latter, for pluralists, are 'numerous, without consistency or predictability of direction', on an audience which is 'fragmented, selective, reactive and active'. Critical theorists, McQuail suggests, see the audience as 'dependent, passive' and 'organized on a large scale' and vulnerable to very powerful ideological effects which are 'confirmative of the established social order'.

McQuail points out that the pluralist model can 'suit more than one perception of the media and more than one set of values'.[52] He goes on to state that

it might represent the libertarian ideal in which there is no control or direction, only the 'hidden hand' of the market working to maximize the satisfaction of changing needs and interests of the customers and clients and eventually the whole society.[53]

Such a statement is considered by some to be sufficient to dismiss pluralism as socially illiterate. Indeed, Hall wrote in 1982 about pluralism in the past tense, as a surpassed paradigm.[54] However appealing this might be, it is premature. It is, nevertheless, the case that pluralism largely fails to acknowledge 'class formations, economic processes, sets of institutional power-relations',[55] and as such, it has a very restrictive and inadequate conception of power. Power is seen as the power of an individual, group, or institution to influence another individual in a way 'which would register as a switch of behaviour'.[56] Given this somewhat narrow conception of power, it would be unrealistic to expect a comprehensive understanding of the power of television to emerge from a pluralist perspective. This point has already been made in the earlier discussion of *Sex, Violence and the Media*. The position adopted by

Eysenck and Nias falls within a pluralist framework in more ways than one. In pluralism, Blumler observes that 'questions about the effectiveness of the media as sources of influence and persuasion loom large'.[57] This is also true of critical approaches. Pluralists, however, in spite of their attempts to overcome the gross oversimplifications of behaviourism in theorising media effects, still submit themselves to the crudities of behaviourist research methodology in testing media effects. Most pluralists continue to seek scientific credibility, and tend to identify the latter rather closely with the methods of behaviourism. It is not clear that those pluralists who reject 'simple behaviourism' as a research model are attuned to its fundamental weaknesses. Thus what became known as the 'uses and gratifications' approach to media research,[58] in rejecting the idea of 'the passive audience' implicit in early media-effects research, went on to reproduce this very idea by employing research methods which confined the research subjects to passivity. Similarly, the empirical methods adopted by Blumler and others, in their studies of the effects of political party campaigns in the broadcasting media, are an untidy mix of non-inferential measures, relatively valid survey methods, and behaviouristic methods.[59]

The common distinction between Marxist or critical perspectives, and pluralist media perspectives, does not sufficiently grasp the extent to which allegiance to the methods of scientific psychology has shaped media-effects research, and the way in which the power of television has been conceptualised as a consequence. It can be suggested that, until the early 1970s, the available methods of scientific psychology, rather than pluralist social theory, dictated the form of media-effects research. Of course, this is perfectly compatible with the liberalism of pluralism. However, more theoretically minded pluralists have been critical of the straightjacketing effect imposed by simple behaviourism. There have been recent attempts to conceptualise more adequately the complex interactions between television and audience from within a pluralist framework.[60] Interestingly, some of these attempts, as we shall see later, connect with Marxist perspective which are themselves critical of Marxist or critical media theory.

Critical media theory

Two of the critical approaches in the classification employed by Curran *et al.* are explicitly Marxist. These are the political economy perspective and the culturalist approach. The third approach, structuralism, borrows from Marxism, but is more indebted to semiotics and Lacan's psychoanalytic theory.

What distinguishes Marxism from both pluralism and structuralism, is its depiction of history as a struggle between contending classes over the resources necessary for the development of societies. For Marxists, the development of advanced capitalist societies, has been, and continues to be, largely a product of the power of the capitalist class's exercise of power over subordinated classes. The power of the capitalist class ultimately resides in its ownership of economic resources. Class domination is thus seen as a central and defining characteristic of capitalist societies. Given this view of society, the task of the media theorist is to depict the role of the mass media in the context of class contradictions, and the continuing dominance of the capitalist class.

This task, however, is an extremely complex one, not least because there are disagreements amongst Marxists on definitions of class, and thus class contradictions, on how capitalist class domination is maintained, on the role of the state in this, and, crucially for media theory, on the role of ideology in maintaining or reproducing class domination. The concept of ideology itself is variously defined and theorised, and some definitions are radically opposed to each other.[61]

Even where there are substantial agreements on key elements of Marxist theory, variation in one's theoretical position can arise from differences in the relative importance of these elements in the total order of things. Here again, the place of ideology in explanations of social reproduction is accorded differential significance amongst Marxists. Thus Marxism provides a range of different responses to contemporary developments in the dominant practices of capitalism, to the exercise of state power, and to the various consequences these practices hold for institutions, for culture, for class configurations, for individuals, and so on. This is the theoretical hinterland of Marxist media theory, and it is one which more or less continuously generates issues for debate. It gives to Marxist media theory a dynamic and lively quality, invariably missing from the more instrumentalist and less critical universe of pluralism.

One of the major preoccupations of Marxist theory is the problem of social reproduction. In critical media theory considerable attention has been given to the role of ideology in social reproduction. As Golding puts it, 'inegalitarian societies continue to reproduce a social order which is not merely tolerated by those receiving least in the distribution of material and cultural rewards, but which also receives their loyalty and acclaim'.[62] The power of television within this view is ultimately an ideological power involved in winning the 'loyalty and acclaim' of subordinated groups to a social order in which they are subordinated. The difference in emphasis between culturalist and political economy perspectives in media theory hinges on differences in explaining how the media perform their ideological service for dominant groups. Critics have argued that the question of how effective the media are as ideological agencies tends to be overlooked. This criticism tends to be advanced by those who are unconvinced that ideology deserves the kind of importance given to it in critical media theory.

Culturalist media theory

Media theory in the culturalist perspective is focused on an examination of media messages, analysing in detail how 'the media become part and parcel of that dialectical process of the "production of consent"—shaping the consensus while reflecting it—which orients them within the field force of the dominant social interests represented within the state'.[63]

The culturalist perspective has been at the centre of debates within critical media theory which, according to Hall, have been guided by two central questions: first, 'How does the ideological process work and what are its mechanisms?' and secondly, 'How is "the ideological" to be conceived in relation to other practices within a social formation?'[64] Hall's own work, and to a lesser extent the work of Raymond Williams, have been criticised by semiotically-orientated structuralists on the first question, and from more 'orthodox' Marxists on the second question. A typical structuralist criticism of the culturalist perspective is that made by Woollacott. 'Semiology or structuralism and in particular the semiological analysis of media texts have been woven into various formulations of a theory of ideology with a range of subsequent problems in the internal coherence of such theories'.[65] Woollacott also refers to Hall's efforts as 'ambitious'. Curran *et al.* state that there are 'some unresolved problems in this approach, not least of which is the unevenness of the theoretical synthesis achieved'.[66]

These can be seen to be rather superficial estimates of the tremendous value of Hall's ability to draw creatively and *selectively* on a formidable range of ideas in addressing the problem of 'how ideology works'. Hall acknowledges a theoretical debt to Gramsci, Poulantzas, Althusser, Marx, to elements of phenomenology, structural anthropology, and to the semiotics of Barthes. Any apparent incoherence in Hall's work reflects not so much the diversity of ideas which constitute his theoretical framework, but rather the fact that the realities which Hall addresses are ones which are not readily resolvable within established theoretical systems. Curran *et al.* pose as a problem in Hall's work what is in fact the way things are. 'Hence, while the media are represented as a "key terrain where consent is won or lost", they are also in other formulations conceived of as signifying a crisis which has already occurred, both in economic and political terms'.[67]

The value of Hall's work for ideological readings of television, in relation to his analysis of ideological shifts currently taking place in Thatcher's Britain, will be discussed later. For the moment, however, it can be noted that the two questions Hall raised above about ideology represent two points around which the power of television has been articulated. I shall argue throughout this book, with Hall, that the two questions need to be considered together. More explicitly than Hall, I shall want to stress that these two questions, though important, need to be placed within a much broader consideration of both the role of the media in reproducing advanced capitalist societies, and a consideration of the role of ideology in the 'total order of things'.

Political economy media theory

In spite of the care taken by Hall to avoid a media- and ideology-centred view of society, it has been pointed out that the culturalist perspective can be interpreted in a way which seriously exaggerates the power of the media in shaping society.[68] One might expect the political economy perspective to counter this view. Thus Murdock and Golding state that: 'Many sociologists, ourselves included, would disagree fundamentally with the proposition that modes of communication "determine what kind of society we are going to have".'[69] However, they merely replace one kind of media-centredness with another when, in their very next sentence they claim: 'On the contrary, sociological analysis should start from the exactly opposite assertion that modes of communication and cultural expression are determined by the structure of social relations.'[70]

The underlying power structure and its impact on the mass media is the primary focus of the political economy approach, whereas culturalists concentrate on the impact of the mass media on society. The political economy of the mass-media perspective is very much 'a political economy *of* the media', and very little attempt has yet been made to place this focus within 'a political economy of society'.

Elsewhere, Golding and Murdock reiterate their basic position.

In our view, the primary task of mass communications research is not to explore the meanings of media messages, but to analyse the social processes through which they are constructed and interpreted and the contexts and pressures that shape and constrain these constructions.[71]

This indicates the recognition of the need to connect the political economy of the media with a political economy of society.

Much of the work arising from the political economy of the mass-media perspective starts from a position which stresses that, on the one hand, economic practices in late capitalism underwrite all forms of social life, including institutions such as the mass media, and, on the other, that the mass media themselves are directly involved in economic practices. This involvement is seen principally in two ways: as an industry producing cultural commodities; and producing services for major power blocs by the selling of information and its accompanying hardware, and by selling audiences to advertisers.[72] Intricately part of ongoing capitalism, the mass media are directly involved in the practices of class domination, and thus in the consequences of class domination for determining the social structure and the social conditions in which people live.

Following the lead of the Frankfurt School, contemporary German media theorists are attempting to formulate the ideological implications of this level of economic analysis. In addition, through broad historical sweeps, they are theorising connections between the standardisation of media products under capitalist ownership and control, and their effects on the structure of consciousness.[73] Much work remains to be done in this area. One promising line of development, which I shall pursue in Chapter 6, is that which sees the electronic media as reinforcing, in their increasingly privatised modes of reception, trends in the privatisation of social life related to crisis tendencies in late capitalism. This suggests one place where the gap between the political economy of the media and the political economy of society can be filled. In Chapter 5, I shall explore another place in which this gap can be bridged, following the Frankfurt School's writings on the manipulation of needs in relation to the activity of television viewing.

In addition to pursuing investigations following the view that 'the mass media are first and foremost industrial and commercial organisations which produce and distribute commodities within a Late Capitalist economic order',[74] Golding and Murdock have been concerned with the ideological nature of the mass media, and its ideological effectiveness. Understandably they argue that 'the production of ideology cannot be separated from or adequately understood without grasping the general economic dynamics of media production and the determination they exert'.[75] Critics have been too ready to dismiss this approach as a crude form of economic reductionism. This is far from the case, as Garnham makes clear.[76] Such a criticism can only arise from incomplete readings which enable critics to ignore Golding and Murdock's response to Smythe, in which they stress the need to recognise the media's *'independent* role in reproducing ideologies'.[77]

Structuralist media theory

For all their emphases on 'sophisticated' ideological readings of media messages, the contribution of structuralists to critical media theory has been a controversial one. Their ideological analyses of television appear, at least to the more sociologically and politically minded media theorists, to be socially naive alongside the analyses from both the political economy and culturalist perspectives. Where pertinent analyses are produced, as in some feminist structuralist work, one is inclined to suppose that it is the underlying feminist perspective, rather than the structuralist methodology which is the source of enlightenment.

On the one hand, structuralists have been concerned with how discourses produce meanings within texts, including television programmes as texts. The ideological effect in this context refers to the meaning or meanings produced. This is normally analysed semiotically.[78] On the other hand, meaning production is involved in the interpretation of texts, and structuralists here have been at loggerheads among themselves as to how best to approach the ideological effect of the text. Among the various positions which have emerged there are two which attribute discourses, and thus television, with an awesome power. The first is best represented by Laclau and Mouffe in which discourses are attributed with a power to effectively shape economic and political practices.[79] Certain aspects of this work are compatible with other critical media-theory perspectives especially with respect to the effects of television's ideological output on dominant groups, that is, on those who have access to the power resources enabling them to practise dominant ideologies. The second position is far more problematic. It is the position most closely associated with a psychoanalytic-semiotic conception of ideology in which discourses are viewed as being sufficiently powerful to 'constitute individuals ideologically' through the unconscious.

Both positions treat discourses as having a material existence, and as working autonomously as ideological practices. In the case of Laclau and Mouffe, meaning production or ideological production is cast in Marxist terms, whereas the concept of ideology employed in the more psychoanalytic-semiotic position is for the most part divested of any critical connotation, with the exception of work which emphasises the role of ideology in the production of gendered subjects.[80] While this position claims to be derived from a particular interpretation of Althusser's work on ideology, on the one hand, and Lacan's theory of the unconscious, on the other, it does borrow freely from the semiotics of Barthes, structural linguistics, the ideas of Derrida and even Foucault, in order to deconstruct texts (including television as text) to reveal the 'play' of ideology. This position, in addition to more traditional perspectives which draw upon the Freudian theory of the unconscious, tends to leave us with a view of the individual as being ideologically thoroughly duped by television.[81]

Changing perspectives on the power of television

We can enumerate some of the major ways in which thinking about television's power has moved beyond the simple behaviourist conceptions.

1. From a focus on the effects of television in terms of changes in isolated aspects of individual behaviour, attention has shifted toward 'ideological effects'.
2. Structuralist theory apart, the source of television's power is no longer isolated to television's messages. Rather television works in

conjunction with other forces, and derives much of its power from its socio-political context.

3.   It is no longer considered appropriate to conceive of televisual messages as embodying isolated stimuli properties. Messages are now treated as more complex phenomena, often as 'coded discourses'.

4.   Again, certain structuralist accounts notwithstanding, it is widely acknowledged that individual audience members may variously interpret television's coded discourses.

5.   More theoretical attention is given to the fact that the individual is subject to a wide range of potential influences other than television and the mass media.

6.   Attention has been drawn to television as a commercial enterprise, involved in, and integral to, the practices of capitalist enterprises.

7.   Attention has been drawn to ways in which television serves the interests of the state and dominant groups by projecting a dominant ideology.

Very generally, we can say that the power of television is now understood in terms of a socio-political model. But the shift from psycho-behavioural effects is far from complete, as I shall indicate below in presenting some of the issues which have a bearing on the power of television in contemporary society.

Behavioural and ideological effects

A widely accepted verdict of behavioural media-effects studies, at least until fairly recently, was that television does not make a measurable difference in terms of changing behaviour, attitudes and opinions. As we have seen, this verdict is quite meaningless on account of the fact that the evidence on which it is based is highly problematic. The rejection of behaviourist methods, which was a central part of what was known as the 'critique of positivism' and the ensuing paradigm shift in sociology in the late 1960s and early 1970s, remains valid. There are some critical theorists for whom this point has not sunk in. Two issues are threatening to make the critical theorists' interest in the ideological effectiveness of television historically continuous with the early behaviourist media-effects studies. In summarising the latter, Klapper suggested that the power-effectiveness of the media could be described in terms of 'conversion' (the greatest change), 'minor change', and 'reinforcement'.[82] Some critical theorists are arguing that the conclusion that the media do not change behaviour may, in fact, represent an important effect, namely that the media reinforce existing patterns of behaviour. Such a view lends support to some of the ways in which television is said to be ideologically effective. Needless to say, in invoking such an argument, critical media theorists are as a consequence endorsing the methods of behaviourism.

The second issue produces an identical consequence. Pluralists are still inclined to attribute behavioural research with an unwarranted validity. They are calling upon Marxists to submit their claims about the ideological effectiveness of television to the test of behaviourist empirical methods.[83] Oddly enough, some Marxists seem willing to comply.[84] As I shall argue, there are ways of empirically testing for television's alleged ideological effect without using behaviourism's methods.

Analysing the message

Televisual messages can be analysed in many ways, from numerical counts of the recurrence of particular types of event or theme, for example, the number of murders shown in a week at prime viewing time, to a more qualitative analysis of the underlying structure of the messages. Do messages, for example, reflect a common value system, and how does this work in relation to technologies peculiar to television production?

Quantitative content analysis can be useful, but most attention nowadays is directed at the ideologies in which televisual messages are coded. There are considerable disagreements about the determinants of televisual discourses, how they affect the messages produced, and how this in turn affects the audience. The various disagreements on how messages should be analysed tend to reinforce the idea that the source of television's power resides in its messages. As we shall see this can lead to a distorted view of television's power.

The audience: active or passive?

In being insensitive to the experience of the viewer, early behaviourist media research conveyed an image of the audience as passive organisms vulnerable to the manipulative power of the stimulus properties of televisual messages. Against this view, those pluralists adopting a 'uses and gratification' model of the relation between media and audience have stressed the 'active' nature of viewing. Rather than being concerned with what television does to the audience, attention was focused on how the audience uses television, and for what purpose. There is genuine concern that critical media theory's preoccupation with the power of television ideologically to manipulate audiences resurrects the idea of a passive audience. If television's messages are believed to be so powerful as to win the consent of the subordinated to the social system in which they are subordinated, then quite clearly this suggests a less than flattering view of the viewers' intelligence.

The issue of the passive or active audience, however, is not a clear-cut one. The notion of an active audience using television in order to meet some self-defined need is a notion which is difficult to reconcile with the observation that much television viewing is a matter of routine, and largely unselective. On the other hand, some elements of critical media theory incorporate the view that the audience does have scope for interpreting messages. Stuart Hall, for example, tends to favour the view that the interpretive capacities of individuals are exercised, for the most part, within a shared consensual framework. In other words, individuals tend to intepret what they see by using a meaning system which is compatible with the way in which televisual messages are coded. He acknowledges that there is always the possibility of interpreting messages through meaning systems other than the dominant ideological framework. Some structuralists, however, consider this flexibility to be relatively unimportant, and stress instead the way in which televisual discourses 'position' the viewer, making the latter vulnerable to ideological manipulation at an unconscious level. To all intents and purposes this does seem like another version of the passive viewer.

There is a real need, which I intend to address, to develop an approach to the audience which attempts to understand the potential psychological consequences of the kinds of social conditions in which subordinated groups live, and which does so in ways which neither belittle human intelligence, nor attribute motive (ideological or otherwise) where it does not exist.

Television, the economy and the state

There is considerable agreement among critical media theorists that television produces and reproduces a dominant ideology. Exactly how this comes about, however, continues to be debated. These debates turn on the relative importance of economic determinants, the explicit and hidden forms of government interference, and the professional ideologies of programmers in determining both the range of output and specific programme content. The impact of the interrelations among these determinants on ideological reproduction is far from clear. Thus while television entertainment involves 'audience maximisation' for advertisers, seeking 'proven' means of being inoffensive to large audiences, promoting certain forms of entertainment known to be popular, and confining less popular programmes outside prime-time hours, there is not always a neat fit between what is popular and a clear expression of elements of a dominant ideology.

Another set of issues concerns the extent to which television reflects the 'real world' as opposed to projecting a media-created reality. Many complexities arise in theorising such a problem in the context of the various interpenetrating determinants of news and current affairs production.

Media-centredness versus social totality

Quite clearly, television is only *one* of several forces impinging upon the individual, and it is ill-advised to explain human action and consciousness solely in terms of what the individual has 'learned' from television. Put in this way, no self-respecting social scientist would ever consider this to be a serious proposition. However, the very media-centredness of all media theory often conveys an impression that the media theorist has lost sight of the fact that individuals do things other than watch television, videos, listen to the radio, and read newspapers. Issues arise around the tendency, for example, to emphasise the connections between dominant ideologies structured into all our major institutions, and the ideologies represented in televisual discourses, and then the tendency to understand individual action as the expression of these ideologies.

Media theorists have increasingly attempted to understand how the social totality affects television production. There is a real need to understand how the social totality affects the individual *prior to* specifying the impact of television.

Notes

1. Denis McQuail, *Mass Communication Theory*, London, Sage, 1983, p. 176.
2. Fred Fejes, 'Critical mass communications research and media effects: the problem of the disappearing audience', *Media, Culture and Society*, vol. 6, 1984, p. 219.
3. See, for example, Alan Gauld and John Shotter, *Human Action and its Psychological Investigation*, London, Routledge, 1977; John Hughes, *The Philosophy of Social Research*, London, Longman, 1980.
4. For a useful summary, see Gordon Westland, *Current Crises of Psychology*, London, Heinemann, 1978.
5. H.J. Eysenck and D.K.B. Nias, *Sex, Violence and the Media*, London, Temple Smith, 1978.
6. Ibid., p. 17.
7. Ibid., p. 84.
8. Ibid., p. 82.
9. Ibid., pp. 90–1.
10. Ibid., p. 99.
11. Ibid., p. 12.
12. Ibid.
13. Ibid.
14. Ibid., p. 41.
15. Ibid., p. 73.
16. Ibid., p. 28.
17. Ibid., p. 75.
18. Ibid.
19. Jack D. Douglas, *Investigative Social Research*, London, Sage, 1976, p. 19.
20. Eysenck and Nias, op. cit., p. 56.
21. See R.D. Laing, *Self and Others*, Harmondsworth, Penguin, 2nd revised edn, 1969.
22. John G. Adair, *The Human Subject*, Boston, Little, Brown, 1973, p. 24.
23. Ibid.
24. See for example, R. Rosenthal and R.L. Rosnow, eds, *Artifact in Behavioral Research*, New York: Academic Press, 1969.
25. Eysenck and Nias, op. cit., p. 74.
26. Ibid., p. 12.
27. Ibid., p. 28.
28. See the compelling case made by R.B. Joynson, *Psychology and Common Sense*, London, Routledge, 1974.

29. Eysenck and Nias, op. cit., p. 42.
30. Ibid., p. 43.
31. Ibid.
32. See, for example, Clarence J. Karier, 'Business values and the educational state' in Roger Dale, Geoff Esland and Madeleine MacDonald, eds, *Schooling and Capitalism*, London, Routledge, 1976, pp. 21–31.
33. Paul Henderson, 'Class structure and the concept of intelligence' in Dale *et al.*, op. cit., p. 147.
34. Ibid., pp. 147–8.
35. See Karier, op. cit.
36. Eysenck and Nias, op. cit., p. 152.
37. Given Eysenck's commitment to the view that approximately 80 per cent of human personality and intelligence is genetically determined, very little room is left for television to exert its influence!
38. Alice Heim, *Intelligence and Personality*, Harmondsworth, Penguin, 1970.
39. Ibid., p. 89.
40. Eysenck and Nias, op. cit., p. 43.
41. In the capacity of an observer of those involved in recording the behaviour of young children at play on a rating scale for 'social adjustment', I was impressed by the way in which more or less identical behaviour was consistently judged radically different behaviour. What for black children was recorded as 'impulsiveness', was strongly recorded as 'creative self-expression' for selected white children. As early as 1936, for example, Canady found that black children scored higher on intelligence tests when the test was administered by a black, rather than a white, person: H.G. Canady, 'The effect of "Rapport" on the I.Q.: a new approach to the problem of racial psychology', *Journal of Negro Studies*, 1936, pp. 208–19.
42. Eysenck and Nias, op. cit., p. 151.
43. See, for example, A.G. Miller, *The Social Psychology of Psychological Research*, London, Collier-Macmillan, 1972.
44. Joynson, op. cit., p. 63.
45. Eysenck and Nias, op. cit., p. 203. Here their target is psychoanalysis.
46. James Curran, Michael Gurevitch and Janet Woollacott, 'The study of the media: theoretical approaches' in Michael Gurevitch, Tony Bennett, James Curran and Janet Woollacott, eds, *Culture, Society and the Media*, London, Methuen, 1982, pp. 11–29.
47. Fejes, op. cit., pp. 219–232.
48. Jay G. Blumler and Michael Gurevitch, 'The political effects of mass communication', in Gurevitch *et al.*, op. cit., p. 261.
49. Ibid.
50. Jay G. Blumler, 'Purposes of Mass Communications Research' in G. Cleveland Wilhoit and Harold de Bock, eds, *Mass Communication Review Yearbook*, *Vol. 1, 1980*, London, Sage, 1980, pp. 33–44.

51. McQuail, op. cit., pp. 67–70.
52. Ibid., pp. 69–70.
53. Ibid., p. 70.
54. Stuart Hall, 'The rediscovery of "ideology": return of the repressed in media studies' in Gurevitch *et al.*, op. cit., pp. 56–90.
55. Ibid., p. 59.
56. Ibid.
57. Blumler and Gurevitch, op. cit., p. 261.
58. For an informed discussion see Jay G. Blumler, 'The Role of Theory in Uses and Gratifications Studies' in Wilhoit and de Bock, op. cit., pp. 201–28.
59. See, for example, Jay G. Blumler and Denis McQuail, *Television in Politics*, London, Faber, 1968.
60. See Fejes, op. cit., pp. 219–32.
61. For a comprehensive and critical coverage, see Jorge Larrain, *The Concept of Ideology*, London, Hutchinson, 1979, and Jorge Larrain, *Marxism and Ideology*, London, Macmillan, 1983.
62. Peter Golding, 'The Missing Dimensions—News Media and the Management of Social Change' in Elihu Katz and Tamas Szecskö, eds, *Mass Media and Social Change*, London, Sage, 1981, p. 63.
63. Hall, op. cit., p. 87.
64. Ibid., p. 65.
65. Janet Woollacott, 'Messages and meanings' in Gurevitch *et al.*, op. cit., p. 110.
66. Curran, Gurevitch and Woollacott, op. cit., p. 27.
67. Ibid.
68. Bob Jessop, Kevin Bonnett, Simon Bromley and Tom Ling, 'Thatcherism and the Politics of Hegemony: a Reply to Stuart Hall', *New Left Review*, vol. 153, 1985, pp. 87–101.
69. Graham Murdock and Peter Golding, 'Capitalism, Communication and Class Relations' in James Curran, Michael Gurevitch and Janet Woollacott, eds, *Mass Communication and Society*, London, Arnold, 1977, p. 13.
70. Ibid.
71. Peter Golding and Graham Murdock, 'Theories of Communication and Theories of Society', in Wilhoit and de Bock, op. cit., p. 72.
72. See for example, James Curran, 'The impact of advertising on the British mass media', *Media, Culture and Society*, vol. 3, 1981, pp. 43–69.
73. See in particular, Franz Dröge, 'Social knowledge and the mediation of knowledge in bourgeois society', *Media, Culture and Society*, vol. 5, 1983, pp. 49–63. Horst Holzer, 'The "use-value" of social communication and the media in West German capitalism', *Media, Culture and Society*, vol. 5, 1983, pp. 89–100. Wulf D. Hund, 'Modes and levels of consciousness', *Media, Culture and Society*, vol. 5, 1983, pp. 75–81. Oskar Negt and Alexander Kluge, 'The context of life as object of production of the media

conglomerate', *Media, Culture and Society*, vol. 5, 1983, pp. 65–74.

74. Peter Golding and Graham Murdock, 'Ideology and the Mass Media: the Question of Determination' in Michele Barrett, Philip Corrigan, Annette Kuhn and Janet Wolff, *Ideology and Cultural Production*, London: Croom Helm, 1979, p. 210.

75. Ibid.

76. Nicholas Garnham, 'Contribution to a political economy of mass-communication', *Media, Culture and Society*, vol. 1, 1979, pp. 123–46.

77. Golding and Murdock, 'Ideology and the Mass Media', p. 210.

78. For an accessible introduction, see Terence Hawkes, *Structuralism and Semiotics*, London, Methuen, 1977.

79. See, for example, Ernesto Laclau and Chantal Mouffe, *Hegemony and Socialist Strategy*, London, New Left Books, 1982.

80. See, for example, Kevin Robins, 'Althusserian Marxism and media studies: the case of *Screen*', *Media, Culture and Society*, vol. 1, 1979, pp. 355–70. For a similar conclusion, see Cliff Slaughter, *Marxism, Ideology and Literature*, London, Macmillan, 1980, especially pp. 200–13.

81. I have argued this at length in Conrad Lodziak, 'The Ideology of the Ideological Deconstruction of Media Products', *Power and Communication*, Nottingham, Trent Papers in Communication, vol. 1, 1983, pp. 4–58.

82. Joseph T. Klapper, *The Effects of Mass Communication*, New York, Free Press, 1960.

83. See, for example, Blumler and Gurevitch, op. cit., especially pp. 260–3.

84. See, for example, Charlotte Brunsdon and David Morley, *The Nationwide Audience*, London, British Film Institute, 1978, Monograph 10; David Morley, *The Nationwide Audience*, London, BFI, 1980, Monograph 11.

2 Ideological Readings of Television

It is true to say that the ideological character of the mass media has been the dominant concern in critical media theory over the past decade. Basically, it is widely believed that television's power is rooted in the social significance of the ideological service it provides for dominant groups. This thesis involves three related aspects which can be summarised as follows:

1. Television is ideological in that its messages are generally supportive of the interests of dominant groups.
2. Television's output is to some extent ideologically effective.
3. Ideology is necessary for the reproduction of capitalist societies, thus television participates, through its ideological effects, in reproducing structures of domination in capitalist societies.

There are, I shall suggest, two major versions of this thesis—a strong version and a weak version. The stronger thesis claims a greater ideological effectiveness for television than the weaker thesis, and gives a greater emphasis to the role of ideology in social reproduction. Both versions of this thesis, however, accept that television programmes, for the most part, are shaped by and reflect ideologies which serve the interests of dominant groups. This view is non-controversial in critical media theory. A host of studies have substantiated this claim. Whether the object of analysis is television drama and entertainment, advertising, or news and current affairs, the message from these studies is rather clear: television produces and reproduces a dominant ideology.

Having said this, it must be emphasised that the production and reproduction of a dominant ideology in televisual discourses occurs *for the most part*. In other words, critical media theorists acknowledge that particular programmes may contest the dominant ideology, and that spaces for contestation may exist within programmes which are framed by a dominant ideology. In their analysis of how British television represents 'terrorism', Elliott, Murdock and Schlesinger distinguish 'official' from 'alternative' and 'oppositional' discourses.[1] Official discourses reflect a dominant ideology. Alternative discourses 'do not offer a fundamental challenge to the claims to legitimacy found in the official discourse. Instead they develop piecemeal challenge...'[2] Indeed, as we shall see later, most conceptions of the dominant ideology allow for that kind of flexibility which enables a range of alternative meanings to be incorporated within it. So, when it is claimed that television, for the most part, produces and reproduces a dominant ideology, it is understood that the dominant ideology itself embodies some ambiguity. However, there is considerable disagreement amongst critical media theorists as to what is meant by 'dominant ideology', whose interests are served by it, and what those interests are. There are, too, ideological analyses of television which proceed without a conception of 'dominant ideology' or an equivalent notion, for example, 'official discourse', or 'preferred reading'. Thus Feuer, for example, refers to 'the ideology of live television', but it is not clear that this ideology serves the interests of any particular group.[3] Similarly, much that passes for 'ideological analysis' in structuralist-semiotic approaches is merely an exercise in uncovering the multiple meanings available in a television programme.

I shall restrict my attention to those studies in which the concept of ideology is closely connected to the interests of dominant groups, in ways which serve to legitimate class, gender and racial domination. The Elliott *et al.* study adopts such a concept in focusing on the relation between televisual discourses on terrorism and ruling-class interests. However, what is particularly useful about this study is that in comparing news, current affairs, documentaries, fictional series, serials and single plays, they are able to make observations about the extent to which ideological closure operates variously throughout these types of programme. Their analysis of fictional forms was limited to a small number of programmes, making generalisations difficult. Nevertheless, some of the conclusions arrived at are in basic agreement with those of other studies. Thus while television fiction allows 'for a range of representations which are largely excluded from actuality programming',[4] popular prime-time fictional forms 'are still subject to a number of pressures and constraints stemming from the forms and genres they employ and from their position within the domestic and international market'.[5] Action-adventure series which are essentially self-contained episodes, focused around the heroic exploits of one or two leading characters common to all episodes, tend to operate firmly within the official discourse. Elliott *et al.* note that 'the upholders of order and the agents of disruption are always unequally represented. We know a good deal about the heroes...but we usually know next to nothing about the villains...they remain drastically undercharacterised, and the action is presented almost exclusively from the heroes' point of view'.[6] These limitations, which make for considerable ideological closure, can be overcome in the popular serial with its 'more relaxed narrative pace'. But Elliott *et al.* consider that the least closed fictional representations of terrorism are most likely to be found outside prime-time viewing and in the less popular form of the single play.

Unlike series and serials, television plays are not in the front line of the battle for audiences or programme exports and so they are not under the same pressure to work with the most prevalent ideological themes or to deliver predictable pleasures to the largest possible number of viewers. On the contrary, the producers of single plays are expected to fulfil the role of 'authors' and to express their own particular viewpoints...[7]

The single play offers scope for the representation of oppositional sentiments, but 'this potential for provocation is not always fully realized of course'.[8] Elliott *et al.* quite rightly point out that 'plays on sensitive issues (such as the situation in Northern Ireland) are subject to political pressures from inside and outside the broadcasting organizations, and cuts and cancellations are therefore a permanent possibility'.[9] They discuss an anti-American imperialism *Pilger Report* as an example of a documentary which atypically uses the licence of authorship to the full. Far less provocative documentaries on the situation in the six northern counties of Ireland have either been banned or heavily censored. This suggests that constraints on programming, and thus on ideological content, are likely to vary in relation to the 'proximity' in time and space of the issue at stake. Thus the American Broadcasting Corporation was able to broadcast a documentary in 1980, entitled *To Die for Ireland*, which began as follows:

For centuries all of Ireland was ruled by Great Britain until the Irish Republican Army took up guns in 1916 to seek independence. To end the bloodshed Britain divided; into a free, largely Catholic republic to the south, and a Protestant dominated British province to the north.

As a result of the division, the Catholics in Northern Ireland became a minority denied equal status in jobs, housing and government.[10]

Philo, Hewitt, Beharrell and Davis observe that this programme 'could simply not be shown in Britain—in fact the British government even protested about it being shown in America'.[11]

The fictional form not discussed by Elliott *et al.*, the soap opera, offers considerable scope for ideological play. Indeed, Lovell applauds the way in which *Coronation Street* makes use of this flexibility. She goes as far as to argue that the 'utopian and oppositional elements of popular culture— those elements which express the hopes, fears, wishes and simple refusals of the dominated—are *not* marginal but defining elements which are essential to the whole meaning and appeal of popular entertainment'.[12] What she applauds, however, others would see as nothing less than the dominant ideology at work, legitimating entrenched structures of women's subordination.

Coronation Street offers its women viewers certain 'structures of feeling' which are prevalent in our society, and which are only partially recognised in the normative patriarchal order. It offers women a validation and celebration of those interests and concerns which are seen as properly theirs within the social world they inhabit. Soap opera may be the opium of masses of women, but like religion, it may also be...a context in which women can ambiguously express *both* good-humoured acceptance of their oppression *and* recognition of that oppression, and some equally good-humoured protest against it.[13]

Lovell does admit that 'this kind of representation presents no particular difficulties in terms of the dominant ideology'.[14] She thus emphasises the scope of soap operas to 'stretch' the dominant ideology. A more common view is that represented by Brunsdon in her analysis of *Crossroads*. She argues that '*Crossroads* textually implies a feminine viewer to the extent that its textual discontinuities, in order to make sense, require a viewer competent within the ideological and moral frameworks (the rules) of romance, marriage and family life'.[15] In a similar vein, Flitterman examines the advertisements during daytime soap operas in the United States. She notes that 'a plethora of household items, defining and delimiting the role of good mother, wife and homemaker, predominate in soap opera advertising'.[16] Significantly, the copyright for many soaps is held by the world's largest television advertiser, Procter and Gamble.

Little wonder, then, that American daytime audiences are treated to approximately six advertising slots of two minutes' duration per hour.

There is a never-ending amount of ideologically relevant comment which can be made about the whole range of television entertainment, advertising and children's programmes. Without being exhaustive, I shall provide a sample of such comment in itemised form.

1.   Some adverts treat women as 'fragments of flesh', and promote male-constructed images of the female.
2.   Adverts suggest that individual happiness is closely aligned with the acquisition of unnecessary goods.
3.   Almost all television entertainment reproduces stereotypes which may be damaging to the self-images of individuals belonging to certain groups, particularly women, non-whites, certain nationalities, gays, and so on.
4.   The highest forms of human achievement are closely linked with technological progress.
5.   The competitive ethic looms large.
6.   Very little attention is given to the sources of major forms of domination, imperialism, class and gender domination. Rather issues and problems arising from these basic social contradictions are invariably translated into individual psychological problems, or interpersonal conflicts.
7.   A dominant moral framework identifies 'goodness' as, amongst other things, pro-Western/anti-communist, makes an idol of law and order, celebrates heterosexism, and criminalises deviance.
8.   Fictional heroes are invariably male, white, macho and the personification of traditional moral values. The action orientation undervalues the quiet, reflective manifestations of human intelligence.
9.   The rare representation, in television entertainment, given to oppositional viewpoints fosters the illusion that television is the embodiment of free speech.

This 'sample of ideological comment' offers examples of the more obvious and relatively non-controversial ways in which television entertainment can be said not to be ideologically neutral. One of the tasks ahead is to show ideological analyses of television can reveal the not so obvious. In pursuit of the not so obvious there is the danger that the analysis may read things into a television programme which 'are not there'. This raises a rather awkward problem. The analysis may be valid, but not received as such. In other words it may be received as 'far-fetched' not because it is 'far-fetched', but because we are unable to see or appreciate what it is that the analyst is getting at. On the other hand the analysis may be ill-founded, and thus actually far-fetched. The following analysis, for example, is based on a particular interpretation of Freudian theory. Whether or not we accept Winship's analysis of the Guinness advert as valid or far-fetched depends very much upon our knowledge of, and assessment of, Freudian theory, and whether or not her application of Freudian theory is appropriate in this particular case.

The ad depends on our knowledge that women do not usually drink Guinness—they are 'ladylike' (and castrated): it depends on the *difference* between women's 'lack' and men's plenitude—the full glass of Guinness. However, that difference is *disavowed* in the condensation of 'ladylike—Guinness': women can and do drink Guinness but remain 'ladylike'. But the future pouring of the commodity Guinness between the as-yet-closed lips—the as-yet-'ladylike' lips—is also a metaphor for the sexual act: man's penetration of the lips, the vagina, which provides affirmation of women's 'castration'. We are dared to drink Guinness, but our daring, after the grounds of 'feminity' have slightly shifted, continues to place us firmly within the conventional bounds of patriarchal relations.[17]

I shall say more about this kind of analysis in Chapter 4. For the moment it will be possible to engage with forms of ideological analysis which seek the not so obvious and yet which remain within the orbit of credibility.

Even though the Elliott *et al.* study, cited earlier, made a number of credible and pertinent observations on ideological aspects of television entertainment, the question has been raised as to whether or not it is appropriate to treat 'entertainment' with the kind of seriousness which an ideological analysis suggests. While there are good reasons to suppose that viewing preferences do not reflect ideological motivations, there are even better reasons to suppose that 'ideologies work' most effectively when our guards are lowered. Television critics may be justified in, for example, a belief that limitations on opportunities create stereotypes and stereotypes limit opportunities in the real world, in pointing to the strong tendency of television fiction to show non-whites, for example, almost exclusively in subordinate positions. Television companies may argue that fictional forms should not be subject to these kinds of considerations, and that television can hardly be held responsible for correcting social inequalities through the production of entertainment.

The relation of television to the real world, however, is a central consideration in news and current affairs production. Indeed, news broadcasters are 'legally bound' to provide objective, truthful and impartial representations of events in the real world. That this is so, and vigorously defended by television news professionals as being so, constitutes an essential condition for the potential ideological potency of news presentations. Needless to say, television news has been subjected to more ideological analysis than any other televisual form.

Television news and ideology

With people becoming increasingly dependent on television as a source of news, and increasingly perceiving television to be a more reliable news source than newspapers, it is important to discuss those claims which depict television news reporting as ideological. To critical media theorists, much of the discussion which follows will appear redundant. It is, after all, as Collins points out, well established that 'information in television news output' is '*produced*; selected, organized, structured and (necessarily) "biased"'.[18] Collins cites the Langs' study of the Chicago MacArthur day television presentation,[19] work by Cohen and Young,[20] the Glasgow University Media Group,[21] Baggaley and Duck,[22] and Schlesinger,[23] as establishing the bias of television news. Since these studies, Collins observes, quite correctly, that the central question occupying media theorists is that concerning the *source* of the bias. If, for example, the power of television is thought of primarily as an ideological power, and further, if it is claimed that it is television journalists who are primarily responsible for producing ideologically distorted news, then presumably, in order to remove this distortion, all we need do is to train our journalists to be non-ideological.

Obviously things are not as simple and straightforward as this. Golding and Elliott,[24] and Schlesinger,[25] have, on the basis of detailed observations of the news-production processes, made it clear that journalists have very little room for manoeuvre. In fact most media theorists are agreed that 'shop-floor' journalists are not to be blamed for ideologically distorted news presentations. The spaces occupied by journalists are already defined by editorial policies, reflecting an ideological stance in relation to the economic and time constraints involved in news production, and in relation to the state, particularly to the government of the day. The news we are presented with could certainly be other than it is. But for radically different forms of news presentations to be in evidence, it would be necessary for radical changes to occur in the underlying economic relations within which editorial policies are formulated, and for these changes to be co-ordinated with compatible changes in state practices.

Perhaps Collins is correct in stating that 'we will not arrive at a theory of the state and television news, capitalism and television news or the autonomy of television news because the reality we are dealing with is constantly in movement'.[26] However, that reality 'is constantly in movement' within the 'logic' of capitalism. While it can be agreed that 'determination operates differentially',[27] Collins makes far too much of the proposal 'that the relations between news producers and the (notionally) determining forces of state and capital are relationships of *bargaining*, the essence of a bargain being that the parties to it resolve the contradictions between their shared and antagonistic interests'.[28] The space for bargaining is already delimited by capital and the state. Further it is generally the case that 'antagonistic interests' share the same ideological framework, and resolve antagonisms within this framework.

No doubt media theorists will continue to advance theories in their attempts to specify the sources of ideological bias in news presentations. What concerns us more here is the systematic nature of this ideological bias, and the more specific ways in which it can be said that television news reflects a dominant ideology.

Most critical media theorists employ a dual concept of the dominant ideology. On the one hand it refers to the ideas and values of dominant groups, and on the other to ideas and values which serve the interests of dominant groups. To the extent that television news production is closely bound up with 'elites' or dominant groups, television news does convey the dominant ideology in the former sense. These expressions of the dominant ideology are explicit and open to contestation from the audience and from fractions of elites. Less easily contested, because of their silence or invisible presence, are those underlying, taken-for-granted elements of the dominant ideology which structure the whole ideological field. It is these elements which best serve the interests of dominant groups. It is not necessary for the moment specifically to define what the interests of dominant groups are. This is a particularly difficult task, not least because there is a certain fragmentation of interests amongst dominant groups. However, as Giddens has pointed out,

> there is one sectional interest, or 'arena of sectional interests', of dominant groups which is peculiarly universal: an interest in maintaining the existing order of domination, or major features of it, since such an order of domination *ipso facto* involves an asymmetrical distribution of resources that can be drawn upon to satisfy wants.[29]

In effect this points us toward identifying elements of a dominant ideology in the representation of ideas and values which protect or legitimate the existing order of domination, and towards identifying ways in which television news fails to represent or misrepresents those ideas and values which could pose an ideological threat to dominant groups.

Given that not all that goes on in the world can be reported, there must be available some means whereby consistent selections from the totality of events can be made. As we shall see, those events about which most information is available to news teams, and the means whereby this information is quickly assessed for its newsworthiness, constitute two sites where ideological distortions operate in the interests of dominant groups.

Ideological aspects of news values

The dependence of news-production teams on news agencies, especially for foreign news, is a dependence on news which has already been selected for them. In their empirical observations of news-production practices, Golding and Elliott note that 'Swedish and Nigerian journalists were concerned, in different ways, at pro-Western bias in the wire agencies, particularly the American agencies'.[30] They go on to mention that Reuters, the British-based agency, widely considered to be the most reliable source of news, 'was regarded with suspicion and it was a house rule at NBC (Nigerian Broadcasting Corporation) that no Reuters stories about Nigeria were to be used'.[31] They are clearly making a reference to Reuters when they refer to 'lingering British imperial undertones'.[32]

The mass of already pre-selected information available to news teams has to undergo further selection procedures on account of the limited time available for news presentations. The very rule-of-thumb routines, whereby available information is transformed into news, invariably involves ideological distortions. The 'news values' proposed by Galtung and Ruge in their pioneering study of the structure of foreign news can be briefly considered in this context.[33] Building upon an earlier study by Östgaard, Galtung and Ruge hypothesised a number of conditions which potential news items generally satisfy prior to becoming actual news.

1. *Frequency.* The frequency of an event refers to 'the time-span needed for the event to unfold itself and acquire meaning'.[34] This is an important source of the ahistorical nature of news reporting. Without the provision of historical background to news stories, the activities of the IRA and other freedom fighters, for example, are largely unintelligible. In his study of BBC news, Schlesinger notes that 'the waiving of impartiality in Northern Ireland coverage...has involved defining some views as illegitimate, which, coupled with an ahistorical approach concentrating on violence, has made much reporting from Ireland largely incomprehensible'.[35] Indeed any group engaged in the long, slow process of historical struggles, cannot find anywhere near an adequate representation in news. The ahistorical nature of news, as we shall see later, refers not only to the lack of representation of 'the long march of history', but also to the disappearance of history on a much shorter time-scale, within an ongoing news item.

2. *Amplitude.* This refers to the 'size' of an event—'there is a threshold the event will have to pass before it will be recorded at all'.[36]

3. *Unambiguity.* 'An event with a clear intepretation, free from ambiguities in its meaning, is preferred to the highly ambiguous event from which many inconsistent implications can and will be made'.[37]

4. *Meaningfulness.* A meaningful event is one which lends itself readily to interpretation 'within the cultural framework of the listener'.[38]

5. *Consonance.* Events or news stories which are consonant with audience expectations are preferred for inclusion in news presentations.

6. *Unexpectedness.* This hypothesis is not a contradiction of the consonance value. It refers to unexpected events 'within the meaningful and the consonant'.[39]

7.   *Continuity*. This refers to following up news items.
8.   *Composition*. An item may become news in order to effect a balance to the total news broadcast, as in balancing coverage between foreign and home news, or serious and light news, for example.

A tremendous amount of ideological play, both in terms of *what* becomes news, and in terms of *how* news is presented, is clearly possible in enacting the values of unambiguity, meaningfulness and consonance. Events which are deemed to be unambiguous and meaningful tend to be those which lend themselves to short and simplistic transformations. Here, perceptions of the audience in conjunction with professional techniques which are well oiled in the art of simplifying and trivialising complex events, intervene directly in what is to be selected as a news item. In other words, anticipating how an event can be presented determines whether or not certain events will get reported. Since events are made meaningful within dominant frameworks of meaning, and since, as we shall see, these frameworks embody entrenched elements of a dominant ideology, we can see that unambiguous, meaningful and consonant events already reflect an ideological selection, prior to the further ideological work involved in their presentation.

Galtung and Ruge go on to hypothesise four further news values which they consider important within the Western media.

9.   *Elite-centred*. 'The more the event concerns elite nations, the more probable that it will become a news item'.[40]
10. *Elite-people*. Similarly events involving elite people are more likely to be reported.
11. *Personification*. 'The more the event can be seen in personal terms, as due to the actions of specific individuals, the more probable that it will become a news item'.[41]
12. *Negativity*. 'The more negative the event in its consequences, the more probable that it will become a news item'.[42]

The two news values concerning elite nations and elite persons, in conjunction with personification, lead to some of the more common forms of ideological distortion. News stories of events of considerable complexity are invariably structured through personification, leading to gross simplifications, misrepresentations, and significant absences in what is reported. Significant absences arise, for example, when industrial disputes are presented as personality conflicts between a union leader and an industrial chief, or when the prospects for ridding the world of nuclear weapons hinges on the idiosyncracies of elite personalities. Western news media present what Sennett calls a 'psychomorphic view of society, one in which questions of class, race and history are all abolished in favour of explanations which turn on the character and motivation of participants in society'.[43]

The most significant of all absences from news stories is an understanding of social power. Concentrated attention on the occupants of powerful positions displaces attention from the fact that power is rooted in positions. The concentration of news presentations on elite political figures, as Golding notes, means that 'power is reduced to areas of negotiable compromise, and politics to a recurrent series of decisions, debates and personalities'.[44] Power is represented in such a way that 'it is removed from the institutions of production; thus news bears witness to the institutional separation of economics and politics, a precondition for the evacuation of power from its account of the world'.[45] In this way television news co-ordinates rather neatly with the interests of big business. The exploitive processes through which the ownership of economic resources is deployed for the maximisation of profits, and which as a consequence produce the social context in which we live, remain unreported. Instead, news reports divert attention to 'the public display of formality, gesture and speech by major political actors'.[46]

News and current affairs presentations are largely about elites. Elites are, of course, members of dominant groups whose practices shape events in the real world. There is, through the interaction of elites and television news production, a strong tendency for the views of dominant groups both to 'frame' and to predominate in news and current affairs presentations. More than this, the presentation of conflicts and disputes amongst elite political figures, as for example during elections, in promoting the idea that television presents a balanced picture of disputes, conceals the common ground which elites occupy. In the example of elections, the whole system of parliamentary democracy is the common ground. In most industrial disputes the common ground is, for example, the acceptance of the divisions between capital and labour, employer and employee, or manager and worker. The common ground is the 'ideological field', as Hall puts it. Some of the most significant absences in television news presentations (and current affairs) are those which fail to address the ideological field, and this failure serves the interests of dominant groups in that the structures through which they maintain their domination receive no challenge. As Westergaard observes, the media 'focuses on diversity of debate, critique and contest within set parameters, but is indifferent to the existence and social shape of those parameters'.[47]

News values, according to Westergaard,

make broadcast news, very largely, an inevitably selective transmission of information about events and incidents accompanied only by interpretations consonant with conventional wisdom; or, with equal significance, by no interpretation, so that conventional interpretation stands by sheer default of any alternative.[48]

It has been widely noted that not only is it extremely difficult for non-elite groups challenging the ideological field to gain access to television news, but when access is achieved, the representation of these groups is, for the most part, seriously inadequate. Thompson argues that 'dissent is scarcely communicated at all. It can never gain access to the media for long enough to present a sustained and coherent image'.[49] Nor is it likely that a coherent image of dissent can be presented, since television news reproduces 'the sheer inertia of understandings of the world of affairs circumscribed by the horizons of those who run affairs'.[50]

There is a partial recognition amongst television professionals that the kinds of constraint to which news production is subjected may lead to significant absences in news bulletins which can be remedied in current affairs programmes. Yet, with a few notable exceptions, most current affairs programmes merely skim the surface, and are similarly circumscribed by the underlying ideological field. Typical of current affairs programmes was the presentation of the Union Carbide disaster in India in 1984. The disaster was portrayed in terms of managerial negligence with no attempt to probe the underlying logic of the practices of multinational corporations. Third World poverty and social inequalities in the advanced capitalist societies are rarely probed far enough to condemn the capitalist system. Indeed what Goban-Klas says of the Western press applies generally to television news and current affairs presentations. There is, he believes,

hostility towards all ideologies of equality, especially those proclaiming the principles of national independence and revolution;

hostility towards the ideology of nationalization and thus towards all economic actions leading to expropriation of great supranational corporations;

hostility towards the ideologies of collectivism and thus towards the policy aiming at securing the interests of the whole society of a given country.[51]

News value, and 'current affairs values',[52] I have argued, produce ideological consequences favourable to the interests of dominant groups. As Golding notes, 'broadcast news is, for historical and organizational reasons, inherently incapable of providing a portrayal of social change, or of displaying the operation of power in and between societies'.[53] This in itself, in its *absence*, is constitutive of a dominant meaning framework, which is also enacted in how news is presented as meaningful, and in focusing 'our attention on those institutions and events in which social conflict is managed and resolved'.[54]

One key, then, to a critical ideological reading of television news and current affairs presentations, is to seek out *the significant absences*, that is, to seek out *what does not get reported*. These significant absences arise from the reproduction of the dominant ideological field, which, as we shall see below, is more or less continuously reproduced in *how* television presents news and current affairs.

The dominant ideology in television news and current affairs

In a detailed analysis of a *Panorama* programme just prior to the British General Election of October 1974, Hall, Connell and Curti argue that television's definition of, and procedures for achieving, objectivity, neutrality, impartiality and balance provides 'a "relatively independent" and neutral sphere' in that no particular bias in favour of any one political party is displayed. Rather, occupancy of this neutral site enables the media to reproduce 'the *whole* terrain of State power,—the underlying idea of the general interest'. This is, they point out, 'the most significant part of the ideological field which the media reproduce'. It involves television in reproducing '*selectively* not the "unity" of any one Party, but *the unity of the Parliamentary political system as a whole*'.[55]

In this way television and the media in general reproduce the appearance of the neutrality of the state. This is of considerable ideological importance in that the 'State is required as a neutral and objective sphere, precisely in order that the long-term interests of capital can be "represented" as a general interest'.[56]

Hall argues that the media help to maintain the hegemony of the state by drawing upon

a very limited ideological or explanatory repertoire; and that repertoire (though in each case it requires ideological 'work' to bring new events within its horizon) will have the overall tendency of making things 'mean' within the sphere of the dominant ideology.[57]

The dominant ideology, according to Hall, is produced over time, is drawn upon to represent events, and elements within it can be redrawn with new elements in order to provide ideological shifts within the dominant framework itself. Much of Hall's work attempts to chart contemporary ideological shifts in what is taken for granted. The media in conjunction with politicians can help to advance the hegemonic projects of a dominant political party. Hall analyses how, by signifying events in line with this project, the media contributes toward the creation of a new 'common sense'.[58] The idea of 'ideological shifts' captures the fact that ideological reproduction is never an exact reproduction. In time, these shifts can add up to substantial changes in the dominant ideology itself, as Williams has recorded.[59]

We have already noted that it is taken for granted by critical media theorists that events do get recurrently signified in ways which serve the interests of dominant groups, and we have seen how news values can contribute to this. But news values or 'the professional code', Hall maintains, 'operates *within* the "hegemony" of the dominant code', even though it is '"relatively independent" of the dominant code, in that it applies criteria and transformational operations of its own'. The dominant code generates dominant definitions of events, and these definitions 'are hegemonic precisely because they represent definitions of situations and events which are "in dominance"'.[60]

To make events meaningful, news and current affairs presentations 'encode' messages within 'preferred' codes. As I noted earlier, perceptions of audience enter into the selection of codes. As Hall observes, the selection of a preferred code is a selection which appears 'to embody the "natural" explanations which most members of the society would accept...[and] casts...problematic events, consensually, somewhere within the *repertoire* of the dominant ideologies'.[61] The 'natural' explanations, which reflect taken-for-granted assumptions, appear (mostly, but not always) in two interconnected forms in televisual discourses. First, television encodes its messages in verbal discourse, but significantly its second form, its visual character, grounds 'its discourse in "the real"—in the evidence of one's eyes'. It thus produces 'nature as a sort of guarantee of its truth'.[62] The verbal and visual discourses, then, work together— the visual confirming the verbal in all its ideological glory.

Sometimes, of course, the verbal and the visual are uncoordinated, as when the 'reality effect' of the visual contradicts the dominant ideology of the verbal discourses. In these circumstances the limits of the range of meanings which can be produced within the dominant ideology are exposed. In late 1984, British television-news teams were anticipating the release of British citizens who had been retained in Libya. Libya had long since been established, through preferred codes, as a 'dictatorship' under the 'unpredictable' Colonel Qadhafi, who was also cast as an eccentric bordering on lunacy. This 'preferred reading' of the Libyan political system, consistent with the negative portrayals of alternatives to our own system, is unable to make meaningful the Libyan experiment with 'direct democracy'. Eventually the television-news cameras were informing us that the lengthy public debates (peoples' congresses), which are central to the democratic process in Libya, were responsible for delaying the return of the British citizens. What viewers were being shown was a direct contradiction of the verbal discourses which were faithfully adhering to the ideological play of the elements: Qadhafi— dictator—unpredictable—lunatic.

Interestingly, this example illustrates how our own ideological under- standing of 'democracy' has become shaped through dominant discourses which have privileged the identification of 'democracy' with 'parliamentary representation' and 'voting' in a system which involves only a basic minimum of participation from the represented. Thus the dominant ideology gives rise not only to preferred readings of events, but these preferred readings become reinforced by the persistent exclusion of explanations of events which fall outside the range of readings avail- able through the dominant codes. Through the dominant ideology, elements are put together to signify events in particular ways, but in so doing it makes it extremely difficult for the elements thus used to be articulated with viewpoints oppositional to dominant interests. Hall refers to the way in which 'freedom' has been articulated and historically established with 'the liberty of the individual, with the "free" market and liberal political values' and disarticulated from 'the "freedom" of the worker to withdraw his labour or the "freedom" of the "freedom-fighter"'. He goes on to note that 'these traditional couplings, or "traces" as Gramsci called them, exert a powerful traditional force over the ways in which subsequent discourses, employing the same elements, can be developed'.[63] Support for this view is to be found in the analysis of 'keywords' made by Williams. He describes the transformation of meaning which a number of ideologically relevant words have undergone over time.[64]

'Established' discourses, too, are drawn upon to structure both news and current affairs presentations as a whole. We rarely, if ever, see interviewers fielding questions to politicians from a position clearly reflecting a socialist consciousness. Rather the base of the whole ideological field is reproduced, and specific elements within it are privileged. As Hall reasons,

When in phrasing a question, in the era of monetarism, a broadcasting interviewer simply takes it for a granted that rising wage demands are the sole cause of inflation, he is both "freely" formulating a question on behalf of the public and establishing a logic which is compatible with the dominant interests in society.[65]

One of the strengths of Hall's work, and what sets it apart from more structuralist-semiological approaches to news and current affairs analyses, is that he always conducts ideological readings of television in a way which gives due weight to the relative role of signifying agents in the 'real' world, on the one hand, and in the media, on the other. He acknowledges that the relationship between what goes on in the real world and how it is represented is not a consistent one. There are instances and periods when television and the mass media play a more primary role in the signification of events, and thus a more active role in generating ideological shifts and establishing dominant discourses. An interesting example which illustrates the active media exercising their relative autonomy to the full is that provided by Cohen's treatment of how the media 'blew-up' out of all proportions a number of violent skirmishes involving rival factions of British youth in the early 1960s.[66] Cohen argues that this media amplification had helped to generate a 'moral panic', which, in turn, was given further excessive media attention. Not only had the media amplified events in the real world, but through a 'spiral of signification' connected their amplification to a whole range of concerns which, Hall *et al*. suggest, were 'stitched together' within a 'law and order' discourse.[67] The spiral of signification extended the moral panic. The latter came to embrace concern over drug abuse, teenage sex, lack of parental authority, indiscipline in schools, the decline of educational standards, mugging, abuse of the welfare system, and so on, and was further broadened out to cast its net over student protests and militant trade-union activity. This was the fodder for the progressive establishment of the law and order discourse convenient for the political interests of the Right.

It would be misleading to suggest that television is more or less continuously involved in amplifying events, but we should nevertheless be alerted to this possibility. But as we become increasingly dependent on television for information on matters beyond our direct experience, media amplification is not always easy to identify. We are in a far better position to comment on the reality–media relation when the media represent those events in which we are experientially involved. In this respect it is useful to consider briefly the representation of industrial disputes as one form of social conflict common to Western societies. The experience of those involved in such conflicts can be drawn upon as a 'reality base' against which we can assess the ideological nature of television's representations.

Television's presentation of industrial disputes

If television, as critical media theorists maintain, performs an ideological service for dominant groups, then one might expect this service to be particularly vigorous when the interests of dominant groups are under threat. Industrial disputes invariably pose a threat to employers and managers. This threat may be localised and relatively isolated, or, depending on the industries involved, it may extend to the capitalist class as a whole. The detailed studies of television's presentation of industrial disputes conducted by the Glasgow Media Group suggest that television assumes a more active role in its coverage, when disputes are prolonged, when they involve 'key' industries, for example, energy, transport, communications—thereby disrupting industrial life in general—and when the conflict is around issues other than or in addition to pay levels.[68] What will be of particular interest here is how it is that television is able to provide an active ideological service for capitalist class interests and yet, at the same time, is able to claim that its presentation of industrial disputes is 'impartial'.

It is widely noted that the privileged access to television enjoyed by industrial owners, high-level managers and members of government enables these elite persons to exercise an undue influence on the presentation of industrial disputes. The information provided by these groups, for example, is invariably treated as 'official', whereas trade-union sources of information tend to be considered suspect in some way. More than this, however, elite persons are the agents of the established discourses of the dominant ideology through which their own interests are projected as universal, and through which opposition to their interests is thus articulated as being against the 'common good'. The articulation of a negative stance toward industrial disputes as the appropriate expression of the interests of the capitalist class keys in very neatly with the news value of major industrial disputes—their 'negativity' (see p. 47). Given that news and current affairs values operate within the dominant ideology, the presentation of industrial disputes is already favourably disposed toward the representation of these disputes advanced by elite persons. One of the most frequently made comments about television's presentation of industrial disputes, amongst other matters, is that television professionals in conjunction with elite persons, through sharing the established discourses of the dominant ideology, focus on a limited range of issues to the relative neglect of issues identified by unions, and thus direct the attention of the public to 'an agenda' firmly established in ways compatible with dominant interests.

The first move in the agenda-setting function performed by the presentation of industrial disputes is to translate 'the dispute' into 'the strike', and this enables 'union militancy' and 'socially disruptive consequences' to become focal points in news coverage. 'The strike' rather than 'the dispute' becomes *the problem* around which news and current affairs presentations are structured. It is very rare for *the problem* to be defined in terms which identifies management as the source of a dispute. As a British politician puts it: 'Unions always "demand" and "threaten", management always "offers" and "pleads"'. He continues:

Or, put it the other way round: take any dispute. You could say that the trade unions are 'offering' to work for eight per cent when inflation is ten per cent, and 'pleading' with their management not to cut their real wages, and management are 'demanding' they work for five per cent, and 'threatening' to sack them if they don't...I have not seen any programme discussing whether it is right for the Government to cut the real wages of health service workers, or to cut the real wages of railwaymen. It is just not put on the agenda by the media.[69]

It is *after* the agenda has been set that television sets about attempting to achieve its 'balanced reporting'. In effect this means that the best that can be achieved is a balanced presentation of a partial definition of a dispute. In other words the agenda-setting practices of news and current affairs presentations result in an editorial slant favourable to dominant interests. This conclusion is vigorously denied by editors. As one former editor asserts: 'In my experience, no such slant is given editorially, but there is socio-centralism'.[70]

'Socio-centralism' in fact is the product of the influence exerted by the dominant ideology on the news value of negativity. Indeed, we are told that this is so.

'socio-centralism'...means that the media tend to reflect the values of the society in which they live; that anything that threatens the peace, prosperity and harmony of that society is likely to attract headlines; and that a reaction of a large part of the audience is likely to be *unfavourable* to those who disturb social harmony.[71]

There is no acknowledgement here that socio-centralism reflects the dominant ideology, rather it is seen as 'the perspective of the average citizen'. Thus news bulletins, it is claimed, '*do* in general reflect a middle-of-the-road approach. And although the headlines and the treatment 49 times out of 50 are factual and detached, they are looking at events with the perspective of the average citizen'.[72] This approach to media impartiality is fraught with difficulties. The 'average citizen', some would argue, is a media-constructed myth. When the average citizen participates in a strike 'he' loses his average-citizen's status, which legitimates the non-representation of 'his views'. As soon as the strike has ended, the worker is restored to his average-citizen status. Even if we go along with the idea that there is such a creature as the average citizen, it might be argued that the average citizen is already ideologically shaped, and that the media themselves have contributed to this process.

In general elections television attempts to achieve 'balance' in its coverage by allocating an equal amount of time to the major contending political parties. It is often claimed that such a principle operates in the coverage of industrial disputes. Indeed, in the 1984–5 coal dispute in Britain, quantitative analyses of exposure time reveal that the union had more television exposure than the management. The obvious difficulty with this approach to media balance and neutrality is that unions are given very little time to express freely their position. They are rather invited to answer questions derived from a pre-established agenda. Very often this means that the union's television exposure is taken up with addressing what, from a union perspective, are irrelevant questions. This does place the union in an awkward position: failure to answer irrelevant questions can be readily perceived as a weakness in their case, yet if irrelevant questions are answered, then the union can be seen to be endorsing the dominant ideological framework underpinning the agenda. This is particularly troublesome in the case of a dispute in which the union's position represents a radical political challenge to dominant interests, and thus to the underlying ideological field. Further, the fact that management can make its position meaningful through established discourses means in effect that they require less time than a union whose position can be made meaningful only through oppositional discourses. The latter, through a long history of non-exposure, have been unable to assume the time-saving taken-for-grantedness automatically available to established discourses.

Television professionals, particularly in some current affairs programmes where the programme format is suggestive of a conscious attempt to represent a balance of opinion, may present themselves as occupying a neutral site between the two sides in an industrial dispute. We have already seen how this self-presentation is deceiving on account of the agenda from which the television presenter orchestrates proceedings. Additionally, 'the style' of presenters often transforms their 'neutral space' into a partisan one. 'Style' is a rather elusive concept to pin down, but a common observation concerning the attitudinal stance of presenters to representatives of either side in industrial disputes goes some way toward capturing what is meant by 'style'. Thus it is often the case that television presenters adopt an 'aggressive questioning' stance towards union representatives (perhaps as noted above, to obtain answers to irrelevant questions), while they tend to treat capitalist class representatives with deference. For this reason, in addition to other reasons discussed above, some critics claim that in major, prolonged disputes many journalists, 'with notable exceptions', become 'cheerleaders for the government'.[73]

It is during prolonged industrial disputes that the neutral space at the centre of many current affairs programmes tends to be progressively used for 'peace-making' rather than refereeing purposes. Both 'the referee' and 'the peace-maker' are traditional roles of impartiality. We have seen that the current affairs presenter as referee observes rules

which favour dominant interests. Hall's analysis of 'ideological processes', in which he draws on the work of Poulantzas, can be used to
specify the kind of ideological work taking place in pursuit of impartiality from the 'neutral space' occupied by the current affairs presenter,
initially in the refereeing role, and later in the role of peace-maker.

In Poulantzas's scheme, 'ideological processes' operate to produce
three 'ideological effects' at the level of discourse. Initially, the current
affairs presenter as referee presides over an agenda reflecting dominant
interests. The industrial dispute is made meaningful within established
discourses so as 'to mask, conceal or repress...the antagonistic founda-
tions of the system'.[74] Then, not so much as referee, but more as the
representative of the public interest, the interventions of current affairs
presenters tend to focus on the negative consequences for all concerned
of the strike itself. These consequences are put to the union representatives, often in terms which highlight 'divisions within the union', 'divisions within the wider labour movement', or even in terms of divisive
tensions within families, and lack of public support which is 'isolating
the union'. The ideological effect produced by these kinds of intervention is described by Poulantzas as that of 'fragmentation or separation'.
This refers to the ways in which 'the collective interests of the working
classes are fragmented into the internal oppositions between strata of the
class'.[75] Finally, in the peace-making role, television presenters attempt
to bring some apparent unity or coherence to the fragmentation which
they have earlier foregrounded. There are often frequent appeals to 'the
good of the union', 'the good of the nation', or 'the peace we all want'.
The peace-maker presenter can be seen to participate in processes which
produce the third ideological effect, according to Poulantzas, in which
'unities are once again produced; but now in forms which mask and
displace the level of class relations and economic contradictions and
represents them as non-antagonistic totalities'.[76]

It would seem, then, that the various means through which television
professionals attempt to achieve impartiality can produce consequences
which are quite the opposite of what is intended. In other words the
'techniques' of media impartiality are actively involved in the reproduction of the underlying ideological field within which news and current
affairs presentations are produced.

So far attention has been focused on television's more active role in the
coverage of industrial disputes. As I noted earlier, however, there is
considerable value for an ideological analysis in that approach which
attempts to specify the significant absences, or what Golding refers to as

the 'missing dimensions'[77] of news and current affairs coverage. This is of particular relevance to the coverage of industrial disputes, in that all disputes expose to varying degrees the basic class contradiction inherent in all capitalist societies. Since 'ideology' in much Marxist thought is defined as 'that which conceals class contradictions', industrial disputes, again to varying degrees, offer opportunities for television professionals to present the challenge to the dominant ideology represented by the union. It is widely noted that most industrial disputes in Western societies, with the possible exception of France,[78] in so far as they are confined to conflicts over pay levels, do not pose a *fundamental* challenge to the dominant ideology. Disputes over wages, however detrimental to the short-term interests of employers, do reproduce the validity of the concept of a 'wage', and as such do not threaten the long-term interests of the capitalist class. Marx expressed this point rather strongly.

An enforced *raising of wages* (disregarding all other difficulties, including that this anomaly could only be maintained forcibly) would therefore be nothing but a *better slave-salary* and would not achieve either for the worker or for labor human significance and dignity.

Even the *equality of wages*, as advanced by Proudhon, would only convert the relation of the contemporary worker to his work into the relation of all men to labor. Society would then be conceived as an abstract capitalist.[79]

Wage disputes, then, can be made intelligible within the established discourses of the underlying ideological field. To the extent that television news and current affairs reporting of industrial disputes achieves this kind of intelligibility, it cannot be accused of ideologically distorting 'the reality' of the dispute. In such a case the reality itself is ideologically distorted.

However, if wage disputes reproduce the dominant ideology, they also contain some challenge to *elements* of the dominant ideology. The various analyses of television's coverage of wage disputes suggest that unions' limited challenge to elements of the dominant ideology is not so much misrepresented, but rather *underrepresented*. Television coverage tends to *foreground* and thus *overrepresent* issues which derive from the 'negativity' attributed to 'the strike', and it tends to *background* issues concerning the justice of the union's case. These issues invariably challenge the fairness of the distribution of rewards, if not the system itself; they challenge the 'workings' of the meritocratic ideology, if not the validity of this ideology; they challenge 'managerial competence' and 'style', if not 'the right of management to manage'; and they often challenge the relation of profits to wages, if not the underlying structural relation between capital and labour. The underrepresentation of these limited challenges to elements of the dominant ideology is yet another way in which we can refer to the ideological service television provides for dominant groups.

The underrepresentation of those issues which are antithetical to dominant interests can shade off into their *non-representation*. Or, to put it another way, issues which are backgrounded can become *significant absences*. This is more likely to happen in television's coverage of industrial disputes which, as Giddens describes them, are 'struggles over control' and 'involve attempts on the part of working-class associations to acquire an influence over, or in the most radical context to gain full control over, the "government" of industry'.[80] Disputes over control create very difficult problems for broadcasters of news and current affairs. Such disputes are potentially disruptive of the close relation between television professional and elite persons, and are a potential threat to the finely balanced relationship of broadcasters to the state. Quite simply,

any sort of major extension of industrial conflict into the area of control poses a threat to the institutional separation of economic and political conflict which is a fundamental basis of the capitalist state—because it serves to bring into the open the connections between political power in the polity as such, and the broader 'political' subordination of the working class within the economic order.[81]

Dominant discourses are inherently incapable of accommodating the representation of radical opposition to the *status quo*. In order adequately to represent the radical stance of the union, television presenters must either be competent in the use of oppositional discourses, or they must allow the union to 'have its say'. Since they are not well practised in the former, television presenters tend to opt for the latter, but rarely in a form which enables the union to have sufficient opportunity to 'freely express' the full range of their opposition. To allow too much of this would in effect constitute the relinquishing of control over the agenda, and would thus bring into question the professional competence of programme presenters and editors. Professional incompetence in this context refers to broadcasters' 'behaving irresponsibly' by virtue of giving time to those 'intent on disruption', that is, to those who from the viewpoint of the state are 'against the public interest'. Given the delicate relationship between the state and broadcasting in Western societies, in which the state attempts to maintain a position of 'non-interfering overseers' of broadcasters, the latter will not want to risk the possibility of having their already limited sphere of professional autonomy eroded. Editors persistently maintain that they are perfectly capable of exercising their autonomy in a responsible manner, and without supervision from the state. The above discussion strongly suggests that editors are justified in adopting this view. For the most part they have shown themselves to be competent servants of the state, and one of the clearest manifestations of this competence is to be found in the coverage of industrial disputes over issues of control.

Industrial disputes which present a direct political challenge to the capitalist state are by no means typical of the kinds of event covered by television news and current affairs programmes. These disputes do, nevertheless, raise serious doubts about the adequacy of techniques intended to achieve impartial and balanced reporting, and they do reveal television in its most ideologically vigorous form as an active defender of the dominant ideology and as an active producer of significant absences. They are, as I shall indicate below, useful for illuminating the 'ideological work' of television, in ways other than those already considered, and in ways which are relevant for ideological readings of all types of television programme.

Ideological forms and levels

Giddens suggests that there are three major *ideological forms* through which 'domination is concealed as domination', and through which 'power is harnessed to conceal sectional interests'.

1.   'The representation of sectional interests as universal ones...'
2.   'The denial or transmutation of contradictions...'
3.   'The naturalisation of the present: reification'.[82]

These three ideological forms are closely related and work in conjunction with each other. When the interests of the capitalst class, for example, are portrayed as being in the public interest, then it follows that the validity of any opposition to those interests must be denied. The following sequence of some elements of the dominant discourse captures the relationship between the universalisation of interests and the denial of class contradictions: profits are good for everybody—profits generate investment capital—investments create jobs—jobs create wealth—wealth means prosperity—we all want prosperity—strikes halt production—strikes reduce profits—therefore strikes are bad for everybody. In television news and current affairs presentations, these elements, and many more to which they are related, are given an explicit airing by elite persons and by television professionals. At an implicit level the dominant discourse, which conceals the exploitive basis of the capital accumulation process, informs the whole conduct of news and current affairs presentations, and in television fiction, often provides the backcloth on which drama unfolds.

The three ideological forms proposed by Giddens can be applied to the concealment of forms of domination other than class domination. Especially in prime-time television, some popular forms of 'law and order' entertainment privilege the universality of the law, often with the effect of criminalising racial tensions and thus reproducing the denial of racism as a source of racial tension. Similarly, sexism as a source of gender contradictions finds little expression in popular television entertainment. Instead we are fed a steady diet of psychological intrigue in which the underlying gender contradictions are translated into problems of romance and interpersonal relationships, often within the universalising appeal of familialism.

It is perhaps through the ideological form of reification that gender and racial forms of domination are most effectively concealed. Reified myths about gender and race are actively reproduced in prime-time television entertainment and advertisements. With respect to reification, Giddens notes that

In so far as reification is understood as referring to circumstances in which social relations appear to have the fixed and immutable character of natural laws, it can be regarded as the principal mode in which the naturalisation of the present is effected.[83]

The 'naturalisation of the present' inhibits an understanding of the 'mutable, historical character of human society', and is 'a phenomenon which thoroughly permeates the taken-for-granted assumptions of lived experience'.[84] Television entertainment, for the most part, reproduces the idea that the subordination of women in Western societies, and the low social status of non-whites, reflect a natural rather than a socially produced state of affairs. Such forms of 'common sense' are by no means confined to television entertainment,[85] or to the reproduction of sexism and racism. We noted earlier that television news and current affairs programmes tend to reproduce in their whole approach that common-sensical taken-for-grantedness which assumes that the socially produced divisions between capital and labour, employer and employee, manager and worker, mental and physical labour, and so on, reflect natural divisions.

The major ideological forms in discourse, Giddens argues, are to be found at two levels. At one level we can recognise 'the use of artifice or direct manipulation of communication by those in dominant classes or groups in furthering their sectional interests'.[86] As Giddens observes, at this level, the ideological aspects of discourse can be readily recognised and identified as ideology. But at the second level ideological analysis involves seeking 'to identify the most basic structural elements which connect signification and legitimation in such a way as to favour dominant interests'.[87] These are 'the most "buried" forms of ideology' and 'are likely to be deeply sedimented in both a *psychological* and an *historical* sense'.[88]

For our purposes here, and by way of summarising the connections between the different emphases of the various ideological analyses of television discussed in this chapter, it is useful to extend the two levels of ideological operations identified by Giddens, to four levels.

Level one. The close relationship between members of dominant groups and television producers of news and current affairs enables presentations to include *direct expressions* of the viewpoints of elites.

Level two. Broadcasters tend to represent events in ways which are derived from the representations used by dominant groups. The viewpoints of dominant groups may be similarly mediated by fictional characters. News and current affairs values are enacted at this level.

Level three. It is at this level that television reproduces the ideological framework underlying the explicit expressions of dominant viewpoints at the first two levels of ideological operations. Both the sources of news and current affairs values and the agenda-setting practices are reproduced at this level. The third level, then, contains the embedded taken-for-granted elements of dominant discourses. To the extent that the third level of ideological operations is rarely foregrounded, the dominant ideology appears to be absent, but in fact it is silently reproduced—it is 'silently present in its absence'.

Level four. Television news, current affairs and prime-time entertainment tend not to represent viewpoints oppositional to dominant interests—the significant absences—or, they underrepresent these viewpoints. There are times, too, when oppositional values are misrepresented by attempts to fit them into the framework of dominant discourses.

This scheme is particularly useful for capturing the ideological complexities of television. Very often in the whole range of television programmes, the third and fourth levels, in conjunction with either the first or second level, are *simultaneously* operative. The 'ideological play' at the first two levels reproduces in a concealed form the ideological operations at levels three and four, where the interests of dominant groups are most adequately served by their absence from the 'field of conflict'.

Notes

1. Philip Elliott, Graham Murdock and Philip Schlesinger, '"Terrorism" and the state: a case study of the discourses of television', *Media, Culture and Society*, vol. 5, 1983, pp. 155–77.
2. Ibid., p. 157.
3. Jane Feuer, 'The Concept of Live Television: Ontology as Ideology' in E. Ann Kaplan, ed., *Regarding Television*, Los Angeles, The American Film Institute, 1983, pp. 12–22.
4. Elliott *et al.*, op. cit., p. 163.
5. Ibid.
6. Ibid., p. 164.
7. Ibid.
8. Ibid.
9. Ibid.
10. Greg Philo, John Hewitt, Peter Beharrell and Howard Davis, *Really Bad News*, London, Writers and Readers Publishing Cooperative Society, 1982, p. 141.
11. Ibid.
12. Terry Lovell, 'Ideology and *Coronation Street*' in Richard Dyer, Christine Geraghty, Marion Jordan, Terry Lovell, Richard Paterson and John Stewart, *Coronation Street*, Television Monograph 13, London, British Film Institute, 1981, p. 52.

13. Ibid., pp. 50–1.
14. Ibid., p. 52.
15. Charlotte Brunsdon, '*Crossroads*: Notes on Soap Opera' in Kaplan, op. cit., p. 81.
16. Sandy Flitterman, 'The *Real* Soap Operas: TV Commercials' in Kaplan, op. cit., p. 85.
17. Janice Winship, 'Sexuality for sale' in Stuart Hall, Dorothy Hobson, Andrew Lowe and Paul Willis, eds, *Culture, Media, Language*, London, Hutchinson, 1980, p. 223.
18. Richard Collins, 'Walling Germany with brass: Theoretical paradigms in British studies of television news', *Media, Culture and Society*, vol. 6, 1984, p. 27.
19. K. Lang and G.E. Lang, 'The Unique Perspective of Television and its Effects', *American Sociological Review*, vol. 18, 1953, pp. 103–12.
20. S. Cohen and J. Young, *The Manufacture of News*, London, Constable, 1973.
21. Glasgow University Media Group, *Bad News*, London, Routledge and Kegan Paul, 1976. Glasgow University Media Group, *More Bad News*, London, Routledge and Kegan Paul, 1980.
22. J. Baggaley and S. Duck, *The Dynamics of Television*, Farnborough, Saxon House, 1976.
23. P. Schlesinger, *Putting Reality Together*, London, Constable, 1978.
24. Peter Golding and Philip Elliott, *Making the News*, London, Longman, 1979.
25. Schlesinger, op. cit.
26. Collins, op. cit., p. 32.
27. Ibid., p. 33.
28. Ibid.
29. Anthony Giddens, *Central Problems in Social Theory*, London, Macmillan, 1979, p. 190.
30. Golding and Elliott, op. cit., p. 104.
31. Ibid.
32. Ibid., p. 105.
33. Johan Galtung and Mari Homboe Ruge, 'The Structure of Foreign News: The Presentation of the Congo, Cuba and Cyprus Crises in Four Foreign Newspapers' in Jeremy Tunstall, ed., *Media Sociology*, London, Constable, 1970, pp. 259–98.
34. Ibid., p. 262.
35. Schlesinger, op. cit., p. 218.
36. Galtung and Ruge, op. cit., p. 263.
37. Ibid.
38. Ibid.
39. Ibid., p. 264.

40. Ibid., p. 265.
41. Ibid.
42. Ibid., p. 266.
43. Richard Sennett, 'Destructive Gemeinschaft' in Robert Bocock, Peter Hamilton, Kenneth Thompson and Alan Waton, eds, *An Introduction to Sociology*, London, Fontana, 1980, p. 97.
44. Peter Golding, 'The Missing Dimensions—News Media and the Management of Social Change' in Elihu Katz and Tamas Szecskö, eds, *Mass Media and Social Change*, London, Sage, 1981, p. 77.
45. Ibid.
46. Ibid.
47. John Westergaard, 'Power, Class and the Media' in James Curran, Michael Gurevitch and Janet Woollacott, eds, *Mass Communication and Society*, London, Arnold, 1977, p. 101.
48. Ibid., p. 107.
49. E.P. Thompson, *Writing by Candlelight*, London, Merlin, 1980, p. 6.
50. Westergaard, op. cit., p. 110.
51. T. Goban-Klas, cited in James D. Halloran and Peggy Gray, *Mass Media, Sport and International Understanding: A Review of Literature and Research*, University of Leicester, Centre for Mass Communication Research, Report, pp. 19–20.
52. See Stuart Hall, Ian Connell and Lidia Curti, 'The "Unity" of Current Affairs Television' in Tony Bennett, Susan Boyd-Bowman, Colin Mercer and Janet Woollacott, eds, *Popular Television and Film*, London, British Film Institute, 1981, pp. 88–117.
53. Golding, op. cit., p. 80.
54. Ibid.
55. Hall *et al.*, op. cit., p. 115.
56. Ibid., p. 114.
57. Stuart Hall, 'Culture, the Media and the "Ideological Effect"', in Curran *et al.*, op. cit., p. 344.
58. Stuart Hall, 'Authoritarian Populism: A Reply to Jessop *et al*', *New Left Review*, vol. 151, 1985, pp. 115–124.
59. Raymond Williams, *Keywords: A Vocabulary of Culture and Society*, London, Flamingo, revised edn, 1983.
60. Stuart Hall, 'Encoding/decoding' in Hall *et al.*, eds, *Culture, Media, Language* p. 136.
61. Hall, 'Culture, the Media and the "Ideological Effect"', p. 343.
62. Stuart Hall, 'The rediscovery of "ideology": return of the repressed in media studies', in Michael Gurevitch, Tony Bennett, James Curran and Janet Woollacott, eds, *Culture, Society and the Media*, London: Methuen, 1982, p. 75.
63. Ibid., p. 84.

64. Williams, op. cit.
65. Hall, 'The rediscovery of "ideology"', p. 88.
66. Stanley Cohen, *Folk Devils and Moral Panics*, London, Paladin, 1973.
67. S. Hall, C. Critcher, T. Jefferson, J. Clarke and B. Roberts, *Policing the Crisis: Mugging, the State and Law and Order*, London, Macmillan, 1978.
68. Glasgow University Media Group, *Bad News*; Glasgow University Media Group, *More Bad News*.
69. Tony Benn, 'Agenda Extra', *The Guardian* (28 July, 1982), p. 14.
70. Alastair Hetherington in Arthur Scargill, Alastair Hetherington, Martin Adeney, Alan Fountain and Keith Harris, 'Scargill takes on the telly men', *New Socialist*, October 1984, pp. 22–3.
71. Ibid., p. 22.
72. Ibid., p. 23.
73. David Jones, Julian Petley, Mike Power and Lesley Wood, *Media Hits the Pits*, London, Campaign for Press and Broadcasting Freedom, 1985, p. 7.
74. Hall, 'Culture, the Media and the "Ideological Effect"', p. 337.
75. Ibid.
76. Ibid., pp. 337–8.
77. Golding, op. cit.
78. Anthony Giddens, *The Class Structure of the Advanced Societies*, London, Hutchinson, 2nd edn, 1981, pp. 207–15.
79. Karl Marx, *Economic and Philosophic Manuscripts (1844)* in Loyd D. Easton and Kurt H. Guddat, eds, *Writings of the Young Marx on Philosophy and Society*, New York, Anchor, 1967, pp. 298–9.
80. Giddens, *The Class Structure of the Advanced Societies*, p. 205.
81. Ibid., p. 206.
82. Giddens, *Central Probelms in Social Theory*, pp. 193–5.
83. Ibid., p. 195.
84. Ibid.
85. 'There are, of course, instances such as the now notorious remark by a government minister, Patrick Jenkin, to the effect that had God intended equality he would not have created men and women'. Michele Barrett and Mary McIntosh, *The Anti-social Family*, London, Verso, 1982, p. 12.
86. Giddens, *Central Problems in Social Theory*, p. 190.
87. Ibid., pp. 191–2.
88. Ibid., p. 192.

3 The Ideological Effectiveness of Television

The dominant ideology thesis

It is, as we have seen, a relatively unproblematic matter to establish that the ideological output of television, for the most part, is supportive of the interests of dominant groups. It is quite another matter to establish that television's output is sufficiently powerful to effectively manipulate the audience ideologically. Yet, as I noted at the beginning of the previous chapter, the most influential ways in which television's power is construed within critical media theory embodies the idea that television is ideologically effective.

It is the very obviousness of television's ideological bias which is used to support the view that television helps to win consent for a dominant ideology. As we shall see, there are a number of objections to this view. Pluralists, placing faith in their own audience research, seriously doubt that television is as effective as critical media theorists claim it is. What some suggest is that critical media theorists ought to climb down from their theoretical perches and submit their claims to the test of empirical research procedures adopted in audience research. Others suspect that critical media theorists have *uncritically* assumed that television exercises an awesome ideological power over the audience. To help critical media theorists 'think through' their unexamined assumptions, a number of behaviourist models of media effects are 'offered' as potentially useful! It will be a relatively easy matter to show that these pluralist objections are misconceived and without foundation.

There are, however, Marxist objections to the view that television helps to win consent for a dominant ideology. These objections arise from what has come to be known as 'the critique of the dominant ideology thesis'. From within this critique there are three challenges to critical media theory. First, it is argued that the working classes do not generally adopt a dominant ideology. By implication, this means that television has been largely ineffectual in ideologically manipulating the audience. The way in which this particular challenge is formulated, however, fails to address what is meant by 'a dominant ideology' within critical media theory, and, further, is dependent on a problematic interpretation of empirical evidence. What evidence there is, does lend itself to the interpretation that the relationship of the working classes and other subordinated groups to the dominant ideology is one of 'indifference'. The second challenge to critical media theory, then, questions the assumption of ideological motivation, which is implied in the idea that the subordinated *give their consent* to a dominant ideology. If the subordinated are generally indifferent in terms of their allegiance to the dominant ideology, then this casts grave doubts about television's power *to win consent* to the dominant ideology.

Critical media theorists have had their reasons for supposing that television and the mass media do win consent to the dominant ideology. These reasons run deep and have become so firmly entrenched that they have enabled critical media theorists to interpret empirical evidence, historical trends and contemporary events in ways which support the idea that the subordinated are ideologically incorporated into the system which subordinates them. We can recall Golding's statement that 'inegalitarian societies continue to reproduce a social order which is not merely tolerated by those receiving least in the distribution of material and cultural rewards, but which also receives their loyalty and acclaim'.[1] What is being hinted at here is that the 'loyalty and acclaim' of subordinates in inegalitarian societies is closely related to the reproduction of these societies. Elsewhere Golding and Murdock state that to be concerned

with the processes of legitimation through which the prevailing structure of advantage and inequality are presented as natural and inevitable...entails exploring the relations between communication systems and the other agencies through which disadvantaged groups are incorporated into the existing social order...[2]

We can compare these statements with what Bottomore understands to be the dominant ideology thesis: 'that modern capitalist society...maintains and reproduces itself through the effects of a "dominant ideology" which successfully incorporates the working class into the existing social system, thereby perpetuating its subordination'.[3] Common to both critical media theory and the dominant ideology thesis is the view that it is through the consent of a vast majority to a dominant ideology that capitalist societies are able to reproduce themselves. It is precisely this view which is the target of the third challenge to critical media theory posed by Marxist critics of the dominant ideology thesis. It is argued that not only are the majority of the subordinated *not* ideologically incorporated into the social order, but that also it is not necessary that they should be, since the reproduction of capitalist societies is achieved principally through means other than ideology. This argument undermines the basic assumption upon which television's power is formulated within critical media theory, namely that television's power is an ideological one, and that it is through ideology that capitalist societies, with all their forms of domination, are legitimated and thus reproduced. Quite simply, if ideology is not as important as critical media theorists assume it is, then it is difficult to entertain notions which emphasise the power of television to manipulate people ideologically in socially significant ways.

On the face of it, it would seem that the Marxist challenge to the role of ideology in 'the total order of things' places critical media theory in deep trouble. It does prise open the media-centredness of media theory, and enables a more realistic assessment of television's power. Not all is lost, however. There are, within the critique of the dominant ideology thesis, a number of spaces remaining for understanding television's power as an ideological one, but it is by comparison with popular and influential formulations a vastly reduced power. Before considering this it will be necessary to examine the Marxist challenge to critical media theory.

The critique of the dominant ideology thesis

In their attack on the dominant ideology thesis, Abercrombie, Hill and Turner develop a set of arguments which involve a critique of what they see as the four elements constituting this thesis. These four elements are:

(1) There is a dominant ideology, the precise content of which is not always carefully specified.
(2) Dominant classes 'benefit' from the effects of the dominant ideology, although not necessarily through their own deliberate activities.
(3) The dominant ideology does incorporate the subordinate classes, making them politically quiescent, though there is considerable disagreement as to

the degree of incorporation and the consequent degree of social stability. The effect of ideology is to conceal social relations.

(4) The mechanisms by which ideology is transmitted have to be powerful enough to overcome the contradictions within the structure of capitalist society.[4]

The dominant ideology thesis (one should say 'theses' since there are several different versions), as Abercrombie *et al.* note, has evolved over the past fifty years or so, principally as a product of the efforts of major Marxist thinkers to explain the continuing stability of capitalist societies. Of course, not all Marxists have adopted this explanation of social reproduction, but significantly those who have exerted the greatest influence on critical media theorists, especially Gramsci and Althusser, are identified by Abercrombie *et al.* as two of the principal advocates of the dominant ideology thesis. What has been most puzzling to Marxists, and indeed to social theorists generally, is not only that in the face of the continuing existence of exploitive forms of domination has a socialist revolution not materialised, but large numbers of the subordinated 'appear to have resigned themselves' to an existence of subordination, and some even 'appear to be so happily resigned' that they align their own interests with those of the dominant class. Working-class consciousness, far from becoming revolutionary consciousness, seemed to be moving in the opposite direction. With the spread of the mass media, and particularly television, this development was seen to be given an enormous boost. Hence the very close correspondence between the dominant ideology thesis and what we might call the stronger version of 'the power of television thesis'—both theses come from the same theoretical stable.

Surprisingly, in view of the kinds of argument presented in the previous chapter, Abercrombie *et al.* question whether or not something akin to a dominant ideology actually exists. They report the absence of a clear formulation of a dominant ideology on which there is widespread agreement. Because of this they 'construct' a dominant ideology in ways compatible with many existing versions, in conjunction with their own analyses of dominant class fractions in late capitalism. This constructed dominant ideology is made up of the 'ideologies of accumulation', 'state neutrality and welfare', 'managerialism', and elements of 'bourgeois culture', for example, 'individualism'. A range of evidence derived from ethnographic studies,[5] interview studies and questionnaire surveys, is considered to determine whether or not there is widespread acceptance amongst the working class for the various elements of the constructed dominant ideology.

With respect to the 'ideology of accumulation', which includes beliefs which justify property rights, ownership, profits, and the means by which these are secured, they find a consistent rejection of much of this ideology amongst the working class. They note that 'in place of accumulation...we find evidence of a fairly coherent and explicit model of social organisation which goes beyond the simple rejection of dominant ideology'.[6] Drawing on a survey conducted by Moorhouse and Chamberlain, they state that the respondents proposed 'that human need should be the *raison d'être* of economic activity'.[7] However, they do concede that there is insufficient evidence to assess the extent to which the underlying economic structure is accepted. Relevant to this is that the evidence supports the existence of a 'consensus' endorsing the occupational structure and its related structure of incomes. This, of course, 'implies some endorsement of the meritocratic version of inequality...an agreement that inequality *ought* to be meritocratic'.[8] Acceptance of the principle of a meritocracy is the acceptance of one of the means whereby accumulation is legitimated. But Abercrombie *et al*. quite rightly point out that acceptance of occupational and income structures does not 'imply acceptance of market principles and functional importance in fixing pay levels'.[9]

To the extent that the structure of the occupational hierarchy is accepted, and that mobility and placement within this structure should be based on 'merit', the existence of a managerial level is endorsed. However, elements of the managerial ideology such as 'presumed technical competence' and 'managerial professionalism' are rejected. It would seem, too, that that aspect of this ideology which denies conflict between managers and managed is also widely rejected.

Abercrombie *et al*. note that there is a very limited amount of evidence pertaining to the acceptance or rejection of the ideology of state neutrality and welfare. *The Dominant Ideology Thesis* was written before the electoral victories of the Right in Europe and the United States. If there had been support for elements of the ideology of state neutrality and welfare, such as the denial that the state promotes the interests of capital, and that it attempts to redress economic inequalities, it is extremely doubtful now that such an ideology could receive any credibility. Relevant here is a recent survey taken in Britain on a sample representative of the total adult population. Eighty-five per cent of those surveyed were opposed to reduced spending on health and education; 64

per cent opposed the development of a two-tier health service; 89 per cent favoured government job-creation schemes; 69 per cent supported 'a programme whose first priority is combating unemployment rather than inflation'; 70 per cent were in favour of price controls; and 72 per cent supported import controls, and believed the gap between high and low incomes to be too great.[10]

Abercrombie *et al.* also review studies which focus on beliefs about the workings of liberal democracy and its responsiveness to 'pressure from below'. They report that 'there is no unanimity within the working class'.[11] However, they note that the studies conducted in this area provide evidence which is insufficiently comprehensive in addressing working-class beliefs about political efficacy.

The extent to which working-class culture is permeated by bourgeois values is again difficult to assess, and the evidence Abercrombie *et al.* draw on is limited and not representative of all fractions of the working class. On the whole they believe that the evidence supports the view that working-class culture is relatively self-contained, and that bourgeois notions of 'individualism', 'respect for hierarchy' and 'deference to authority' are largely rejected. But, drawing on studies of working-class boys, they state that 'the glorification of manual against mental labour allows the boys to feel that they are rejecting the dominant ideology, even at the moment in which they accept the nature of the economic system and their place in it'.[12]

Abercrombie *et al.* conclude, on the basis of their extensive review of studies on working-class beliefs, that sociologists, amongst others

have overestimated the degree of social integration...that value dissensus can be found throughout the working class and concerns, in varying degrees, most of the range of ideological elements which we identified earlier...that social order cannot be explained primarily by ideological incorporation and value consensus.[13]

It would seem, on the face of it, that the critique of the dominant ideology thesis refutes stronger versions of the power-of-television thesis. In his stronger tones, for example, Hall appears to go as far as assuming the complicity of the psychological realm in subordinate groups consenting to their subordination. The process of 'structuring and reshaping of consent and consensus', for Hall, is one of 'constantly structuring the sum of what individuals in society think, believe and want'.[14] Indeed, when Hall states that 'the weakness of the earlier

Marxist positions lay precisely in their inability to explain the role of "free consent" of the governed to the leadership of the governing classes under capitalism',[15] he is assuming that the governed *do* freely consent to their rulers. It is precisely this assumption which Abercrombie *et al.* argue is *the* problem which has plagued Marxism, and it is this assumption which is the target of their critique. From within this assumption Hall reasons that the mass media, through the processes of 'masking— fragmenting—uniting' (see pp. 58–9), are involved in '*securing* the legitimacy and *assent* of the subordinated to their subordination'.[16]

In the light of the critique of the dominant ideology thesis Hall's position on the ideological effectiveness of the mass media is without foundation. Indeed, Abercrombie *et al.* are agreed that the mass media are 'partial'. This suggests that they would go along with much of the thrust of the discussion in the previous chapter. But their analyses of studies on working-class beliefs and values suggest to them that the mass media are not particularly influential. Even so, they do also consider 'the evidence' pertaining to media influence. In an extremely sparse discussion, in which they rely on McQuail's review of studies on the effects of mass media,[17] they conclude that the 'evidence of media influence is so thin and subject to so many caveats that our conclusion must be that the media are not significant except in the most isolated instances'.[18] The problem, as I was at pains to point out in Chapter 1, is that 'the evidence' provided by McQuail is derived from poorly conducted and fundamentally invalid studies. But even if we take 'the evidence' at face value, it actually supports the idea that the mass media do not *change* people's attitudes and beliefs. This cannot be taken as evidence that the mass media are non-influential in *reinforcing* existing beliefs. Abercrombie *et al.* do concede, however, that 'it is probable that beliefs are influenced by the media in some way when people have *no* other basis on which to form an opinion'.[19] It is on these grounds that 'the media may account, for example, for the unpopularity of Soviet-style socialism'.[20]

As I mentioned earlier, there are difficulties with some aspects of the critique of the dominant ideology thesis. Five objections can be raised and concern, first, the validity of the empirical evidence on working-class beliefs; second, the failure to consider the evidence of results of General Elections; third, the failure to consider data other than on the British working class; fourth, the failure to consider race and gender ideologies; and finally, Abercrombie *et al.*'s limited conception of 'ideology'. The first three objections, I shall argue below, do not pose a serious threat to the critique of the dominant ideology thesis.

The critique of the dominant ideology thesis: unwarranted objections

With respect to the problem of the evidence relating to working-class attitudes, values and beliefs, it is maintained that this evidence is suspect. Basically the data derived from questionnaires is notoriosuly unreliable, and from interviewing even more so. Obviously the prompting of interviewees by interviewers manipulates the opinions elicited. Similarly, ethnographic studies are open to all kinds of research biases, and rarely form an adequate basis from which generalisations can be drawn. I shall say a little more about ethnographic studies later since in spite of their difficulties they do provide the best bet for social research. Nevertheless, the objections concerning the problematic nature of the evidence surveyed by Abercrombie *et al.* are generally sound, particularly when the evidence is used to support rather precise claims, and when such evidence is attributed with an unwarranted validity on account of its scientificity, which is in fact a 'bogus scientificity'. An example of the latter are the questionnaire surveys conducted by professional organisations such as Gallup. The relatively accurate predictions of opinion polls on the outcome of elections are invariably used as a 'guarantee' of the validity of opinion surveys. Asking people how they intend to vote in a restricted choice and action situation is clearly a different matter from that involved in asking them for the extent of their agreement or disagreement with propositions which they may not be particularly bothered about. Not all such surveys need take this form, although the vast majority do. In every month of 1981, for example, Gallup conducted an open-ended question survey, in Britain, asking: 'What would you say is the most urgent problem facing the country at the present time?'[21] In every month 'unemployment' was given as by far and away the most common response—for nine of the twelve months of the survey, more than 70 per cent of those surveyed gave 'unemployment' as the answer. We can have far more confidence in open-ended question surveys than in the more typical closed propositional ones, such as: 'Generally speaking, and thinking of Great Britain as a whole, do you think trade unions are a good thing or a bad thing?'[22]

With respect to the critique of the dominant ideology thesis, Abercrombie *et al.* are very cautious in their interpretation of survey data. They treat the evidence as a very rough and crude indicator of working-class values (which at best is all that it can be), *and this is all that is required* given that they are using the evidence to raise doubts about the extent to which the working class accept the dominant ideology, as assumed in the stronger versions of the dominant ideology thesis. While we cannot use the survey data to declare *precisely* what the values of the working class are, we can use this data in a rough and ready way to cast doubts on those views which theorise the working class as being thoroughly ideologically integrated into the capitalist social order.

But what of the objection to the critique of the dominant ideology thesis which bases itself on the evidence of the results of general elections? Electoral victories by right-wing political parties would seem to suggest that a proportion of the working class are supporting the dominant ideology, and that this may be indicative of a wider trend amongst the working class. As Hall puts it:

Formally, the legitimacy of the continued leadership and authority of the dominant classes in capitalist society derives from their accountability to the opinions of the popular majority—the 'sovereign will of the people'. In the formal mechanisms of election and the universal franchise they are required to submit themselves at regular intervals to the will or consensus of the majority.[23]

Hall echoes what has become a popular view amongst some sections of the Left when he states that the mass media are involved in shaping 'the consensus of the majority', so that 'it squares with the will of the powerful'.[24] He argues that media institutions 'powerfully secure consent precisely because their claim to be independent of the direct play of political or economic interests, or of the state, is not wholly fictitious'.[25]

We may want to grant the possibility of a limited media influence which has some impact on the outcome of general elections, but before we rush into making connections between television's ideological output and right-wing electoral victories, it is necessary to consider other factors. There are, for example, no grounds to suppose that there are substantial differences amongst Western democracies in terms of television's production and reproduction of a dominant ideology. Yet social democratic political parties continue to win elections. This suggests that the relationship between the ideological output of the mass media and the outcome of general elections is not a consistent one. *Some* of this inconsistency can be hypothetically due to differences in the abilities of political parties to use their access to television effectively. In such cases, however, electoral victories can be said to be the product of politicians' communicative power, rather than television's ideological power. This, in fact, is the direction pursued by Hall in his more recent work in which he attempts to account for the 'ascendancy of the Right' in British politics.[26] His focus is very much on the 'hegemonic project' of the Right, and how this project takes advantage of ideological shifts in post-war Britain—ideological shifts in which television has been centrally involved (see above, pp. 53–4). While similar shifts have taken place in other Western societies, it may well be the case that the 'rightward drift' on the back of the media-amplified law and order discourse has been more marked in Britain than elsewhere. If this is so, it suggests a qualification to my observation, above, that there are no substantial differences in the ideological output of television amongst Western democracies. To follow Hall, we would have to acknowledge a few specific differences. This would appear to be perfectly reasonable. Thus while one might expect all Western democracies to embrace the enduring 'core elements' of the dominant ideology, it would be reasonable to also expect each society to show some variation in the ways in which core elements are articulated with historically and culturally specific elements.

If we accept that it is necessary to examine the particular manifestations of the dominant ideology peculiar to each society, there still remains the question of whether or not it is valid to use electoral victories as evidence of the power of television to *win consent* for the dominant ideology of a particular society. Here there are essentially three problems.

If an electoral victory reflects consent to the dominant ideology, then it is rarely the consent of the *majority*. The party-political systems of Western democracies are such that electoral victories are more often than not obtained with the votes of less than half of the eligible voters. More than this, and somewhat damaging to Hall's claims, votes cast for the victorious Right in Britain have actually declined.[27] However, Hall has argued that the rightward drift in British politics applies to all political parties. To argue this diverts our attention away from the specific 'success' of the Right, and more toward its general influence on the party-political system. A majority of the eligible voters do vote, and a majority of the votes, except in the United States, go to ostensibly, even if rightward moving, social democratic parties. Is Hall suggesting that the act of voting in a general election reflects the consent of a majority to the dominant ideology? If he is suggesting this, then we encounter the second major problem.

Offe notes that 'although the overwhelming majority of citizens does vote in general elections, this behaviour often seems to be more of a ritualistic rather than a purposive nature'.[28] In support of this view, Offe draws on the evidence of surveys conducted in Western societies which suggest 'a great increase in distrust and even cynical views that people hold about political parties'.[29]

Two comments relevant to television's ideological power can be made here. First, in spite of being subjected to intensive advertising/electioneering campaigns on television, sizeable minorities choose not to vote in general elections (approximately 30 per cent in Britain, and almost 50 per cent in the United States), and many who do vote do so reluctantly. The coercive efforts employed by political parties to 'get out the vote' hardly conjures up an image of people voluntarily consenting to the system which governs them. Television, it would seem, fails to stir the reluctant voter. It is relevant to be reminded that the reluctant voter, in the main, comes from the ranks of the highest viewers of television, and while the reluctant voter may be disinclined to watch political party campaigns, the viewing alternatives are nevertheless steeped in the dominant ideology. The highest viewers tend to be found amongst the poorer and more powerless groups in society where the most alienation from the party political system is experienced. Here, we can make a second comment on television's power, or at least its use by political parties. The increasing use of television for party-political campaigns has coincided with 'the overextension of the strategy of the "catch-all party" which tries to win votes from wherever they come, denying any class-specific base of its programme and politics'.[30] This is no innocent coincidence. It leads, 'in the eyes of the voter, to a loss of party-identities, and to the impression that the differences contained *within* any of the parties are greater than those *between* parties'.[31] In competing for the middle ground of public opinion, the use of television by political parties may have contributed significantly to that state of affairs in which the political parties, taken as a whole, do not represent the total range of public opinion. This observation is compatible with Hall's identification of a rightward drift. It suggests that political parties may have changed through their use of television, and that their projection of their 'catch-all' strategies on television, confirms for the reluctant voters that they are without political representation.[32]

Of the majority who do vote in general elections, and bearing in mind Offe's observations, it is difficult to describe their vote in terms which emphasise voluntary consent to a dominant ideology. I shall discuss the problem of consent in some detail later.

The biggest problem by far with using electoral victories as evidence either of the effectiveness of the dominant ideology, or of the ideological effectiveness of television, or both, is that it cannot be assumed, particularly in the era of 'catch-all' parties, that the individual's vote is a clear reflection of ideological motive. People vote the way they do for all kinds of reasons. Ideology-centred and media-centred interpretations of the outcome of elections are manifestations of the dominant ideology thesis at work.

The third objection to the critique of the dominant ideology thesis— Abercrombie *et al.*'s exclusive attention to the *British* working class—is not a serious one. What comparative evidence there is tends to suggest a greater acceptance of elements of the dominant ideology among the British working class than among their European counterparts.[33] To focus on Britain is to focus on a society where the evidence suggests a higher degree of ideological incorporation of subordinates than elsewhere, with the exception of the United States, and possibly, on some elements of the dominant ideology, West Germany. In view of this, the exclusive attention to the British working class is methodologically valid.

A more serious and fundamental challenge to the critique of the dominant ideology thesis is contained within the final two objections to the critique. These objections are discussed below.

The critique of the critique of the dominant ideology thesis

The fourth objection to Abercrombie *et al.*'s critique focuses on their failure to consider racism and sexism as part of the dominant ideology. In one sense this objection is not as serious as it might seem at first, but in another sense it opens up a far more serious weakness in their conception of 'ideology', which I shall discuss shortly. In defence of Abercrombie *et al.*, we need to bear in mind the specific, and thus limited, task they set themselves.

The apparent success of capitalism in surviving periodic crises and the absence of violent revolutionary struggle of the Western working class against the exploitive conditions of modern industrial production have led a variety of Marxist writers to argue that, especially in late capitalism, the coherence of industrial society is to be explained primarily by the *ideological* incorporation of the labour force. There exists a widespread agreement among Marxists...that there is a powerful, effective, dominant ideology in contemporary capitalist societies and that this dominant ideology creates an acceptance of capitalism in the working class. It is with this dominant ideology thesis that our book is concerned.[34]

Given the way in which 'this thesis' is stated, Abercrombie *et al.* are quite justified to limit their attention to the possible ideological effects of the dominant ideology in class-relevant terms only. Class domination is *the* defining characteristic of *capitalist* societies. They set out to falsify the idea that the reproduction of class domination is primarily attributable to the working class adopting capitalist class ideologies.

The objection that the critique of the dominant ideology thesis fails to consider gender and race ideologies is an objection relevant to the particular dominant ideology thesis which Abercrombie *et al.* address, and not appropriate to their critique.

While gender and race domination might be convenient for, and helpful for the reproduction of, class domination, they are not essential for it. Further, while the reproduction of capitalist societies involves the reproduction of gender and race domination, it only *necessarily* involves the reproduction of class domination. The *transformation* of a capitalist society into a socialist society necessarily involves the abolition of class domination. But it would surely be an incomplete socialism which did not also abolish gender and race domination. In this sense gender and race domination, apart from being evils in and of themselves, are major obstacles to the development of a libertarian socialism. In this sense, too, there is merit in adopting a broader conception of the dominant ideology—one which includes race and gender ideologies. This broader conception derives its logic from a concern to identify the major obstacles to the development of a libertarian socialist society. Such a concern includes but is not restricted to explaining the reproduction of capitalist society. It is through confining their attention to the latter problem that Abercrombie *et al.* miss out on ways in which there may yet be significant ideological effects. This constitutes a serious weakness in their critique of the dominant ideology thesis.

If we set out to answer the question, 'What are the major obstacles to the development of a libertarian socialist society?', then not only are we likely to give full consideration to sexism and racism, but we are also likely to give consideration to ideas, beliefs and values other than capitalist class ideologies, which may prevent the development of opposition to capitalism, and which may thus also contribute to the reproduction of class domination. This brings us to the final objection to the critique of the dominant ideology thesis, namely that Abercrombie *et al.*, for the most part, restrict their attention to ideological effects arising from what I have referred to earlier as the first and second levels of ideological operations (see pp. 63–4). Yet it is at the third and fourth levels that the dominant ideology is likely to be most effective.

What this suggests then, is that ideological effects may be sought at different levels corresponding to the levels of ideological operations. The kind of evidence required to establish the existence of ideological effects is that which is relevant to:

1. The extent to which the views of dominant groups are also the views of the public (level one). Abercrombie *et al.* are primarily concerned with the extent to which the views of the capitalist class have been adopted by the working class.
2. The extent to which the public make sense of events consonant with the manner in which these events are made meaningful by dominant groups and their mediators, for example, television presenters (level two).
3. The extent to which the public reproduce the *underlying* elements of the dominant ideology within which agendas are set, issues defined and priorities established; and the extent to which the public reproduce ideas, beliefs and values which serve the interests of dominant groups (level three).
4. The extent to which there is an absence of views which are opposi-tional to the interests of dominant groups (level four).

In reviewing the evidence pertaining to the extent to which the working class accept elements of capitalist-class ideologies, Abercrombie *et al.* fail to give sufficient consideration to the fact that some elements belong to level three, the 'total ideological field or framework', as Hall puts it. Significantly, the evidence does suggest that there is something akin to a 'consensus' at this level. This can be illustrated with examples from Abercrombie *et al.*'s critique. They argue, drawing on the research of Moorhouse and Chamberlain,[35] and Goldthorpe, Lockwood, Bechhofer and Platt,[36] that the working class do not support 'existing principles of accumulation'. They suggest that wage bargaining itself indicates that 'many workers clearly question the basis on which surpluses are distributed between labour and capital, wanting more to go, as wages, to labour, and this is true even of workers who are not particularly radical in other respects'.[37] While this does reflect a rejection of an element of the dominant ideology, it also gives legitimacy, not to the 'ideology of accumulation', but to the domination of labour by capital which is reproduced through wage bargaining. There is an *underlying* ideology, then, within which wage bargaining operates. It is an ideology which accepts the idea of a 'wage', and in so doing reproduces the legitimacy of the idea of the division between employer and employee, that is, it reproduces the representation of a structural feature of class domination.

In a similar vien, Abercrombie *et al.* note that there is widespread dissatisfaction with the workings of the meritocratic system,[38] and that this is connected to a rejection of many elements of 'managerial ideology'. But here again, while many workers may contest 'managerial professionalism' and remain unconvinced about 'managerial competence', these sentiments are about styles of management, rather than the existence within the occupational structure of a managerial level. The latter would seem to be endorsed, and with it the idea that the occupational structure should be based on meritocratic principles.

When Abercrombie *et al.* declare that the 'conduct of industrial relations reflects value dissensus, the rejection of hierarchy and submissiveness, an appreciation of the virtues of collectivism in place of bourgeois individualism...',[39] they again fail to relate these observations to the ideological framework which is reproduced. The 'rejection of hierarchy' is in practice the manoevring for position and 'getting the best deal possible' *within* a hierarchical occupational structure. The 'appreciation of the virtues of collectivism' does not replace 'bourgeois individualism', but operates *within* many elements of it, particularly the self-interest of 'possessive individualism'.

'Sociological studies of "achievement motivation"', Mann writes, 'have shown that almost all persons, of whatever class, will agree with statements like "It is important to get ahead"'.[40] The value of 'achievement', in most Western societies, is defined in such a way that the ideological criteria underpinning notions of 'merit' and 'ability' are the means by which most people judge their own self-improvement, and assess their own worth. Abercrombie *et al.* note that 'large numbers of people agree...on the significance of education, training and skill as criteria of economic worth and social honour'.[41] Again, these are the very criteria which underpin the opportunity structure, and which define the meritocratic ideology which legitimates the opportunity structure. In measuring their own progress in terms of material rewards and/or level of position in the status hierarchy, members of subordinate groups are reproducing an element of the dominant ideology which legitimates the existing structure of rewards and their unequal distribution.

We can probe this particular example a little further to illustrate the value of considering, within the orbit of the dominant ideology, ideas, values and beliefs which *serve the interests of dominant groups*, including the capitalist class. It is doubtful, for example, that capitalists, given their profit-making preoccupations, have given much consideration to the meaning of 'intelligence'. Yet the dominant meanings of intelligence have served the capitalist class in ways which the capitalist class would never be able to orchestrate. What is meant by 'scholastic achievement', 'ability' and 'merit' is shot through with dominant definitions of intelligence. These definitions are enacted in ways which determine school careers, and the latter are heavily influential in the development of self-concepts and future expectations. The majority of working-class youth emerge from schooling with very limited horizons concerning their immediate and long-term prospects, and with views of of themselves as not particularly 'bright', 'clever' or 'intelligent'. These self-attributions are the product of internalising alien and impoverished criteria of 'intelligence/ability' which are inscribed in schooling practices and embedded in working-class culture. (see pp. 14–16)

We would not want to refer to the 'ideology of intelligence' as a 'capitalist class ideology', but we can certainly see that the 'ideology of intelligence' serves the interests of the capitalist class, not only in terms of legitimating and structuring the meritocratic ideology, but also in limiting potential working-class resistance to exploitation by fashioning working-class expectations.

The arguments presented above suggest that Abercrombie *et al.* construct the dominant ideology so as to capture its contradictory elements, but fail to identify the ideological framework within which these elements are located. The distinctions between different levels of ideological operations enable us to agree with Abercrombie *et al.*'s conclusion that 'value dissensus can be found throughout the working class and concerns, in varying degrees, most of the range of ideological elements'[42] of their constructed dominant ideology, *at the first two levels only*. The third level of ideological operations, in which the underlying ideological field is located, and where the legitimation of the total social order occurs, is of far greater social significance than the first two levels. Their argument that 'broad endorsement of dominant values about inequality of income therefore conceals disagreement on a number of issues concerning fairness and allocative mechanisms',[43] should, in the light of the arguments presented above, be reversed to read as follows: 'disagreement on a number of issues...conceals broad endorsement of dominant values'.

The dominant ideology: the problems of 'consent' and 'consensus'

The critique of the critique of the dominant ideology thesis might suggest that critical media theorists advocating a stronger version of the power-of-television thesis are now back in business. There would seem to be, after all, a broad acceptance of a dominant ideology by a majority of the public. Without attempting to be exhaustive, we could say that the dominant ideology includes a cluster of elements involving at least: the acceptance of the existing framework of capital–labour relations, including the legitimacy of the divisions between employer and employee, manager and worker; the acceptance of unequal economic rewards based on existing meritocratic principles; the acceptance of the idea that the state should be actively involved in welfare provision (this certainly applies to Europe, if not the United States)—the welfare consensus serves the long-term interests of the capitalist class; the acceptance of myths about race and gender; the acceptance of elements of nationalism; the acceptance of the 'cold war ideology', including anti-Soviet and anti-communist sentiments.

This 'minimal form' of a dominant ideology might not be as far-ranging and comprehensive as the dominant ideology critical media theorists have in mind when it is claimed that television helps 'to win the consent of a majority to the dominant ideology'. Nevertheless, if we are able to uphold this claim in relation to the minimal form of the dominant ideology, then we would still be justified in supporting stronger versions of the power-of-television thesis. Before we can give our support to such a thesis, it is necessary to ask what is meant by 'consent' or equivalent notions such as 'acceptance' or 'endorsement'. Here it must be said that critical media theorists have given insufficient attention to this question, and this negligence is one of the sources responsible for the extravagant claims which have been made about television's ideological power.

As Giddens observes, 'most elements of social practices are not directly motivated',[44] and the whole idea of 'consenting' to a dominant ideology implies a degree of motivation which just does not exist.

We have to regard as suspect any theory that holds that every relatively stable society necessarily rests upon a close parallelism between, or 'interpenetration' of, the value-standards involved in legitimation and the motives co-ordinated in and through the conduct of the members of that society.[45]

The evidence of the studies reviewed by Abercrombie *et al.* and Mann,[46] lend themselves to an interpretation which suggests that subordinate groups are generally ideologically indifferent. To talk of a 'consensus' of a majority to a dominant ideology, or even a 'dissensus' of opinion, is to attribute a relevance to ideology, ideas, values, beliefs, opinions, and so on, which is not shared by that majority.

Mann notes that 'the precise meaning of this word "accept" has greatly troubled Marxists'. He goes on to make a valuable distinction.

We must distinguish two types of acceptance: *pragmatic* acceptance, where the individual complies because he perceives no realistic alternative, and *normative* acceptance, where the individual internalizes the moral expectations of the ruling class and views his own inferior position as legitimate. Though pragmatic acceptance is easy to accommodate to Marxism, normative acceptance is not, and the unfortunate popularity of the latter concept has contributed to the inadequacies of much modern Marxist theory.[47]

We can add to this that the concept of normative acceptance has contributed to the inadequacies of much critical media theory. Mann concludes that the ordinary citizen's 'normative connections with the vast majority of fellow citizens may be extremely tenuous, and his commitment to general dominant and deviant values may be irrelevant to his compliance with the expectations of others'.[48]

The ideology-centredness of critical media theory has led to far too much weight and importance being given to the role of ideology as a motivating force governing people's actions. If we accept that the vast majority are not ideologically motivated, then the social significance of television's ideological power has to be radically rethought. There may well be evidence of the ideological incorporation of subordinates into the social system, but this incorporation is unlikely to be achieved through eliciting a commitment to a dominant ideology strong enough to ensure the reproduction of capitalist society. Here we can agree with Abercrombie *et al.*, for reasons which I shall make clear later, that the reproduction of capitalist society is achieved *primarily* through means other than ideological incorporation. It is because this is so, that the stronger versions of the power-of-television thesis must be rejected.

It needs to be made clear that what is being contested here is *not* the existence of a dominant ideology which a majority 'go along with', but that this 'going along with' is of sufficient strength throughout that majority to justify referring to it as a 'consensus'. This is not to deny that minorities may be committed to some elements of a dominant ideology. Indeed, both Mann and Abercrombie *et al.* agree that this is the case. In support of this view, Giddens reasons that 'the level of normative integration of dominant groups within social systems may be a more important influence upon the overall continuity of those systems than how far the majority have "internalised" the same value-standards'.[49]

This is an extremely important observation for critical media theory. It implies that the attempts to theorise the power of television in terms of its ideological effects on subordinate groups is misplaced. There is considerable empirical support for the view that 'among middle-class subordinates...dominant values are more universally accepted'.[50] Whether or not this acceptance arises from the power of agencies of ideological transmission, for example television, or from the rewards available to the middle classes, as Marcuse has argued,[51] raises a number of issues relevant to locating the site of television's ideological impact.

Television and ideological shifts

Critical media theory does contain within it an approach to theorising television's power in ways which avoid all the difficulties involved with the dominant ideology thesis. The approach in question is that which draws on Hall's analyses of media amplification (see pp. 51, 53–4). However, these analyses are often embedded within a framework which assumes the ideological incorporation of subordinates to the dominant class. In what follows, I shall tease out of Hall's work on media amplification and its relation to shifts in the 'ideological climate', what I consider to be the most plausible account available of television's ideological power. In doing this, I shall steer clear of what, in the light of the arguments presented in this chapter, are problematic aspects of Hall's views—the power of television in the shaping and the winning of the consent of a majority to a dominant ideology. I shall not be concerned, then, to *represent* Hall's views, but rather to use those ideas which enable us to formulate the strongest *acceptable* version of television's power.

Hall, following Gramsci, notes 'that often, ideological shifts take place, not by substituting one, whole, new conception of the world for another, but by presenting a novel combination of old and new elements'.[52] Hall, along with Marxists, sociologists and other social critics, believes that the ideological climate throughout Western capitalist societies has undergone a major transformation since the Second World War. This transformation constitutes an ideological shift which is most clearly evident in the general direction of changes in state policies.

The particular shift in question is that involving the gradual break-up of the 'corporatist–social-democratic–welfare consensus', and its replacement, not so much by a new consensus, but by a more authoritarian state which 'was pioneered by, harnessed to, and to some extent legitimated by a populist groundswell below'.[53] Perhaps more so in Britain than elsewhere, the populist sentiments, Hall argues, had been to some extent shaped by 'a sequence of "moral panics"' during the 1960s and 1970s, 'around such apparently non-political issues as race, law-and-order, permissiveness and social anarchy'.[54] While the particular form taken by the 'moral panics' may have been peculiar to Britain, they nevertheless demonstrate television's capacity, through media amplification, to initiate crises which can be discursively exploited by sectional interests. The emergence of the authoritarian state in Britain was certainly helped by the scene which had been set by television and the media. But perhaps more important is the fact that television provides a stage on which *crises*, media-generated or real, are addressed, and thus further amplified in a spiral of signification. Television provided the stage for politicians to 'flex their ideological muscles' in response to the economic crises of the 1970s, which hit, to a varying degree, the whole of the Western capitalist world.[55]

The economic crisis was very much a crisis of capitalism, and thus ready-made for oppositional discourses. Even so, the lack of a history of exposure does place oppositional discourses at a disadvantage in relation to established discourses (see p. 57). Sensitive to the possible effects of the 'jarring' sounds of left-wing analyses on the public, the leaders of social democratic parties, with the possible exception of in France, divested themselves of any clear socialist commitment, and entered the stage of television ready to address the economic crisis in terms other than through oppositional discourses. As members of elites with privileged access to television, the leaders of social democratic parties shied away from influencing the 'crisis agenda' in ways favourable to the Left. The debates turned, not on capitalism versus socialism, but on different approaches to managing the crisis within a capitalist framework.[56] In this context the voices of the Left became marginalised. Both right-wing and social democratic parties became advocates of the need for a 'strong state' to manage the economic crisis, hence the rightward drift in Western politics.

Perhaps too much can be made of both television's handling of the economic crisis and the persuasiveness of particular right-wing politicians. The cause of the Right was given a boost by television's tendency to seize upon divisions in the social democratic ranks, and the disarray on the Left. But it was the strategy of the social democratic parties' leadership which launched them further to the Right, and which placed them in a disadvantageous position in relation to right-wing parties. It was this strategy, too, more than television, which fuelled the fragmentation of social democratic parties. Having accepted the terms of reference of the debates over crisis management, they had in fact placed themselves in a position from which they could not win. Having failed in government to manage the crisis, their own proposals lacked credibility, and, more than this, any proposals from the Left were seen to be criticisms of both of the past record of social democratic governments and of the efforts of the leadership to regain credibility with a disillusioned public. In these circumstances it was relatively easy for the Right to make ideological gains. Whether or not these gains were enough to secure electoral victories is to some extent irrelevant. The discourses of the Right became dominant throughout the capitalist West. Hall notes that in the late 1970s 'Poulantzas attempted to characterize a new "moment" in the conjuncture of the class democracies'.[57] According to Poulantzas this 'new moment' was formed by

intensive state control over every sphere of socio-economic life, combined with radical decline of the institutions of political democracy and with draconian and multiform curtailment of so-called 'formal' liberties, whose reality is being discovered now that they are overboard.[58]

The 'new moment', descriptive of the political-ideological climate which had emerged in capitalist democracies, was referred to by Poulantzas as 'authoritarian statism'. For Hall, 'authoritarian populism' is a more apt description, capturing the ideological self-representations of the authoritarian state as 'anti-statist', and the way in which the ruling political forces were able to 'harness to its support some popular discontents, neutralize the opposing forces, disaggregate the opposition and really incorporate *some* strategic elements of popular opinion into its own hegemonic project'.[59]

In emphasising that the shift in the ideological climate incorporates '*some* strategic elements of popular opinion', Hall is in fact distancing himself from both the dominant ideology thesis and stronger versions of the power-of-television thesis. It is thus difficult to uphold Jessop *et al.*'s criticism that Hall's treatment of authoritarian populism 'generates an excessive concern with the mass media and ideological production'.[60] In a reply to Jessop *et al.*, Hall explicitly rejects their view that 'although Hall and others have raised the question of the audience's reception of ideologies, the danger remains of assuming that the "message" as emitted is identical to the message as received and understood'.[61] Hall believes that such a misunderstanding of his work arises from insufficient attention being paid to the way in which he uses the concept of 'hegemony'. He states quite emphatically that 'in my own work, I have consistently struggled *against* any definition of hegemony which identifies it as exclusively an ideological phenomenon'.[62] Instead, Hall believes that dominant groups secure their dominance 'not by ideological compulsion, but by cultural leadership', which is accomplished 'not without the due measure of legal and legitimate compulsion'.[63] Hegemony, for Hall, involves the coercive practices of the state in its attempt to win consent. In achieving hegemony, the dominant ideologies are 'modified', without comprising the essential interests of dominant groups, to incorporate some populist sentiments. As for the role of television in the achievement of hegemony, Hall states that

We can speak only of the *tendency* of the media—but it is a systematic tendency, not an incidental feature—to reproduce the ideological field of a society, in such a way as to reproduce, also, its structure of domination.[64]

There is perhaps a tendency in Hall's work to emphasise the contradictory nature of dominant ideologies as being in some way instrumental to the hegemony of dominant groups. Indeed, authoritarian populism is a 'deliberately contradictory term precisely to encapsulate the contradictory features of the emerging conjunction'.[65] Be that as it may, I want to emphasise more strongly than Hall, that the ideological shift which has produced the ideological climate common to most Western capitalist societies has far more to do with the imposition of authoritarian practices than with the appeal of the contradictory ideology.

The significance of the discourses of the Right in changing the ideological climate does *not* reside in their potential influence in winning popular consent, but rather in their influence on those who occupy positions which provide them with the power to enact the discourses. Further, the social impact of the discourses of the Right does *not* inhere in the 'power of the discourses' themselves, but in the *force of the material practices* in which they are inscribed and through which they are *materialised*. What I am proposing, then, is that the 'shift', which Hall, Poulantzas and others have addressed, is best characterised as a modification in the material context in which we live. To be sure, we can understand changes in the material conditions of everyday life in Western societies as a product of the materialisation of ideological shifts. But to say this, is to emphasise that dominant discourses are likely to be effective in so far as they fall on and influence those with the material power to put these discourses into practice. It is these practices as practices, rather than the discourses themselves, which have an impact on the majority. It is, too, as I shall argue in later chapters, through the effects of material practices rather than the effects of ideology that societies are reproduced.

My emphases on the power-effectiveness of material practices over ideological representations is not to be seen as a product of an exclusive concern with specific changes in Western societies. What I want to suggest is that noticeable shifts in a society's material life and ideological climate are in many respects 'condensed-time' forms of the changes which take place in more stable periods of social reproduction. During times of noticeable shifts, the relation between the practices which modify the texture of everyday life, and their underlying discourses, is thrown into sharp relief. The law and order discourses through which the media-generated moral panics were articulated and addressed, rather quickly found their material expression in repressive legislation, and were seen to have an influence on police policy, and thus on policing practices, on magistrates, and on professions such as teaching. Similarly, the discourses of the Right, which exploited the economic crisis of the 1970s, soon materialised in the form of extending the coercive practices of the state to intervene in almost all aspects of contemporary life.

Periods of crisis are by definition periods in which routine social reproduction is disrupted. Crises 'call for' immediate practical solutions. The practices which normally sustain economic and political life are expected to undergo some change. In these circumstances 'the crisis' provides opportunities for heightened power struggles amongst dominant groups, and a specific focus for the more normally dispersed attentions of politicians, other dominant groups and the mass media. But, just as the dominant discourses addressing 'the crisis' fetch up in material practices, so too with the dominant discourses in periods of routine social reproduction. In periods of relative stability, the dominant discourses are no less connected to power-effective practices, whose effects are to reinforce, consolidate, sustain, maintain and generally reproduce the existing state of affairs.

What this suggests, then, is that the condensed-time of noticeable material and ideological changes is an exaggerated form of the relation between material practices and the dominant ideology. It enables us to see the processes of ideological production in operation, and the effects of ideology on dominant groups and their middle class subordinates. In time, and through their materialisation, the dominant discourses constitute embedded elements of the dominant ideology, and as such are routinely reproduced by dominant groups in their daily conduct.

In the above discussion, I have moved a considerable distance away from the focus of the dominant ideology thesis on the ideological incorporation of the working class as necessary for the reproduction of capitalist societies. By implication, I have also distanced myself from the stronger versions of the power-of-television thesis. This is not to say that television has no significant role either in producing ideological effects, or in social reproduction.

Television's capacity to generate crises has been noted. Whether in times of crisis (media-generated or otherwise), or in periods of stability, television is the principal medium through which dominant discourses are represented to the public. But whereas advocates of the dominant ideology thesis might want to stress that the effect of television's representation of dominant discourses is one of winning the consent of a majority to the dominant ideology, I have, in keeping with earlier arguments (see pp. 84–6), emphasised that dominant discourses are more likely to have their greatest impact on dominant groups and middle-class subordinates. This is not to say that many of the working class do not go along with aspects of dominant discourses, but we cannot refer to this 'going along with' as a form of ideological incorporation of sufficient strength to secure the reproduction of society.

In so far as dominant discourses are materialised we can say that television participates in those practices centrally involved in social reproduction and capitalist-class domination. This is to acknowledge television's representation of dominant discourses 'works on' those with the power to enact the discourse. In contrast to the dominant ideology thesis, what is being stressed here is television's involvement in *material* effects. It is through material rather than ideological effects that society is reproduced. The importance of this point can be illustrated by the fact that myths about gender, routinely reproduced in all forms of television, fall on the male population, a substantial proportion of whom enact these myths, and it is this enactment which constitutes male domination.

We can also note, with Hall, that television reinforces many populist sentiments, but these, unlike myths, do not automatically serve dominant interests although they are exploitable by dominant groups.

More importantly, as far as the working class is concerned, there is little evidence to suggest the existence of a consensus around viewpoints oppositional to the dominant ideology. Abercrombie *et al*. state that 'this obviously reduces the threat to social order that would have resulted should subordinates have developed such an oppositional ideology'.[66] It would be far too media-centred to point an accusing finger at television for this state of affairs. Clearly, working-class associations and political parties have a major responsibility in this area. It could even be argued that in so far as the education system is a public institution it ought to educate people in the full range of ideas and practices. However, it has been noted that the long history of television's underrepresentation, non-representation and misrepresentation of oppositional discourses not only makes it difficult for opinion to be mobilised around oppositional viewpoints, but it makes it difficult for agents of opposition to make themselves understood. Television, through its significant absences and missing dimensions, participates in the production of what can be referred to as 'negative' ideological effects, corresponding to the fourth level of ideological operations. (see p. 81).

The Pluralist challenge

I noted at the beginning of this chapter that pluralists suspect that critical media theorists too readily assume that television has a powerful ideological impact on the audience. We have seen that there are Marxists and critical social theorists who share this suspicion.

Pluralists have quite correctly maintained that questions about the ideological effectiveness of television and the mass media cannot 'remain on the realm of high-pitched polemic and high-flown (and unsubstantiated) speculation'.[67] Blumler reasons that the 'speculative hypotheses' of 'grand theory' (critical media theory) should be operationalised so that 'their validity can be independently checked against a set of relevant facts'.[68] The 'relevant facts' are, for Blumler and Gurevitch, to be derived from 'an adequately founded investigation of audience response'. Without this, they claim, 'the study of mass communication as a social process...is like a sexology that ignores the orgasm!'.[69]

Fejes, in a similar vein, commenting on critical media research, suggests that 'as more and more research is focused towards message content and production, the audience will become more and more invisible in the theory and research of critical scholars'. A major consequence of this is 'a distinct danger of a disappearing audience'.[70] In going on to discuss the value of a number of behaviourist models for conceptualising the relation between television and audience, Fejes implies that 'the disappearing audience' reflects an absence of the concept of audience in critical media theory.

In response to these kinds of criticisms of critical media theory, it can be agreed that empirical observations of the effects of television on the audience are essential in assessing television's ideological power. But much hinges on what is meant by 'empirical observation', and more specifically, 'empirical observations of audience response'. I want to suggest that critical media theory, at least in the political ecomony and culturalist perspectives, *is* rooted in empirical observations, and that it embraces a concept of the audience which is methodologically superior to that employed by pluralists. However, the major problem with critical media theory, in keeping with the arguments of this chapter, is that the *interpretation* of the empirical evidence indicative of television's ideological power has been conducted, in the main, from within the framework of the dominant ideology thesis. It is this interpretation which both reflects and reinforces the media- and ideology-centredness of critical media theory.

The kind of evidence required to test the ideological effectiveness of television on the audience is that derived from a continuous monitoring of what people think, and what they deem to be important. In practice this translates into what people say—preferably what they say when unsolicited—even though we know that the total range of what we say does not necessarily correspond with the total range of our thoughts. Quite clearly these requirements alone are well beyond the resources and capabilities of the information gathering and storage facilities available for the surveillance practices of the state, let alone the meagre resources available to social scientists. In addition to this ideal evidence, that is, unobtrusive ethnographic evidence, we would need surveys of what people watch on television. In pursuing the relationship between television viewing and the total range of concerns and thoughts held by individuals, we would need ethnographic evidence of an historical variety, which would enable us to assess the *sources* of the concerns and thoughts.[71]

The non-availability of ideal empirical evidence which can be used to assess the ideological effectiveness of television means that we have to use evidence which is less than ideal. The major difficulty with using audience-response data, as the critique of traditional media effects research reveals, is that as soon as one attempts to investigate audience response to specific programmes, the audience is no longer a typical audience. One consequence of participating as a research subject in audience-response research is that the individual is transformed from being a 'typical' audience member, into a 'critical' one. This is particularly important in considering ideological effects, since members of the audience may be most vulnerable to ideological manipulation when they are not 'on their guard', as they would have to be as participants in audience research. As Wren-Lewis has argued, 'this problem will be almost impossible to circumvent'.[72] There is, then, the distinct possibility that audience-response research fails to investigate those kinds of audience and their reactions which are normally associated with non-selective routine forms of television viewing.

By contrast, critical media theory focuses on 'the public' as audience, and draws upon surveys of public opinion, ethnographic studies, election results, and other forms of social observation indicative of the ideological climate, in order to assess 'ideological effects'. They thus avoid the methodological difficulties which attend those research attempts to specify a causal relation between specific programmes and their effects. If the precise relation between specific television programmes and the variable responses of specific audiences is not amenable to scientific investigation, then we have to settle for a characterisation of this relation in more general terms. In doing this, critical media theory has not so much ignored the public but has rather interpreted the available data on the public in ways which exaggerate the ideological incorporation of the working class into the social order. Having interpreted the empirical evidence in this way, it is but a short step to assume then that television and the mass media generate powerful ideological effects. I have argued that it is the ideology-centredness of critical media theory which is primarily responsible for the stronger and unwarranted versions of television's power to manipulate audiences.

The ideology-centredness of critical media theory finds its strongest expressions in structuralist perspectives. It is here that the general intent of the concerns of Blumler, Fejes and others is most appropriate. In structuralist approaches to the ideological effectiveness of the mass media, as I shall argue in the next chapter, 'there is a danger that...the audience will be regarded as passive'.[73]

Notes

1. Peter Golding, 'The Missing Dimensions—News Media and the Management of Social Change' in Elihu Katz and Tamas Szecskö, eds, *Mass Media and Social Change*, London, Sage, 1981, p. 63.
2. Peter Golding and Graham Murdock, 'Theories of Communication and Theories of Society' in G. Cleveland Wilhoit and Harold de Bock, eds, *Mass Communication Review Yearbook, Vol 1, 1980*, London, Sage, 1980, p. 73.
3. Tom Bottomore, 'Foreword' in Nicholas Abercrombie, Stephen Hill and Bryan S. Turner, *The Dominant Ideology Thesis*, London, George Allen and Unwin, 1980, p. ix.
4. Abercrombie *et al.*, op. cit., p. 29.
5. This generally refers to 'theoretically informed' observations of 'self in relation to others', of social interaction, as 'lived' in everyday social contexts. The researcher may be a 'natural' member of the group under study, or as an 'outsider' may use a range of techniques to understand 'the world as it is experienced and understood' by those being studied. Such techniques include: participant observation, 'just being around', group discussion, 'unfocused interview', everyday conversation, and so on. For a brief and useful discussion, see Paul Willis, 'Notes on method' in Stuart Hall, Dorothy Hobson, Andrew Lowe and Paul Willis, eds, *Culture, Media, Language*, London, Hutchinson, 1980, pp. 88–95. For a more comprehensive account, see Jack D. Douglas, *Investigative Social Research*, London, Sage, 1976.
6. Abercrombie *et al.*, op. cit., p. 144.
7. Ibid.; see also H.F. Moorhouse and C. Chamberlain, 'Lower-class attitudes to property', *Sociology*, vol. 8, no. 3, 1974, pp. 387–405.
8. Abercrombie *et al.*, op. cit., p. 145.
9. Ibid., p. 146.
10. *British Social Attitudes: the 1984 Report*, cited in James Curran, 'Rationale for the Right', *Marxism Today*, February 1985, p. 40.

11. Abercrombie *et al.*, op. cit., p. 148.
12. Ibid., pp. 150–1.
13. Ibid., p. 153.
14. Stuart Hall, 'Culture, the Media and the "Ideological Effect"' in James Curran, Michael Gurevitch and Janet Woollacott, eds, *Mass Communication and Society*, London, Arnold, 1977, p. 339.
15. Stuart Hall, 'The rediscovery of "ideology": return of the repressed in media studies' in Michael Gurevitch, Tony Bennett, James Curran and Janet Woollacott, eds, *Culture, Society and the Media*, London, Methuen, 1982, p. 85.
16. Hall, 'Culture, the Media, and the "Ideological Effect"', pp. 338–9.
17. Denis McQuail, 'The influence and effects of mass media' in Curran *et al.*, *Mass Communication and Society*, pp. 70–94.
18. Abercrombie *et al.*, op. cit., p. 152.
19. Ibid., pp. 151–2.
20. Ibid., p. 152.
21. Norman Webb and Robert Wybrow, *The Gallup Report: Your Opinions in 1981*, London, Sphere, 1982, p. 68.
22. Ibid., p. 78.
23. Hall, 'The rediscovery of "ideology"', p. 86.
24. Ibid., p. 87.
25. Ibid., p. 86.
26. Stuart Hall, 'Authoritarian Populism: A Reply to Jessop *et al.*', *New Left Review*, vol. 151, 1985, pp. 115–24.
27. Ralph Miliband, 'The New Revisionism in Britain', *New Left Review*, vol. 150, 1985, pp. 5–26.
28. Claus Offe, (ed. John Keane), *Contradictions of the Welfare State*, London, Hutchinson, 1984, p. 168.
29. Ibid.
30. Ibid., p. 169.
31. Ibid.
32. This is perhaps most noticeable in the United States, where the costs of campaigning for president can only be met if the candidates have the backing of big business, and this obviously compromises any candidate seeking office in order to enact radical, progressive social policies. Whatever electoral bargains may be struck to secure 'the black vote', the black population itself passes judgment on these deals by its low turn-out at presidential elections. For a more 'optimistic' interpretation of electoral deals, see Chuck Stone, *Black Political Power in America*, New York, Delta, 1970.
33. Michael Mann, *Consciousness and Action among the Western Working Class*, London, Macmillan, 1973.
34. Abercrombie *et al.*, op. cit., p. 1.

35. Moorhouse and Chamberlain, op. cit.
36. John H. Goldthorpe, David Lockwood, Frank Bechofer and Jennifer Platt, *The affluent worker in the class structure*, vols 1-3, London, Cambridge University Press, 1968, 1969.
37. Abercrombie *et al.*, op. cit., p. 147.
38. See T. Veness, *School Leavers: Their Aspirations and Expectations*, London, Methuen, 1962; and R. McKenzie and A. Silver, *Angels in Marble: Working-Class Conservatives in Urban England*, London, Heinemann, 1968.
39. Abercrombie *et al.*, op. cit., p. 147.
40. Michael Mann, 'The Social Cohesion of Liberal Democracy' in Anthony Giddens and David Held, eds, *Classes, Power, and Conflict: Classical and Contemporary Debates*, London, Macmillan, 1982, p. 378.
41. Abercrombie *et al.*, op. cit., p. 145.
42. Ibid., p. 153.
43. Ibid., p. 146.
44. Anthony Giddens, *Central Problems in Social Theory*, London, Macmillan, 1979, p. 128.
45. Ibid., p. 102.
46. Mann, *Consciousness and Action*; Mann, 'Social Cohesion'.
47. Mann, 'Social Cohesion', p. 375.
48. Ibid., p. 388.
49. Giddens, op. cit., p. 103.
50. Abercrombie *et al.*, op. cit., p. 143.
51. Herbert Marcuse, *One Dimensional Man*, London, Abacus, 1964.
52. Hall, 'Authoritarian Populism', p. 122.
53. Ibid., p. 118.
54. Ibid., p 116.
55. Ibid.
56. For a detailed account, see Ernest Mandel, *The Second Slump: A Marxist Analysis of Recession in the Seventies*, London, Verso, 1978.
57. Hall, 'Authoritarian Populism', p. 116.
58. Ibid., pp. 116–17.
59. Ibid., p. 118.
60. Bob Jessop, Kevin Bonnett, Simon Bromley and Tom Ling, 'Thatcherism and the Politics of Hegemony: a Reply to Stuart Hall', *New Left Review*, vol. 153, 1985, p. 37.
61. Ibid., pp. 37–8.
62. Hall, 'Authoritarian Populism', p. 120.
63. Hall, 'The Rediscovery of "ideology"', p. 85.
64. Hall, 'Culture, the Media, and the "Ideological Effect"', p. 346.
65. Hall, 'Authoritarian Populism', p. 118.
66. Abercrombie *et al.*, op. cit,. p. 153.
67. Jay Blumler, *Mass Communication and Society*, DE353, Unit 8, Milton

Keynes, Open University, 1977, p. 6.

68. Ibid., p. 41.
69. Jay Blumler and Michael Gurevitch, 'The political effects of mass communication', in Gurevitch *et al.*, *Culture, Society and the Media*, p. 265.
70. Fred Fejes, 'Critical mass communcations research and media effects: the problem of the disappearing audience', *Media, Culture and Society*, vol. 6, 1984, p. 222.
71. An ethnographic focus on sources of influence would overcome some of the difficulties raised by critics of Gerbner's 'media cultivation theory'. See George Gerbner, 'Cultural Indicators—The Third Voice' in G. Gerbner, L. Gross and W. Melody, eds, *Communications Technology and Social Policy*, New York, Wiley, 1973, pp. 553–73.
72. Justin Wren-Lewis, 'The encoding/decoding model: criticisms and redevelopments for research on decoding', *Media, Culture and Society*, vol. 5, 1983, p. 196.
73. Fejes, op. cit., p. 222.

4 The Maligned Audience

The thrust of the discussion in the previous chapter led to two connected conclusions: that members of subordinate groups are not 'successfully' ideologically incorporated into the society in which they are subordinated, and that the reproduction of capitalist societies is achieved primarily through means other than the ideological incorporation of subordinate classes. These conclusions suggest that the ideological effects of television and the mass media are not as powerful as many critical media theorists would have us believe, and this in turn suggests that the social significance of television has been exaggerated. But in approaching 'ideological effects', whatever their source, in terms of the opinions or beliefs held by individuals, indicators of 'opinions' and 'beliefs' were treated as 'evidence' of the existence of ideological effects. It can be argued that beliefs and opinions are inappropriate indicators of ideological effects. Thus Abercrombie *et al.* recognise that 'against the evidence we have presented, there may be clear, persistent attempts to preserve the validity of the dominant ideology thesis which involve the suggestion that the dominant ideology has its effects in primarily indirect, undercover, even unseen, ways'.[1]

Within structuralist media theory there is just such an attempt, and it involves a conception of ideology somewhat different from that embodied in the discussion of the previous chapter. Ideological effects are formulated in ways which make them 'indispensible' for the reproduction of all societies, and television is one agency which is deemed to be centrally involved in producing these ideological effects. What we are faced with here is the power-of-television thesis in its strongest form. In order to understand how this thesis has developed it is necessary briefly to consider some aspects of Althusser's theory of ideology.

The Althusserian conception of ideology

The relations of production, which in a capitalist society reflect the subordination of the working class to the capitalist class, are, as Althusser recognises, 'first reproduced by the materiality of the processes of production and circulation'. These material processes are also the realisation of the dominant or ruling ideology. Thus Althusser reminds us that 'it should not be forgotten that ideological relations are immediately present in these same processes'.[2] Indeed all social practices, for Althusser, are the realisation of ideologies, although the reproduction of the ideologies thus realised is not necessarily the primary purpose or function of all practices. The earlier discussion on the materialisation of the discourses of the authoritarian state is illustrative of Althusser's emphasis on 'material practices being inscribed with a dominant ideology' (see pp. 89–92). Consistent with my emphases in that discussion, Althusser argues that 'the (Repressive) State Apparatus functions massively and predominantly *by repression* (including physical repression), while functioning secondarily by ideology'.[3] There are, however, in Althusser's scheme, a whole range of practices which 'function massively and predominantly *by ideology*', but which also 'function secondarily by repression'.[4] These practices constitute the 'Ideological State Apparatuses' (ISAs). These include the practices of the institutions of religion, education, the family, the legal system, the political system, trade unions, sport, the arts, cultural institutions and the mass media. Each of the ISAs contributes, 'in the way proper to it', to the reproduction of the relations of production. The 'communications apparatus' makes its contribution to the reproduction of capitalist relations of exploitation 'by cramming every "citizen" with daily doses of nationalism, chauvinism, liberalism, moralism, etc., by means of the press, the radio and television'.[5]

According to Althusser, the most ideologically effective of all the ISAs, that is, the ISA which provides the greatest ideological service for the dominant class, is the education system. As he puts it, 'no other ideological State apparatus has the obligatory (and not least, free) audience of the totality of the children in the capitalist social formation, eight hours a day for five or six days out of seven'.[6] The ideological effectivity of the education system resides not so much in the ideas which are taught, but more in the fact that children are 'inserted' in the practices which form their experience of schooling. Individuals 'live in ideology', and ideology has a material existence. Schooling is 'an apprenticeship in a variety of know-how wrapped up in the massive inculcation of the ideology of the ruling class'.[7] We have already noted how living in and through the practices of schooling may shape the expectations and motives of working-class children (see pp. 82–4), and how this serves the interests of the dominant class. Indeed it could be said that many working-class children come to 'represent' themselves, and their relation to their conditions of existence, with 'ideas' which *serve the interests* of dominant groups, that is, in ways which contribute to the reproduction of the relations of production. Since these ideas are derived from the practices in which individuals are inserted, and since these practices 'are governed by the *rituals* in which these practices are inscribed, within the *material existence of an ideological apparatus*',[8] we can say that these ideas are ideologically distorted. Thus, for Althusser,

all ideology represents in its necessarily imaginary distortion not the existing relations of production (and the other relations that derive from them, but above all the (imaginary) relationship of individuals to the relations of production and the relations that derive from them. What is represented in ideology is therefore not the system of the real relations which govern the existence of individuals, but the imaginary relation of those individuals to the real relations in which they live.[9]

Here we can begin to see how Abercrombie *et al.*'s focus on the dominant ideology as made up of elements of 'capitalist class ideologies' is much narrower than Althusser's conception of the ideological. Althusser is more concerned with 'ideas' in general which might be used to represent 'the imaginary relation' of individuals to their conditions of existence. Consequently ideological effects cannot be confined to a consideration of the extent to which individuals adopt capitalist class ideologies as beliefs.

It is precisely because of the assumption that 'the "ideas" of a human subject exist in his actions,…and if that is not the case, it (ideology) lends him other ideas corresponding to the actions (however perverse) that he does perform',[10] *and* because television and the mass media are major sources of ideas as 'ideological representations', that critical media theorists generally, not just structuralists, are able to refer to television as producing ideological effects. Thus Hall argues that

the ways in which men come to understand their relation to their real conditions of existence, under capitalism, are subject to the *relay of language*: and it is this which makes possible that ideological displacement or inflection, whereby the 'real' relations can be culturally signified and ideologically inflected as a set of 'imaginary lived relations'.[11]

The ideological effect, in this view, is that individuals 'will "think"' their relation to their conditions of existence 'within the limits of a *dominant ideology*'.[12] This ideological effect, which can be said to be produced by television, amongst other agencies relaying language, performs 'a pivotal role in the maintenance of capitalist relations and in their continuing domination within the social formation'.[13]

At this point it would seem that we have restored a rather strong version of television's power, based on the necessity of its ideological effect for social reproduction. The evidence for television's ideological effect is to be found in the individual's actions in which the discourses of television exist. If we go along with this view (I shall argue later that there are compelling reasons for rejecting it) then it would be reasonable to ask how it is that television's discourses find their way into the action of individuals. Althusser begins to answer this question in his theory of 'ideological interpellation'.

The *theory of ideological interpellation* expresses Althusser's view that '*all ideology has the function* (which defines it) of "constituting" concrete individuals as subjects'.[14] He goes on to state that 'the "obviousness" that you and I are subjects—and that that does not cause any problem—is an ideological effect, the elementary ideological effect'.[15] For Althusser this is so on account of the double meaning of 'subject'. On the one hand 'subject' refers to 'a free subjectivity, a centre of initiatives, author of and responsible for its actions', and on the other hand to 'a subjected being, who submits to a higher authority, and is therefore stripped of all freedom except that of freely accepting his submission'.[16] The obviousness of the first meaning of 'subject' is widely recognised, enabling us 'to work by ourselves'. But the reverse side of this recognition of ourselves as free subjects is that we misrecognise or fail to recognise that we are freely subjecting ourselves to structures of domination. Althusser argues that 'the reality which is necessarily *ignored* (*méconnue*) in the very forms of recognition (ideology = misrecognition/ ignorance) is indeed, in the last resort, the reproduction of the relations of production and the relations deriving from them'.[17]

From here, we can understand how Althusser's theory of ideology can be connected to those ideas which stress that 'it is language which provides the possibility of subjectivity because it is language which enables the speaker to posit himself or herself as "I", as subject of a sentence'. Belsey goes on to say that 'it is through language that people constitute themselves as subjects'.[18] Here again it is the power of language which enables a consideration of television's discourses as being powerfully involved in producing 'the elementary ideological effect'.

The power of television's discourses

Central to much structuralist media theory, is the view that television's discourses are ideological in that they provide 'subject positions' to which audience members are said to be 'recruited'. Thus, as Belsey notes, the individual 'learns to recognise itself in a series of subject-positions...which are the positions from which discourse is intelligible to itself and others'.[19] This recognition is the ideological effect, which is at the same time, a misrecognition.

It can be objected that the viewer is not compelled to take up a subject position, or alternatively, that several conflicting subject positions may be discursively offered by any television programme. In either case it would seem that the ideological effect remains within the discourse and does not translate to the individual viewer. The simple answer to the first objection is that the viewer will not be able to make sense of what she/he sees other than by identifying with, and adopting, a subject position. The second objection poses no real problem in that contradictory subject positions are still subject positions which are taken up. Their contradictions can be seen either to reinforce the ideological effect by emphasising the plurality of 'free subjectivities', or, as some structuralists argue, to consolidate the primary ideological effect by reproducing conventions of 'realism' in which 'subjectivity is a major—perhaps the major— theme'.[20] Drawing extensively on the work of Heath[21] and MacCabe[22], Belsey claims that 'classical realism'—the dominant popular mode in television drama—

performs...the work of ideology, not only in its representation of a world of consistent subjects who are the origin of meaning, knowledge and action, but also in offering the reader (viewer), as the position from which the text is most readily intelligible, the position of subject as the origin both of understanding and of action in accordance with that understanding.[23]

Thus, as an 'ideological practice', Belsey concludes, classical realism addresses viewers as subjects 'interpellating them in order that they freely accept this subjectivity and their subjection'.[24] It must be said that not all structuralists place as much emphasis on classical realism as an 'ideological practice'. What is important to structuralists, however, is the view that 'texts and social experience are both made and understood by discourses, and...subjectivity, the site of this understanding, is equally a discursive product'.[25] Consequently, as Fiske reasons, 'the structured relationship of discourses in both text and society' is 'of greater importance than the individuality of any reader'.[26]

The power attributed to television's discourses by structuralists is of such an order that it is assumed that 'the images conveyed by the media have...become so sophisticated and persuasive that they now organise our experiences and understanding in a crucially significant way'.[27] Structuralists have provided detailed analyses of the whole range of television programmes, including advertisements, to advance their claims about television's ideological power. Thus, in relation to the representation of women in advertising in general, Winship offers the following.

The signifier 'woman' always signifies woman: we recognise ourselves in *any* representation of woman, however 'original', because we are always already defined by our gender. Having recognised ourselves in the ad., we are then 'freshly' positioned as specific feminine subjects in an identification achieved through a misrecognition of ourselves—the signifier 'woman' can never in fact represent us as individual women. It is through this process of misrecognition that ads are effective in producing and reproducing the particular ideological modes in which we live.[28]

Such an analysis enables Williamson to state that 'advertisements...in providing us with a structure in which we, and those goods, are interchangeable...are selling us ourselves'.[29]

Most structuralists would agree with Thompson that 'to pose the problem of the effectivity of a programme...it is necessary to recognise that programmes of themselves are constitutive of the viewer in a particular way'.[30] However, not all structuralists are prepared to treat 'the ideological constitution' of the social individual in terms which extend to the determination of the viewer's thinking, as in Thompson's analysis of an educational television programme. In this analysis of a programme on unemployment, Thompson argues that the particular programme presented a very restricted view of the causes of unemployment, and 'since the causes of unemployment other than in these terms are nowhere raised, the viewer also perceives unemployment in this manner'.[31]

Althusser's theory of ideological interpellation, as I have intimated, can give rise to a stronger and a weaker formulation of the ideological power of television, although both formulations will strike non-structuralists as rather 'strong'. The key to understanding the stronger structuralist positions is to be found in the influence of Lacan's theory of 'the unconscious'.

Television, discourse and the unconscious

Bennett writes:

in speaking of the impact of the media on the terms in which we see the world, we are speaking of an ideological process which, in so far as it concerns the formation of consciousness, is one which those subjected to it—you, me, all of us—tend to be unconscious of. It escapes our consciousness inasmuch as it constitutes the framework within which our consciousness is produced. This is not to say that the operations of ideology are necessarily invisible; but it is to say that their invisibility is a condition of their effectiveness.[32]

It is this kind of view which has proved to be particularly attractive to structuralists. That television produces ideological effects via some kind of manipulation of the unconscious tends to conjure up notions of a powerful medium penetrating the deep-seated psychic core of individuals. The analysis of television programmes, or 'textual deconstruction' as structuralists often refer to it, is directed at making the ideological operations within the programmes visible. Since it is these operations which ultimately produce the ideological effects which are assumed to be necessary for the reproduction of capitalist society (or patriarchal society), then we can appreciate why it is that many structuralists consider the ideological deconstruction of texts to be a form of political practice.

Lacan's theory of the unconscious is especially useful for structuralist accounts of the ideological effectiveness of television, in that it readily connects the idea of television's discourses 'recruiting' the audience to subject positions with unconscious processes, and it understands the primary effect of the unconscious in terms more or less identical to Althusser's primary ideological effect. 'The obviousness that you and I are subjects...', as Althusser depicted the fundamental ideological effect, is, in Lacan 'the illusion of autonomy to which the individual entrusts itself'.[33] This illusion, according to Lacan, is the most significant of all our misrecognitions (*méconnaissances*); *méconnaissance* is the product of the unconscious, and the unconscious is the product of 'the discourses of the Other'. By the latter, he means that the unconscious is structured by the universal structures of language. Indeed, Lacan reasons that the infant's unconscious begins to develop at the point when she/he begins to use language.

To understand the unconscious, in Lacan's theory, is essentially to understand how the structure of language generates meaning—'what the psychoanalytic experience discovers in the unconscious is the whole structure of language'.[34] For Lacan, the source of meaning is not to be found in the relation between the word (signifier) and the object it names (signified), but in the relation between signifiers. Language is made up of interconnected 'chains of signifiers'.

What this structure of the signifying chain discloses is the possibility I have, precisely in so far as I have this language in common with other subjects, that is to say, in so far as it exists as a language, to use it in order to signify *something quite other* than what it says.[35]

The relations between signifiers—which makes language 'signify *something quite other* than what it says'—are structured, in Lacan's scheme, by metaphor and metonymy. Metaphor ('one word for another') is the linguistic equivalent of 'condensation' whereby the repressed contents of the unconscious, according to Freud, are misrepresented. Metonymy, which is descriptive of the displacement or 'slide' of meaning along a signifying chain, corresponds to the Freudian concept of 'displacement', which is 'the most appropriate means used by the unconscious to foil censorship'.[36]

'The particular effects' of the mechanisms of language, Lacan claims, are 'anterior to any possible link with any particular experience of the subject'.[37] This is important for structuralist media theory, in that it enables the effects of television to be specified without any reference to the viewer—the effects can be derived from the analysis of television's discourses alone. Though these effects are theorised without reference to actual audience members, they are nevertheless about viewers. Specifically, the effects of television's discourses 'constitute individuals' in ways unbeknown to the individual.

The signifying game between metonymy and metaphor, up to and including the active edge that splits my desire between a refusal of the signifier and a lack of being, and links my fate to the question of my destiny, this game, in all its inexorable subtlety, is played until the match is called, there where I am not, because I cannot situate myself there.

…I think where I am not, therefore I am where I do not think.

What one ought to say is: I am not wherever I am the plaything of my thought; I think of what I am where I do not think to think.[38]

Our refusal to accept the validity of this formulation is itself the product of langauge mediated through the unconscious. For such a refusal would be indicative of the power of 'the illusion of the autonomous ego' to which we have succumbed.

The ideological effectiveness of television's messages, Heck argues, is to be found at 'a level of "deep structure", which is "invisible" and "unconscious", which continuously structures our immediate conscious perceptions in this distorted way. This is why, in ideological analysis, we must go to the structuring level of messages'.[39] We have seen an example of such an analysis (see p. 42). In a similar vein, commenting on an advertisement for gold, Dyer tells us that much of the advertisement 'works at an unconscious level where a connection is being made between a gold bracelet (signifier) and an intimate (sexual) relationhip between two people (signified). The significance of the message lies in its implicit narrative'.[40]

The structuralist response to those criticisms which accuse critical media theorists of ignoring audience response to television in its portrayals of the ideological power of television can now be explicitly stated. Since the ideological impact of 'the language of television' occurs at an unconscious level, and since this level is revealed in the operations of language itself, it follows that there is no need to record audience response. As Bennett argues,

the proposition that the media are influential in proposing certain ideologically derived definitions of reality is one that cannot be dependent for its validation solely upon the subjective reports of those whose consciousness is said to be produced, without their being aware of it, by this process. It is a proposition that would automatically lose its theoretical power were it to be operationalized in this way.[41]

Although estimates vary as to how influential structuralist approaches to the ideological impact of television are, it is important to recognise that the core connections between language and the unconscious do enable a diversity of approaches which exploit these connections. Thus different semiotic approaches to the analysis of discourses provide different ways of revealing the ideology in television programmes, and the ideology thus exposed can be assumed to be effective at an unconscious level. So, the close relationship between the unconscious and language can be attractive to the whole range of 'textual analysts' other than those who might be referred to as 'structuralist'. Similarly there are those outside of the orbit of critical media altogether, who engage in 'psychoanalytic' readings of television programmes. Very often the validity of these readings rests on the validity of elements of Freudian or Jungian theory, and their significance trades on the assumption that the unconscious controls us in 'weird and wonderful' ways. The value of this assumption for critical media theorists who want to maintain that television exerts a very powerful ideological control over audiences is made clear by Dichter. He claims that 'it has been proved beyond any doubt that many of our daily decisions are governed by motivations over which we have no control and of which we are often quite unaware'.[42]

It is worthwhile to follow some of Dichter's claims because they suggest an approach to the ideological effectiveness of television, which avoids the linguistic emphasis in structuralism. Dichter tells us that 'the reliability of a lighter is important because it is integrally connected with the basic (read "unconscious" here) reasons for using a lighter'. The unconscious reason is 'the desire for mastery and power'.[43] In a manner fairly typical of those well practised in putting the theory of unconscious motivation to use, Dichter elaborates: 'the capacity to summon fire inevitably gives every human being...a sense of power...Fire and the ability to command it are prized because they are associated not only with warmth, but also with life itself'.[44] This speculation is 'validated' by 'the Greek legend of Prometheus and many other myths', which according to Dichter, confirm that 'the ability to control fire is an age-old symbol of man's conquest of the physical world he inhabits'.[45]

A cigarette lighter provides conspicuous evidence of this ablity to summon fire. The ease and speed with which the lighter works enhances the feeling of power. The failure of a lighter to work does not just create superficial social embarrassment, it frustrates a deep-seated desire for a feeling of mastery and control.[46]

The articulation of myth and desire finds its expression in popular interpretations of Freudian imagery.

Research evidence suggests that at a still deeper level the need for certainty that a cigarette lighter will work matters as much as it does because it is also bound up with the idea of sexual potency. The working of the lighter becomes a kind of symbol of the flame which must be lit in consumating sexual union.[47]

Berger, apparently convinced by Dichter's analysis, agrees that 'cigarette lighters are important to people because they take care of powerful but unconscious strivings and needs'. But, more relevant here, Berger claims that 'the same can be said of many of the films we see...and...television programs we watch', and the reason that this is so is that television programmes 'feed our unconscious lives, our psyches, in ways that few people understand'.[48]

Berger cites Lesser, who points out that psychoanalysis 'offers us a systematic and well-validated body of knowledge' about 'non-rational forces which play so large a part in determining our destiny as well as the part of our being which tries, often in vain, to control and direct them'.[49] Thus

psychoanalytic concepts...make it possible to deal with a portion of our response which was not hitherto accessible to criticism—permit us to explain reactions which were intuitive and often non-verbal, and supply the key to the elements in the story responsible for those reactions.[50]

The structuralist approach to theorising the ideological effectiveness of television and the mass media, as we have seen, would seem to pose a direct challange to the conclusions reached in the previous chapter. We are faced with two quite different accounts of social reproduction, and these differences are rooted in alternative conceptions of ideology and ideological effects. Are we, following Abercrombie *et al.*, to explain the maintenance of capitalist class domination primarily in terms of the power of economic compulsion and state coercion? Or, following structuralists, are we to see the reproduction of capitalist societies as secured through the ideological manipulation of individuals at an unconscious level? The attractiveness of the structuralist position for critical media theory is not difficult to identify. In privileging the signifying practices of the mass media as being centrally involved in constituting individuals, and in theorising how this occurs, structuralism offers a way of formulating a very powerful media. Even so, non-structuralist media theorists have raised a number of objections to the way in which structuralist media theory has advanced its claims. I shall discuss some of these objections prior to engaging in a more radical critique of the structuralist perspective.

Culturalist objections to structuralist media theory

Structuralist media theory has been widely criticised by media theorists working within culturalist and political economy perspectives. Golding and Murdock question the centrality given to texts in ideological production. However, since their arguments are more relevant to matters concerning the sources of ideological production rather than the effects of ideology, they are not of prime concern here.[51] Much the same can be said of the criticisms made by Hall and Morley, although both do make some pertinent comments about the problem of the ideological effectiveness of the mass media, as it is treated by structuralists.

The tendency of structuralists to focus on the way in which single texts/programmes position the reader/viewer, Morley argues, isolates 'the encounter of text and reader from all social and historical structures *and* from other texts...which *also* position "the subject"'.[52] Morley implies that the ideological effectiveness of particular television programmes is exaggerated by structuralists. The individual, for Morley, is ideologically constituted through time, through being positioned in social practices and in 'interdiscursive spaces', and comes to specific texts/programmes 'already constituted as a subject'. The way in which the subject is already constituted 'may be seen to have a structuring and limiting effect on the *repertoire* of discurvise or "decoding" strategies available to different sectors of the audience'.[53] But, 'it does not follow that because the reader has "taken the position" most fully inscribed in the text, sufficient for the text to be intelligible, he/she will, for that reason alone, subscribe to the ideological problematic of that text'.[54] Implicit here is a criticism of the tendency in structuralism to conflate 'the subject of the text and the social subject'. This 'unjustified conflation' enables structuralists to assume that the ideological constitution of the subject in the text is automatically effective in the ideological constitution of the empirical social subject as reader/viewer. This effectivity, as we have seen, is theorised by means of Lacanian theory, which Hall argues, is an abstract, universalist theory of the 'subject-in-general', and fails to address specific historically located subjects.

It does not follow that a theory of how the 'subject-in-general' is formed offers, *in itself*, without further determinations, an adequate explanation of how historically specific subjects, already 'positioned' in language-in-general, function in relation to particular discourses or historically specific ideologies in definite social formations.[55]

While these criticisms suggest that specific television programmes may not be as ideologically effective as we are led to believe by structuralists, they do not constitute a serious threat to the structuralist perspective. Structuralists can argue that the social subject, in representing herself/himself in relation to the social conditions of existence, must necessarily use language, and thus falls prey to the power of language in structuring the unconscious. Each television programme, in this view, would contribute to the overall ideological effectiveness of language. Hall's criticisms of structuralism's use of Lacanian theory, it could be argued, reflect Hall's underestimation of the significance of the unconscious in the total theoretical space of 'the subject'. Such an argument is difficult to counter, but in view of the explanatory work required of the concept of 'the unconscious' in structuralist media theory, it is necessary to give some attention to its status in order to assess its significance for theorising the ideological impact of television.

The problem of the unconscious

For our purposes here it is useful to distinguish between two conceptions of the relation between the unconscious and consciousness, both of which are to be found in the writing of Freud. On the one hand, this relation is depicted in ways which suggest that the 'contents' of the unconscious are always potentially available to consciousness. On the other hand, there is a conception of the unconscious, or at least its most deep-seated and mysterious aspects, which stresses that it is permanently cut off from consciousness in the sense that it cannot be fully represented in the self-consciousness of the individual. If we can become conscious of our unconscious, as the first conception suggests, then presumably we can free ourselves from the control of our unconscious. By contrast, the radical consciousness–unconsciousness split of the second conception allows for the possibility of individuals being controlled by forces beyond their control, that is, by unconscious forces residing in the unconscious. It is this view which Lacan favours, and it is this view which is particularly difficult to contest.

Essentially there are two types of argument which confront the significance attributed to the deep-seated, dynamic unconscious by structuralist media theory. Since unconscious forces and motivations are treated as universal, critics can argue that the range of human diversity in action and consciousness is of such an order that the universal mechanisms of the unconscious have a limited effect. Hall's argument is of this type. But, as I noted, structuralists can merely assert that such an argument overestimates the significance of 'human difference'. Besides, there is nothing to prevent structuralists from arguing that differences themselves are the product of universal mechanisms. Of course this is not to say that structuralists are correct—we simply have no way of resolving the dispute.

The second type of argument emphasises that we do not have to be dependent on the concept of the unconscious in order to explain the phenomena which are normally explained by it in psychoanalysis. In a radical form this argument attempts to develop an alternative explanation for the evidence which Freud assumed was indicative of the existence of the unconscious. Structuralists might wonder why their critics should want to avoid using the concept of unconscious control. Quite simply there is the need to avoid the unnecessary mystification of human experience, as is the case when, as Laing argues, 'imagined experiences are explained by processes that are themselves doubly imaginary'.[56] This is consistent with Sartre's comment that 'the hypothesis of the Oedipus complex, like the atomic theory, is nothing but an "experimental idea"'.[57] There is a strong suspicion amongst clinical psychologists other than psychoanalysts, that Freudian concepts are often used unproblematically as explanatory concepts frequently with the effect of obscuring what is to be explained. Rogers, for example, 'claims no greater personal perceptiveness' than Freudians, but thinks that 'with a lighter baggage of preconceptions' he 'is more likely to come to an understanding of the phenomenal world of an individual as it exists'.[58] Similarly, Van Den Berg argues that 'the "unconscious" is the product of a premature cessation of the psychological analysis of human existence'.[59]

The common retort to these kinds of argument (and this is why Popper has characterised psychoanalysis as unscientific on account of its self-protection against falsifiability) is that those who fail to see the value of the concept of the dynamic unconscious are themselves the product of this unconscious. Thus Jacoby, in his critique of Laing and Cooper, states that they 'succumb to unresolved and unconscious contradiction which they do not, like Freud, articulate; rather...they fall prey to them'.[60]

It would seem that in the final analysis we are faced with a theoretical stalemate. Structuralists can always resort to the ultimate defence against their critics. But such a move is a paradoxical one for those structuralists who identify themselves as Althusserian or broadly Marxist, 'unless, of course, one is content with an unconscious subject'.[61] As Brooks goes on to argue, the unconscious is a way of obscuring the dialectic between how one sees the meaning of one's behaviour and how others see it...In both the therapeutic situation and in everyday life, the unconscious is used to obscure the power relations between people by locating the dynamics and issues of intersubjective life inside of the individual...The unconscious, then, is one of those mysticisms that lead astray, with a quite definite political end for the situations in which they are employed.[62]

This kind of argument is taken a stage further by Timpanaro and Logan.[63] Psychoanalytic discourse, it is maintained, is most appropriately seen as the product of the asymmetrical power relations between client and therapist, and what Freud took to be evidence of the existence of the unconscious can be best understood as the reaction of his patients to their relative powerlessness in his presence. It is worth citing Timpanaro at length here. Commenting on a particular case reported by Freud, Timpanaro writes:

Here we are presented with that compound of curiosity and fear which typifies the state of mind of someone entering analysis—and must have done so even more at the beginning of the analytic movement. I do not think that it would be an exaggeration to say that the young man feels 'bewitched'. He knows he is face to face with the fearsome Doctor Freud, who, they say,—and it seems true from what he has read himself—is able to extort confessions even of what is least confessable. He is intrigued as to whether Freud will succeed in this respect with him too, though he is already half convinced that he will...Before the analysis has proceeded very far, the young man asks: 'Have you discovered anything yet?' It is the creation of this sort of fatalistic conviction—that 'one cannot oppose Freud', that no matter how strong one's resistance, one's secret will certainly be extracted—which, more than any of the specific promptings we have noted, is the most powerful means of suggestion at Freud's disposal.[64]

Timpanaro devotes much of his attention to 'slips of the tongue', which he believes are evidence of a 'heightened consciousness', rather than evidence for 'the unconscious speaking'. During the course of conversation it is quite normal to consider whether or not to introduce new information of a private nature. In therapy the individual's expectation that private matters are to be addressed, alerts the individual to her/his most private thoughts, and to considerations of how much private matter should be disclosed to the therapist. In these circumstances fragments of private matter may slip out during the course of therapeutic dialogue—these fragments arise from consciousness. Similarly resistance to suggestion—another indication, for Freud, of the existence of the unconscious—it is argued, is typically no more than the unwillingness of the client to disclose private matters to a more powerful other (the therapist). Again, this implies that the client is conscious of the private information in question. Freud's insensitivity to the influence of his own power-position in determining the course of the therapeutic discourse made him 'extraordinarily unaware of any of the subleties of "superficial psychology"'.[65] Rather than understanding the client's utterances as the product of consciousness responding to an asymmetrical power relation, Freud 'over-psychologised' these utterances.

It is this hyper-psychological bias which is, I think, the principal cause of the arbitrary interpretations to which Freud subjects the 'slip', the dream, and everything we do. It is the effort to penetrate *at all times* to an underlying, unpleasant reality arrived at only by dint of a victory over the subject's resistances, which makes him opt in the majority of cases for the interpretation which is most intriguing—and most improbable.[66]

The hyper-psychological bias in Freud, which is even more evident in Lacan, involves the *premature* attribution of causation to some psychological agency, whether it be the repressed unconscious, penis envy, the castration complex or the rerouting of lost desires in chains of signification, and so on. It is premature in the sense that less arbitrary and more probable explanations of behaviour are not sought. If, for example, human action can be understood as an intelligible response to the present and past opportunities *and* lack of opportunities available to an individual, then it is clearly misleading to explain action primarily in terms of psychological causation, and even more misleading to explain it in terms of the agency of the unconscious.

Timpanaro argues that the concept of the repressed unconscious itself is the product of Freud's hyper-psychological bias. This is not to deny the usefulness of the concept of 'repression'. Indeed, the important point to make about repression is that it involves the blocking of an act intended to express desire. The 'censor' in the first instance is a more powerful other. Freud recognises this, but then goes on to over-psychologise the consequences of the act of repression, allowing no space for the possibility that the lack of opportunity to act, the blocking of an act, may not necessarily remove the original desire. Further, Freud, under his hyper-psychological bias, attributed an enormous significance to the hypothetical consequences of repression, primarily because the psychological significance of our original desires, he supposed, is based on their strength. Yet if our desires, whether original or not, are as strong as Freudians suggest, then their removal from consciousness would seem most unlikely. Similarly it can be argued that the loss of desire occurs when the desire is not particularly strong, and thus not of psychological significance.

The implications of this argument for structuralist media theory are quite far-reaching. The ideological effectiveness of television, for structuralists, is based on the significance of the operations of language on lost desires. If these desires lack significance, then the operations of language are displaced in importance, and any effects which may ensue are likewise relegated in importance.

Against this, Freudians can argue that the critique of the repressed unconscious fails to consider the theory that our underlying biological instincts give rise to 'ideas' which are represented in the dynamic unconscious. In other words there are 'representations' of desire which never achieve an undistorted representation in consciousness, and it is these representations in the unconscious which cause the distortions (*méconnaissances*) of consciousness, and much of what we do. But, as Archard points out, this counter-argument 'raises a problem of verification'. He notes that 'Freud is obliged to argue that unconscious processes' can only be known through 'conscious experiences or behaviour—be they dreams, slips or symptoms...'[67]

Now an unconscious wish or idea becomes known to us only by being subjected to a degree of distortion or disguise which renders it acceptable to consciousness. Thus, it is not just that Freud's inference of the unconscious is indirect; it is that the experience or behaviour from which we infer the unconscious thought is taken to be none other than the latter's disguised representation of itself to consciousness.[68]

That part of the unconscious, which works powerfully in conjunction with language, to secure the ideological effectiveness of television and the mass media, is inferred from ambiguous evidence. Archard concludes that

some of Freud's most important explanatory terms, ones which give his theory its overall coherence and plausibility, cannot easily survive the perpetuation of this ambiguity. For instance, if terms like 'energy', 'tension', 'mnemic trace' are understood as having purely psychic referents, then much of the cited evidence in favour of their existence and concerning their mode of functioning must be discounted.[69]

The way in which Lacan deals with this argument is far from satisfactory, and, as we shall see below, structuralists' claims about the ideological effectiveness of television suffer accordingly.

The power of language: shaky foundations

The Freudian concept of the dynamic unconscious, as many philosophers have noted, holds radical implications for theories of knowledge and truth. Very briefly, since 'knowing' occurs in and through consciousness, and since consciousness for Freudians is distorted by the universal dynamic unconscious, then it follows that knowledge as the product of knowing must bear the mark of distorted consciousness. One might wonder then, as Archard implies above, how it is that Freudians are able to develop a valid knowledge of the unconscious. In Lacan's estimation only a few psychoanalysts, and he includes Freud and himself amongst the few, are sufficiently 'qualified' to 'know' the unconscious.

As a witness called to account for the sincerity of the subject, depositary of the minutes of his discourse, reference as to his exactitude, guarantor of his uprightness, custodian of his testament, scrivener of his codicils, the analyst has something of the scribe about him.
But above all he remains the master of the truth of which this discourse is the progress.[70]
Lacan's elitism, Wilden argues, is based on an illusory expertise, and is potentially oppressive.

So long as the High Priests are the only ones who can read and write, or who can interpret the sacred texts, or who can read the messages of auguries and dreams, the people at large will be forced to trust in the "leadership" of those whose values can never be the values of humanity at large...[71]

Structuralist media theory in its approach to the ideological effectiveness of television and the mass media reproduces Lacan's illusory expertise. Additionally, however, in privileging their own particular interpretation of texts/programmes, structuralists introduce another source of elitism, which may be based on an expertise no less illusory than Lacan's. In promoting semiotic textual analysis, Dyer tells us that the semiotician 'has a particular expertise in analytic methods', which sets the analyst apart from the ordinary audience member. This expertise enables the 'qualified' analyst to 'explain what a text means...and bring out hidden meanings'.[72]

It is the 'hidden meanings' buried in television programmes which are presumed to be ideologically effective. But since these meanings are identified by means of a particular form of textual analysis, there is the real danger that the 'exposed' meanings are more a product of the method of analysis than of a particular television programme. Much depends, of course, on the method of analysis. Useful here is the distinction which Williams makes between 'open' and 'closed' textual deconstruction. Open deconstructionism is that form of textual analysis which,

whether it is analysing literature or television or physical representation...is looking not for the academically explanatory system, but for the system as a mode of formation, which as it becomes visible can be put into question or quite practically rejected. In that sense the whole impulse of this radical semiotics is very different from the structuralist version...which has been much more widely influential...[73]

Closed deconstructionism which sees texts 'as produced by the system of signs' under 'the operation of systematic rules'[74] is the form of structuralism with which we have been concerned in this chapter, since it is this form of analysis in which the strongest claims about the ideological effectiveness of television are theorised. In closed deconstructionism,

the recipient of the text too frequently remains, as in much bourgeois criticism, a cipher, assumed and untheorised. Two tendencies play into this: a notion of the reader as wholly and inflexibly constituted elsewhere, and a contrasted but, in effect, similar view of the reader as a mere effect of the text...both reduce the process of reading to the mechanical reproduction of elements always already composed, in either the text or the subject.[75]

This argument is identical to that advanced by Morley in his critique of structuralism (see pp. 110–11).

The power which controls the viewer, in deconstructionism, is ultimately reducible to 'the structure (however defined) of language'. This structure is privileged as the producer of the 'structure of the programme/text/discourse', and as the producer of the ideologically effective 'hidden meanings'. Thus, as Veron stresses, 'ideology becomes autonomous in relation to the *consciousness* or *intention* of its agents'. The latter 'may be conscious of their points of view about social forms, but not of the semiotic conditions (rules and categories of codification) which make possible those points of view'.[76]

Here, Veron provides an explicit justification for ignoring audience response, thereby validating some of the concerns expressed by pluralists (see pp. 000–0). In conjunction with the power attributed to the unconscious, structuralism in fact embraces a double justification for ignoring audience response in theorising the ideological effectiveness of television. But just as the privileging of unconscious processes involves a lack of consideration of more important ways in which it can be said that individuals are constituted, so too, many critics have observed that structuralists have ignored what is most significant about language. Instead, the ideological power of language is identified with its conditions of possibility. What this adds up to is the very real possibility that in structuralism, the ideological power of television rests on, at worst fictional forces, and at best relatively trivial forces. Either way, the viewer as victim of these 'forces' is portrayed as being ideologically duped in terms which would seem to do a grave injustice to her/his intelligence. The lack of attention given to non-textual forces impinging upon the individual, by manifesting an insensitivity to the material power relations in which individuals are located, reinforces structuralism's misrepresentation of the subject.

Open deconstructionism overcomes many of the weaknesses noted in structuralist media theory. As Foucault expresses it:

If I suspended all reference to the speaking subject, it was not to discover laws of construction or forms that could be applied in the same way by all speaking subjects, nor was it to give notice to the great universal discourse that is common to all men at a particular period. On the contrary, my aim was to show what the differences consisted of, how it was possible for men, within the same discursive practice, to speak of different objects, to have contrary opinions, and to make contradictory choices...[77]

For structuralists favouring open deconstructionism, the ideological effectiveness of television is not dependent on hidden meanings manipulating the audience at an unconscious level, but derives more from the idea of the power of the materiality of discursive practices.

One of the strengths of Althusser's theory of ideology is that attention is drawn to the material embeddedness of ideas in social practices. As I argued earlier, it can be appreciated that 'living in' the practices of schooling and the family does involve being subjected to social practices which do realise elements of the dominant ideology. The question arises as to whether or not the *effects* of living in these practices derive from the power of the materiality of the practices, or from the power of the ideas embedded in them. Or, to put it another way: are the ideological effects of living in schooling and the family dependent on the fact that the ideologies inscribed in these practices are embedded in power-effective material practices? A hint of an answer to these questions is provided by Althusser. He says 'of course, the material existence of the ideology in an apparatus and its practices does not have the same modality as the material existence of a paving-stone or a rifle'.[78]

Critical media theorists have not been as observant as Althusser in distinguishing between different modalities of materiality. The ideas of an individual, Althusser states

are his material actions inserted into material practices governed by material rituals which are themselves defined by the material ideological apparatus from which derive the ideas of that subject. Naturally, the four inscriptions of the adjective 'material' in my proposition must be affected by different modalities: the materialities...are not one and the same materiality.[79]

This enables us to recognise differences in the power-effectiveness of material practices consonant with differences in the modality of materiality of these practices. Thus while it is true that 'signs are the material registration of meaning,[80] and that we can legitimately refer to 'the materiality of the sign', to 'the materiality of language', or to language being 'a special kind of material practice',[81] it is important not to lose sight of the fact that we are referring to a materiality which is essentially different from being subjected to the material practices of work, travel, schooling, family, and so on.

Hall argues that 'we must think of language as *enabling things to mean*. This is the social practice of *signification*: the practice through which the 'labour' of cultural and ideological representation is accomplished'.[82] The stronger versions of the power-of-television thesis trade on there being an equivalence between the ideological effectiveness of living in material practices and the ideological effectiveness of discursive practices. It is assumed that the materiality of language is of the same order as the materiality of our conditions of existence. In its extreme form this assumption is represented in Lacan's statement that 'it is the world of words that creates the world of things'.[83] The significance of this kind of view, according to Hawkes, is that the sign is freed 'from its subservience to that "reality" (or *presence*) which it was supposed to serve...it can be seen to *cause a new reality to come into being*'.[84]

These kinds of view, which are supportive of the stronger claims about television's ideological effectiveness, are arrived at through conflating the distinction Althusser makes between 'living in ideology', for example living in the practices of schooling, and the way we *represent* this 'living in'. The material forms of representation are then attributed with the power which forces us to live in the relations to our conditions of existence. Children are legally compelled to attend school, and have no choice as to the family into which they are born, and on which they are initially dependent for their survival. It is misleading to attribute the discursive practices of television with the kind of power associated with forms of compulsion and coercion.

Interpellation and subjection

I have devoted considerable attention to an examination of the theoretical bases in structuralist media theory which support the strongest versions of the power-of-television thesis. The focus up to now has been on 'how television exerts its power'. But what of the actual effect of this power? How widespread is 'the illusion of the autonomous ego'? How obvious, and for whom is it obvious, that 'you and I are subjects'?

The individual may well be 'interpellated as a free subject', but the effects of this are far from clear. Structuralists, following either Althusser or Lacan, accept the validity of the illusion of the 'free individual'/autonomous ego, or that

the individual *is interpellated as a (free) subject...in order that he shall (freely) accept his subjection*, i.e. in order that he shall make the gestures and actions of his subjection 'all by himself'. *There are no subjects except by and for their subjection*. That is why they 'work all by themselves'.[85]

Althusser states that 'it *has* to be so...if the reproduction of the relations of production is to be assured'.[86]

It would be very useful for dominant groups if individuals believed themselves to be free agents, since this would clearly legitimate their subjection. In reality though, it is doubtful that this belief is sufficiently widespread to account for the reproduction of structures of domination. Much contemporary writing on women's experience[87] challenges Althusser's depiction of the elementary ideological effect. As for the working class, Jacoby observes that 'the notion of the free individual was always a sham'.[88]

Individuals would seem to 'work all by themselves', but the reasons for this may have little to do with illusions of consciousness. Similarly individuals are indeed subjecting themselves to structures of domination, but hardly 'freely'. Rather, individuals may be powerless to do otherwise, and this powerlessness is more real than ideological. As Adorno put it, 'the social power structure hardly needs the mediating agencies of the ego and individuality any more'.[89] All the signs indicate that in modern societies the vast majority are increasingly perceiving themselves as relatively powerless to change the conditions of their own existence. At best the free subject is operative in rather tight power-bound spaces.

Television programmes, in offering subject positions through which its discourses can be understood, can be seen to be involved in inter-pellating individuals. Much structuralist media theory has unproblematically assumed that the interpellating power of television is effective in ideologically constituting individuals. Not only is it question-able that many believe themselves to be free agents, but the production of identities, while involving ideology, is principally rooted in the material practices of family and school. In view of this, the ideological power of television in the formation of identities is at most a power which works on ground already materially prepared. But this power is insuffi-cient to fulfil the theoretical demand that individuals develop identities which enable them to 'freely accept their subjection' to structures of domination.

The necessity of ideology

The difficulties attending Althusser's theory of ideological interpellation have been widely noted within critical media theory. It does not provide a satisfactory basis for theorising the ideological effectiveness of televi-sion, and it gives far too much weight to the influence of discourses in identity formation. The amount of work *required* of ideology in Althusser's formulations derives from the assumption that 'ideology is necessary for social reproduction'. Even those media theorists who reject Althusser's theory of ideological interpellation nevertheless tend to share his assumption that ideological effects, in some form, are necessary for the maintenance of capitalist society (see pp. 101–2).

Given the significance attributed to 'necessary ideological effects', it is understandable that Althusser should want to distance himself from a notion of ideology as 'mere ideas in people's heads'. It is inconceivable that mere ideas could be powerful enough to secure the reproduction of structures of domination. In this respect 'mere ideas' appear to be less suited to this task than beliefs—beliefs suggest a degree of commitment. In order to overcome these problems Althusser gives ideas a material existence, and with the power of materiality behind it, ideology is considered to be sufficiently powerful to shape identities which accept their subordination to the prevailing social order. While I have argued that things do not quite work out in the way Althusser suggests, he does get close to identifying a plausible way in which we can understand at least one aspect of social reproduction. It can be supposed that the willingness or otherwise of individuals to engage in practices intended to remove structures of domination is highly relevant to social reproduction and change. To the extent that progressive forms of social change are dependent upon the actions of particular kinds of individual, the constitution of subjects is important. Western societies are not producing 'bad subjects'[90] in sufficient numbers. In this sense the necessity-of-ideology assumption can be given some substance and credibility.

Unwilling to take this route, critical media theorists settle for a far less substantial and less credible version of necessary ideological effects. What transpires is an account of the ideological effectiveness of television which attributes 'mere ideas' with the power to secure the reproduction of capitalist class and patriarchal domination.

As we have already seen, there is a tendency amongst critical media theorists to equate the materiality of 'living in ideology', for example, living in the practices of the family and school, with the materiality of the *representations* of this 'living in'. But when compared with the ideology of the ideas embedded in material practices in which individuals are inserted, representations *are* mere ideas, even if these mere ideas are registered in material signs, and relayed through the material apparatus of a television set. Now, since capitalist societies are being reproduced through the actions of individuals in social practices, and since human action is not mechanical or automatic, that is, it is 'conscious action', it would seem that there could be a connection between the consciousness of individuals and social reproduction. This possible connection is addressed by Althusser. All individuals *do* represent 'their imaginary relation to their real conditions of existence', and 'the "ideas" of a human subject exist in his actions'. Both of these statements are true. But, under the assumption that ideology is necessary for social reproduction, critical media theorists who follow Althusser this far tend to assume that the actions of the individual are *governed* by the ideas which exist in them. These ideas, furthermore, are those with which individuals represent their imaginary relation to their real conditions of existence. Since television is a major supplier of ideological representations, it can be seen to be centrally involved in producing and reproducing the ideological effects sufficient for maintaining structures of domination.

In formulating television's ideological power in this way, critical media theorists are in fact doing what Althusser most wanted to avoid, namely attributing mere ideas with a power they do not possess. If the ideas people hold are to account for why it is that individuals continue to participate in practices in which they are subordinated, then one would expect a considerable degree of commitment to such ideas. This raises again the problem of motivation, and as we saw in the previous chapter there is very little evidence that members of subordinate groups are sufficiently motivated in relation to a set of ideas such that forms of domination can be sustained (see pp. 84–6). We could say that people are acquiescing to forms of domination because 'they fear losing their jobs', or because 'they see no other means of surviving', or because 'they want to avoid making things more difficult for themselves and their families', and so on. But then these ideas are hardly ideological, and they do point to a reality. It is that reality which needs to be explained, and it is more likely that the explanations will revolve around questions of power and powerlessness, that is resources or the lack of resources available for individuals, than around ideas.

Whether we follow structuralist media theory in its emphasis on the ways in which television's power is enmeshed in the dual powers of language and the unconscious in ideologically constituting subjects, or whether we follow the interpretations of Althusser provided by cultural-ist media theory, we do not encounter an account of television's ideological power which suggests that we ought to revise the conclusions reached in the previous chapter.

What we do find is a media- and ideology-centred approach to social reproduction which pays scant regard to the material forces impinging upon individuals. Attention to the lived experience of actual individuals and to the routines of everyday life would enable a greater sensitivity to the reasons why individuals acquiesce to the conditions of their existence. Ironically, structuralist media theory's emphasis on subjectivity is theorised 'behind the backs' of real individuals, and this cuts off the theory from those, the actual viewers, whose experience both as viewers and as social subjects is a correctional source for the theory's excesses. Structuralist media theory makes the strongest claims about television's ideological manipulation of the audience, but it does so without any reference to actual audiences. In providing instead, a 'theoretical knowledge' of the audience, structuralist media theory 'speaks for the audience', but in ways which seriously malign it.

Moores asks:

This strand of ideological-mythological criticism favours the domain of the textual in any explanation of the social role of the media, but might it be that broadcasting's work in producing compliance lies largely outside this domain?...Is it possible that the social cement of broadcasting might be located in its position within the geography and routine of everyday life in the domestic sphere?[91]

It is to these questions that we shall now turn.

Notes

1. Nicholas Abercrombie, Stephen Hill and Bryan S. Turner, *The Dominant Ideology Thesis*, London, George Allen and Unwin, 1980, p. 189.
2. Louis Althusser, *Essays on Ideology*, London, Verso, 1984, p. 22.
3. Ibid., p. 19.
4. Ibid.
5. Ibid., p. 28.
6. Ibid., p. 30.
7. Ibid.
8. Ibid., p. 42.
9. Ibid., pp. 38–9.
10. Ibid., p. 42.
11. Stuart Hall, 'Culture, the Media and the "Ideological Effect"', in James Curran, Michael Gurevitch and Janet Woollacott, eds, *Mass Communication and Society*, London, Arnold, 1977, p. 329.
12. Ibid., p. 331.
13. Ibid.
14. Althusser, op. cit., p. 45.

15. Ibid., p. 46.

16. Ibid., p. 56.

17. Ibid., pp. 56–7.

18. Catherine Belsey, *Critical Practice*, London, Methuen, 1980, p. 59.

19. Ibid., p. 61.

20. Ibid., p. 73.

21. See, for example, Stephen Heath, 'Narrative Space', *Screen*, vol. 17, 1976, pp. 68–112; Stephen Heath, 'Film and System, Terms of Analysis', Part 1, *Screen*, vol. 16, no. 1, 1975, pp. 7–77; Part 2, *Screen*, vol. 16, no. 2, 1975, pp. 91–113.

22. See, for example, Colin MacCabe, 'Theory and Film: Principles of Realism and Pleasure', *Screen*, vol. 17, no. 3, 1976, pp. 7–27.

23. Belsey, op. cit., p. 67.

24. Ibid., p. 69.

25. John Fiske, 'Popularity and Ideology: A Structuralist Reading of *Dr. Who*' in Willard D. Rowland and Bruce Watkins, eds, *Interpreting Television: Current Research Perspectives*, London, Sage, 1984, p. 186.

26. Ibid.

27. Gillian Dyer, *Advertising as Communication*, London, Methuen, 1982, p. 82.

28. Janice Winship, 'Sexuality for sale' in Stuart Hall, Dorothy Hobson, Andrew Lowe and Paul Willis, eds, *Culture, Media, Language*, London, Hutchinson, 1980, pp. 218.–9.

29. Judith Williamson, *Decoding Advertisements*, London, Marion Boyars, 1978, p. 13.

30. Grahame Thompson, 'Television as Text: Open University "Case-Study' Programmes'" in Michèle Barrett, Philip Corrigan, Annette Kuhn and Janet Wolff, eds, *Ideology and Cultural Production*, London, Croom Helm, 1979, p. 165.

31. Ibid., p. 176.

32. Tony Bennett, 'Media, "reality", signification' in Michael Gurevitch, Tony Bennett, James Curran and Janet Woollacott, eds, *Culture, Society and the Media*, London, Methuen, 1982, p. 298.

33. Jacques Lacan, *Écrits, A Selection*, London, Tavistock, 1977, p. 172.

34. Ibid., p. 147.

35. Ibid., p. 155.

36. Ibid., p. 160.

37. Ibid., p. 64.

38. Ibid., p. 166.

39. Marina Heck, 'The ideological dimensions of media messages' in Hall *et al.*, op. cit., p. 122.

40. Dyer, pp. 118–9.

41. Bennett, p. 298.

42. E. Dichter, *The Strategy of Desire*, London, Boardman, 1960, p. 12.

43. E. Dichter, *Handbook of Consumer Motivations: The Psychology of the World of Objects*, New York, McGraw-Hill, 1964, p. 341.
44. Ibid.
45. Ibid.
46. Ibid.
47. Ibid.
48. Arthur Asa Berger, *Media Analysis Techniques*, London, Sage, 1982, p. 72.
49. Simon O. Lesser, *Fiction and the Unconscious*, Boston, Beacon Press, 1957, p. 15.
50. Ibid.
51. Peter Golding and Graham Murdock, 'Ideology and the Mass Media: The Question of Determination' in Barrett *et al.*, op. cit., pp. 198–224. Similarly, because they are not specifically addressing the structuralists' approach to ideological effects, I am not drawing upon the excellent critiques of structuralist media theory provided by Tomlinson and Robins; see John Tomlinson, 'Habermas and Discourse', *Trent Papers in Communication*, vol. 1, *Power and Communication*, Nottingham, Trent Polytechnic, 1983, pp. 59–107; and Kevin Robins, 'Althusserian Marxism and media studies: the case of *Screen*', *Media, Culture and Society*, vol. 1, 1979, pp. 355–70.
52. David Morley, 'Texts, readers, subjects', in Hall *et al.*, op. cit., p. 163.
53. Ibid., p. 173.
54. Ibid., p. 167.
55. Stuart Hall, 'Recent developments in theories of language and ideology: a critical note' in Hall *et al.*, op. cit., p. 161.
56. R.D. Laing, *Self and Others* Harmondsworth, Penguin, 1969, p. 29.
57. Jean-Paul Sartre, *Being and Nothingness*, London, Methuen, 1957, p. 51.
58. T.W. Wann, ed., *Behaviorism and Phenomenology*, Chicago, University of Chicago Press, 1964, p. 138.
59. J.H. Van Den Berg, *The Phenomenological Approach to Psychiatry: An Introduction to Recent Phenomenological Psychopathology*, Springfield, IL, Thomas, 1955, p. 83.
60. Russell Jacoby, *Social Amnesia: A Critique of Conformist Psychology from Adler to Laing*, Hassocks, Harvester, 1975, pp. 132–3.
61. Keith Brooks, 'Freudianism is not a Basis for a Marxist Psychology' in Phil Brown, ed., *Radical Psychology*, London, Tavistock, 1973, pp. 336–7.
62. Ibid.
63. Josephine Logan, 'Problems Inherent in Analyses of Discourse in the Power-Asymmetrical Therapeutic Relationship', *Trent Papers in Communication*, vol. 3, *Power and Communication: Discourse Analysis*, Nottingham, Trent Polytechnic, 1985, pp. 145–70.
64. Sebastiano Timpanaro, *The Freudian Slip: Psychoanalysis and Textual Criticism*, London, New Left Books, 1976, p. 52.
65. Ibid., p. 59.

66. Ibid., p. 179.
67. David Archard, *Consciousness and the Unconscious*, London, Hutchinson, 1984, p. 32.
68. Ibid.
69. Ibid., p. 31.
70. Lacan, op. cit. p. 98.
71. Anthony Wilden, *Systems and Structure: Essays in Communication and Exchange*, London, Tavistock, 1980, p. 475.
72. Dyer, op. cit., pp. 87–8.
73. Raymond Williams, 'Marxism, Structuralism and Literary Analysis', *New Left Review*, no. 129, 1981, p. 64.
74. Ibid.
75. Ibid.
76. E. Veron, 'The semanticization of political violence' in E. Veron *et al.*, eds, *Lenguaje y communicación social*, Buenos Aires, Nueva Visión, 1969, cited in, and translated by Heck, op. cit., p. 123.
77. Michel Foucault, *The Archaeology of Knowledge*, London, Tavistock, 1972, p. 200.
78. Althusser, op. cit., p. 40.
79. Ibid., p. 43.
80. Hall, op. cit., p. 328.
81. Raymond Williams, *Marxism and Literature*, Oxford, Oxford University Press, 1977, p. 165.
82. Hall, op. cit., p. 329.
83. Lacan, op. cit., p. 65.
84. Terence Hawkes, *Structuralism and Semiotics*, London, Methuen, 1977, p. 149.
85. Althusser, op. cit., p. 56.
86. Ibid.
87. See, for example, Christine Delphy, *Close to Home*, London, Hutchinson, 1984; Josephine Logan, 'Ontological Insecurity in Women', *Reflections*, no. 52, 1985; Peter Leonard, *Personality and Ideology: Towards a Materialist Understanding of the Individual*, London, Macmillan, 1984, especially Chapters 3, 4 and 7.
88. Jacoby, op. cit., p. 38.
89. Theodor Adorno, 'Sociology and Psychology', *New Left Review*, no. 47, 1968, p. 95.
90. Althusser, op. cit., p. 55. He writes: 'subjects…"work by themselves" in the vast majority of cases, with the exception of the "bad subjects" who on occasion provoke the intervention of one of the detachments of the (repressive) State apparatus'.
91. Shaun Moores, 'Review of Len Masterman, editor, *Television Mythologies: Stars, Shows and Signs* (London: Comedia/MK Media Press, 1984', *Media, Culture and Society*, vol. 7, 1985, p. 391.

5 Television and Leisure Time

The arguments of the previous two chapters suggest that television's power, in so far as it is an ideological power, is not as strong as critical media theorists have portrayed it. The assumption that capitalist societies can only be reproduced by ideologically incorporating subordinate groups has led critical media theorists into a preoccupation with the ideological effectiveness of the mass media on the subordinated. Although we have been able to support some ways in which it can be said that television and the mass media produce ideological effects, critical media theory's focus on the ideological incorporation of subordinate groups, as the overall ideological effect of the mass media, gives it a misplaced focus and emphasis. As Urry has argued, 'if we consider what would have been the case, were that effect not to have occurred, then in general we would find that the society would still have been reproduced'.[1] This suggests that forces other than ideology are primarily responsible for social reproduction.

The task of this and the following chapter is to assess television's relationship to those forces which are most influential in reproducing structures of domination. In particular we shall be concerned with addressing the questions raised by Moores: Is television's 'capturing of time and space' a primary means through which Western capitalist societies are reproduced? Or, is television's capturing of time and space a consequence of more powerful social forces?[2]

First, however, it is necessary to consider the extent to which television does capture our time, and thus also our space in the private-domestic sphere.

Television and the colonisation of leisure

Data on television viewing in Western societies are somewhat patchy.

Even so, some clear points emerge.

First, by the mid to late 1970s, more than 90 per cent of the households in Western societies had at least one television set.

Second, comparative estimates of viewing hours suggest that television viewing is highest in Japan, closely followed by the United States, with Britain leading the way in Europe.[3] In the United States, for example, it has been estimated that the average viewing time per head of population is close to 30 hours per week, whereas in Britain the figure is just over 20 hours per week.[4]

Third, viewing tends to be approximately 5 hours more per week in winter months than during the summer.[5]

Fourth, while estimates of average viewing time per head of the viewing public provide a very crude picture of the extent of television viewing, a closer examination of how these averages are attained reveals considerable variation between different social groups. In an American survey, for example, 40 per cent more viewing was reported for highschool dropouts than for college graduates.[6] Generally higher than average viewing is reported for the poor, the retired, the unemployed and for housewives not in paid labour. The latter, for example, it has been estimated, watch 60 per cent more television than women in the paid labour force.[7] Approximately two-thirds of the time available to high viewing groups is taken up with watching television.[8]

Fifth, of the time given to viewing, approximately 70 per cent of it goes to entertainment programmes, a little over 20 per cent to informational programmes and about 5 per cent to 'cultural programmes'.[9] This does not reflect the actual availability of the programmes broadcast. In France, for example, only 40 per cent of the programmes available to the viewer are classified as 'entertainment', and 20 per cent are deemed to be 'cultural'.[10]

Sixth, although the rate of increased viewing appears to be tailing off, television viewing has nevertheless increased during a period when leisure-time, for some groups at least, has been decreasing. Since this last point contradicts the widely held view that we are living in an era of increased leisure, some explanation is in order. There has been, since the early 1970s, a slight increase in the length of holiday periods from employment. Weekly hours of work in paid employment have decreased a little for men, but increased at a similar rate for women. But the numbers actually employed have increased at a faster rate than the escalation in unemployment. Women have been entering paid employment at a rate more or less equivalent to the decline in male employment. Now the crucial statistic is that the average number of persons in paid employment, in proportion to the average number of persons per household, has increased. In effect this means that the time available per average household for unpaid domestic labour and for leisure has decreased. The rate of these changes has not been matched by male participation in and responsibility for child-care activities and domestic labour. This suggests that for a majority of women the leisure age has yet to arrive.[11]

The response from media theorists

The limitations of the media-centredness of media theory become apparent in the general lack of attention given to the social significance of television's colonisation of leisure-time. With one or two notable exceptions, media theorists have not seriously attempted to explain why it is that television viewing is the dominant leisure activity of a majority of those living in Western societies. Rather, television's stranglehold on leisure-time is itself treated as evidence supportive of the importance of television. This still begs the question: In what ways is television viewing important? Merely to cite estimates of the amount of time we give to viewing is to remain *descriptive*, whereas some *explanation* is required. This is not to say that descriptions of patterns of viewing are without merit. One useful observation, for example, is that made by Tunstall in his distinction between 'primary', 'secondary' and 'tertiary' viewing. Television viewing as a 'primary' activity refers to attentative viewing to the exclusion of all other activities. 'Secondary viewing' refers to viewing which is attentative, but not singularly so, as when we watch television while eating meals, for example. The estimates of viewing hours, cited above (p. 129), are for primary and secondary viewing. Much higher estimates are available for 'tertiary viewing', but since these estimates include hours when the television set just happens to be on regardless of whether or not it is actually being watched, they tend grossly to exaggerate television usage.[12]

Typically media researchers have been interested in identifying the activities which have been replaced by television viewing. It is widely observed, for example, that radio listening has sharply declined. But the popular view that cinema- and theatre-going and the reading of newspapers and magazines have suffered as a consequence of increased television viewing is more difficult to support. Thus, Curran and Tunstall note that there has been a marked decrease in cinema attendance in Britain, but they stress that even at its peak cinema going was never a major leisure-time activity. They also note that the decline in reading newspapers, magazines and books has been negligible. Television consumption, they suggest, has been largely at the expense of household chores, 'resting', 'sitting' and 'doing nothing in particular'.[13] Without an underlying social theory by which we might be able to make sense of the total pattern of leisure-time use, these observations tend to suggest that television has merely displaced less attractive activities.

A potentially more useful line of inquiry, and one which connects directly with the ideological emphasis in critical media theory, is that which examines the role of television viewing in the socialisation of children.[14] However, consistent with the preoccupations of media theory in general, much of the literature on television as a socialising agency focuses on programme content, to the relative neglect of historical changes in the pattern of parent–child interaction, and the displacement of 'traditional' childhood experiences. One might also ask why it is that parents should find in television such a convenient aid to their child-minding chores.

I shall discuss television's role in socialisation more fully later on in the chapter. Helpful to that discussion will be a consideration of how television has come to occupy a position of prominence within families. A common assumption in media theory is that television's colonisation of leisure and family life is closely connected to its 'attractiveness'. While this assumption has remained, for the most part, unexamined, media researchers in the 'uses and gratifications' tradition, have conducted audience research which begins to explore the question of television's attractiveness.

The attractiveness of viewing television

McQuail has developed a typology of media uses, and the gratifications audiences claim to derive from these uses. Four main areas of uses and gratifications are identified: information; personal identity; integration and social interaction; and entertainment.[15] McQuail's typology suggests that personal identity needs are met through television viewing in that the latter enables audience members to find 'reinforcement for personal values', to find 'models of behaviour', to gain 'insight into one's self', and to identify 'with valued others (in the media)'. Audience members have reported that television use promotes their integration into society and facilitates social interaction. Although television viewing is an essentially privatistic affair not requiring social interaction, audiences have claimed that viewing enables them to 'carry out social roles', 'to connect with family, friends and society', to identify with others and gain 'a sense of belonging', to achieve 'insight into the circumstances of others', and to find 'a basis for conversation and social interaction'. But these findings may make sense given that audiences have reported that television provides 'a substitute for real-life companionship'.

Somewhat less problematic is the use of television for information seeking and entertainment purposes. The attractiveness of television tends to be closely associated with audience needs for diversions from the problems of the real world, and for relaxation. McQuail's typology also identifies the use of television for entertainment with obtaining 'intrinsic cultural or aesthetic enjoyment', with 'emotional release' and 'sexual arousal', and with it being a 'time filler'.

Uses and gratifications research would seem to suggest that the attractiveness of television and 'thus the "causes" of media use lie in social or psychological circumstances that are experienced as problems and the media are used for problem resolution (the meeting of needs)'.[16] On the basis of an audience survey, Blumler suggests that the high television user is seeking 'sources of satisfactions blocked...by frustrating features of his environment'.[17] He reports that the two major groups using television for diversionary purposes were 'women professing an instrumental rather than an expressive orientation to their work and older people who felt dissatisfied with their jobs'.[18]

Although much of the uses and gratifications research is cast in terms which portray television as performing 'positive' social functions, Blumler's findings do connect with the more 'pessimistic' appraisals which identify the diversionary attractions of television as serving the interests of the dominant class. In this view, television consumes energies which might otherwise be mobilised in forms of political action against dominant groups, and involves people not so much in problem resolution as in 'problem-avoidance'.

Other attempts to explain the attractiveness of television centre on either the nature of the technology itself (colour, cable, and so on), or on programme availability, scheduling and choice, or both. By and large it has been difficult to attribute increases in viewing to technological improvements—subscribers to pay-TV and cable, for example, tend to come from the ranks of the already higher viewers. Similarly, extra programme availability does not result in increased viewing, unless it also constitutes the offering of a wide range of entertainment hitherto unavailable.[19]

It is commonly observed that television planners do attempt to sequence their programmes in ways which 'parallel as closely as possible the temporal structure of daily life for the greatest number of people'.[20] The underlying economics of television production, particularly as it relates to the need to attract large audiences for advertisers, is, as political economists of the media have stressed, essential to understanding the range and scheduling of television's output. Such considerations, however, are fundamentally irrelevant to explaining the attraction of television. However powerful the economics of media production, the individual nevertheless has the choice not to view television. Further, there is evidence which places television's attractiveness in doubt.

Not only has widespread dissatisfaction been reported with respect to the quality and choice of programmes available,[21] but, more significantly, viewers are more than ready to exercise their choice not to view television when given the opportunity to participate in a 'more enjoyable' activity. In a survey conducted by Sahin and Robinson, television viewing was widely reported to be one of the least enjoyable of all leisure-time activities. They conclude that 'once again, viewing emerges as the most expendable or least important of daily activities', but 'once people are in their homes, however, the set appears to have an irresistible hold on their time'.[22]

Sahin and Robinson's findings merely support those consistent sentiments expressed about television during the course of everyday conversations. In spite of the large amounts of time given to viewing, and in spite of the increasing use of video to record 'missed programmes', the gratifications viewers claim to derive from viewing are, by their own admission, of little importance. In other words it would seem that the reported satisfactions derived from television use are *trivial*. This does raise serious problems for uses and gratifications research. Not only is television's attractiveness contested, but there are difficulties with the way in which 'needs' are conceptualised. What uses and gratifications research fails to do is to address the question of the *significance* of the needs which are supposedly met through television viewing.

Much television viewing would seem not to reflect a use purposefully intent on meeting needs, but rather a routine use in which the selectivity of programmes is extremely low. Thus McQuail notes that 'there are many indications that people allocate a certain amount of time to viewing in general, irrespective of what is on'.[23] Although much that we do is a matter of routine, it has occurred to some media theorists that it is the passive nature of television viewing which makes it a 'relatively attractive' routine. This raises again the hotly debated issue of 'audience passivity'.

Curran and Tunstall reason that increased 'mass media consumption does not necessarily denote...increased "passivity" amongst the adult population'.[24] Significantly, most of their examples in support of this claim are derived from the 'benefits' which may accrue from reading newspapers. There are, of course, as Blumler has indicated, a variety of ways in which the audience, as essentially passive or active, can be construed. What Curran and Tunstall are opposed to is a notion of a passive audience which suggests a positive correlation between television's fare and the intellect of high viewers. They are thus opposed to those views which 'cavalierly dismiss the offerings of the mass media as trivial expressions of the lowest common denominator of taste, intellect and even interest among the national audience'.[25] They argue against what they see as Robinson's elitism, in the latter's reference to the role of television as 'that of electronic innkeeper to the less active minds of society'.[26] Curran and Tunstall stress instead the 'importance of the mass media in gratifying audience dispositions and personality needs'.[27] But given that viewers are most ready to dispense with viewing in favour of some more enjoyable activity, the use of television for diversion and personality needs would seem to be an unsatisfying one, providing, at best, pseudo-gratifications. Yet there must be something other than television's limited attractiveness which is powerful enough to tie people to their television sets. Are there ways of understanding television's hold on leisure-time without invoking speculations about the quality of viewers' intellect? Such explanations are available, but in order to avail ourselves of them it is necessary to break away from the media-centred-ness of media theory.

Necessity and the temporal structure of daily life

The value of Blumler's research cited above (see p. 132), resides in his attempt to link media use with the individual's life-situation and the opportunities available therein. This, too, is the strength of Sahin and Robinson's discussion of increased television viewing. Reiterating a point forcibly made by Adorno and Horkheimer, Sahin and Robinson observe that 'much free time must be spent either recuperating from or preparing for work'. They describe television viewing as occupying 'a residual "sink" of time not usable for other purposes'.[28] This suggests that one key to understanding why it is that people watch so much television, is to be found in an analysis of the temporal structure of daily life. Additionally, I shall argue that we need to consider the availability of opportunities to participate in alternative leisure activities. Both considerations, taken in conjunction with each other, point us toward a 'political economy of time'.

Giddens notes that

the economic order of capitalism depends upon the exact control of time labour-time becomes a key feature of the exploitive system of class domination. Time remains today at the centre of capital–labour disputes, as the employers' weapon of time-and-motion studies, and the workers' riposte of go-slows, readily attest. The control of time as a resource employed in structures of domination, however, may be historically more significant than even Marx believed...[29]

That we have time left over for matters beyond necessity is not in dispute. 'By and large', Sahin and Robinson argue, 'the realm of necessity casts its shadow over the realm of freedom'.[30] For Sahin and Robinson, the realm of necessity includes 'pledged time', that is, paid labour time, 'compulsive time', by which they mean time given mainly to domestic functions, and 'personal time', which refers to time for sleeping, eating, and so on. The scheduling of paid labour-time orders our own scheduling of compulsive and personal time, that is, *when* we eat, sleep, travel, or whatever. Leisure-time is not only time left over after we have attended to necessity, it is also 'fragmented time' in the sense that it is made up of 'bits and pieces' of time in between 'necessary time'. As a basic resource for human activity, fragmented time severely restricts its usability. The absence of lengthy continuous tracts of leisure-time is a characteristic of the temporal structure of our daily lives. As such it is particularly suited to the activity of watching television along with other activities which can be pursued with 'closure' (we watch a programme from beginning to end), in relatively short periods of time.

Paid labour-time, or at least our dependence, direct or indirect, on paid work, provides the temporal pattern for our lives, both in the short term (week, month, year), and in the long term (lifetime). Thus, participating in the occupational structure involves being available for work for 'tomorrow', 'next week', 'next month', and so on. The significance of the annual holiday, of the week-end, of public holidays, of Saturday night, and so on, derives directly from the realm of necessity. If the relative absence of lengthy tracts of free time is a feature of day-to-day life, it is only marginally less a feature of life in the short and long term. Ironically those with lengthy periods of more or less continuous free time are unable, for one reason or another, to use it to the full. Time as a resource for human activity is of little value unless it is available in conjunction with other resources.

In capitalist societies the major resource for survival and action in general is money. The vast majority are forced into a relationship of dependency on an employer and/or, partner, spouse or parent who is employed, and/or on the State, in order to obtain their means of survival. It is also a feature of capitalist societies that, in their relationships of forced dependency, some fare better than others. Although estimates vary, at least one quarter of the populations in most Western capitalist societies are classified as 'poor', that is, at the survival or sub-survival level of existence. Television's high audiences among the poorer sections of society can be seen to be directly linked to its relative cheapness, and to the poor being unable to afford to participate in more expensive leisure activities. The unemployed, for example, have time on their hands but lack the major resources to use it. By contrast, the more affluent employed may have money to spare, but limitations on their time govern the ways in which money can be used. The forced dependence of children on adults confines their free-time uses to particular spaces. The retired, another high viewing group, have more free time than most, but even those with money are restricted in their leisure activities on account of their depleted physical resources. The very house-bound nature of being an economically dependent housewife seriously limits her range of leisure-time use.

An increasingly common observation is that which characterises our participation in the realm of necessity, as 'dull, monotonous and routinised'. Modern work processes and household gadgets may have removed much of the sweat and toil once experienced by the working class. But the dull routines of necessity produce their own forms of weariness, which not only impede our leisure-time use, but may actually generate the need for relaxation and rest. The 'appropriation of alien labour', Adorno writes, 'weighs on it (free time) like a mortgage'. Thus 'free time remains the reflex-action to a production rhythm imposed heteronomously on the subject, compulsively maintained even in the weary pauses'.[31] Television may be not so much the 'electronic innkeeper to the less active minds', as to the more weary bodies. The sparkling insights of Adorno and some of his colleagues suggest that the uses and gratifications approach to the study of television viewing (see pp. 131–4) does not go far enough in its understanding of the relation between needs and action. The tendency to attempt to make a connection between the watching of a particular programme, or type of programme, and a particular need (identity, knowledge, diversion, relaxation, and so on,) experienced by audiences, belies the complexity of the needs–action relationship. It is through a consideration of this relationship that we will be better able to explain television's grip on leisure-time.

Needs and action

To understand why people use time in the way they do, it is necessary, according to Sève, to understand what it is that people *must* do in order to secure their survival. This enables Sève to stress that an individual's *total* activity is first and foremost 'a product of the structures of this social world'. Only after first understanding how the realm of necessity determines our total range of action, can the psychology 'of individual activity...be undertaken with some chance of success'.[32] This is a particularly important point to grasp. Not only is it consistent with what we have already said about the structuration of time, but it constitutes a radical break with the hyper-psychological bias of structuralist media theory, and the psychologism inherent in much critical media theory. The individual–society relation, and thus explanations of social reproduction, are, for Sève, to be primarily focused on social practices and individual action, and only secondarily on consciousness and ideology. To understand what an individual does as primarily the product of the individual's consciousness/ideas, as much media theory tends to, is to ignore the more powerful determinations of the range of actions available to the individual. To understand what an individual chooses to do, like watching television for example, it is first necessary to have some knowledge of what the individual is not free to choose.

Sève believes that psychological theorising, if it is to avoid psychologism, must be undertaken within a political economy of use-time. He approvingly cites Politzer, who in 1929 argued that

Psychological determinism in itself is not a sovereign determinism: it does not and cannot act except within the limits, so to speak, of economic determinism...

Psychology does not therefore hold the 'secret' of human affairs, simply because the 'secret' is not of a psychological order.

As far as the fundamental orientation and organisation of psychology are concerned, it is the meaning of economics which is truly fundamental.[33]

It needs to be understood that Sève is not replacing psychology with economics, rather he develops ways of understanding the psychological consequences of the realm of necessity for individuals, and how these consequences in turn, influence action. It is worthwhile discussing Sève's theory further, since it leads to a more comprehensive account of television's colonisation of leisure, and to an account of television's role in social reproduction, understood as a process which is not dependent on the ideological incorporation of subordinate groups to structures of domination.

Sève emphasises that 'every act is, on the one hand, the act *of an individual*, an aspect of his biography, a self-expression; but on the other, is the act *of a determinate social world*, an aspect of social relations, an expression of objective historical conditions'.[34] This 'fundamental duality' is the site of innumerable contradictions, of which, following Marx, that between 'concrete' and 'abstract' labour is basic to understanding the human personality. For Sève, abstract labour involves us in 'socially productive labour', whereas concrete labour involves us in 'activities directly relating to oneself'. While both concrete and abstract labour are 'psychologically productive activities', in that they constitute 'the ensemble of activities which produce and reproduce the personality',[35] Sève insists that, in capitalist society, concrete personal activity is subordinated to abstract social activity. The 'infrastructure of the personality', he maintains, 'is the temporal system of relations between the two broad categories of activity'.

The temporal structure of daily life, which is conducive to viewing television, is also, as Sève suggests, fundamentally involved in the production of personalities. We are 'beings-in-time'. What we do influences what we become, which in turn influences what we do—a point I shall develop later specifically in relation to television viewing. Sève continues:

> The need for time for living is only comprehensible if one is able to account theoretically for the radical difference which exists between time to be lived and time for living, a difference which is by no means a psychic *given* but a social *result* affecting the personality to its core.[36]

As 'a general rule...the existing social relations *impose from without* a use-time...against which the individual will by itself is totally powerless'.[37] Gorz makes a similar point in more explicit language:

> Work...does not belong to the individuals who perform it, nor can it be termed their own activity. It belongs to the machinery of social production, is allocated and programmed by it, remaining external to the individuals upon whom it is imposed.[38]

The distinction between concrete and abstract activity is not an absolute one. Interpersonal and domestic relations, personally satisfying work and certain leisure activities constitute 'intermediary psychologically productive activities'. Sève recognises that some of our leisure activities are 'assimilated to efforts to compensate for the moral depreciation of the value of labour-power'.[39]

One way in which Sève attempts to develop a framework for theorising the consequences of the realm of necessity for 'being-in-time' is by means of another distinction—between what he refers to as 'sector I' and 'sector II' activity. Sector I activity is essentially 'learning' activity contributing directly to the development of capacities, whereas sector II activity involves the exercise of some capacity without necessarily developing it further. Thus 'the increase in learning of new capacities, simplifying in the extreme and taking all conditions to be constant, requires an increase in time set aside for sector I of activity and consequently a decrease of time available for sector II'.[40]

In this scheme, television viewing can be located within a zone of activity which is personal/concrete on the one hand, and intermediary on the other. Some television viewing can be considered as sector I activity in that it may lead to gains in information, which is one type of learning potentially useful to the development of capacities. However, television viewing itself takes time away from the exercise of learning capacities, as in the practical development of skills, and in this respect can be seen to be sector II activity.

There is a need here to emphasise, more than Sève does, that the ability to carry out an act is not solely dependent on 'the ensemble of "actual potentialities", innate or acquired', nor on this in conjunction with the availability of time, but *also* on the availability of other resources necessary for the accomplishment of the act in question. Thus while television viewing keys in rather neatly with fragmented leisure-time, and while it does consume time, however fragmented, potentially available for a more productive development of capacities, viewing alone cannot be identified as the 'cause' of the underdevelopment of human capacities. The capacity to play a violin, to ski, to grow one's own food, to programme a computer, and so on, cannot be developed in the absence of the availability of some necessary material resources. The totality of resources available to an individual is descriptive of that individual's power-to-act. As Giddens puts it, 'resources are the media through which power is exercised', and significantly 'through which structures of domination are reproduced'.[41] The highest television viewing groups tend to be found amongst the least powerful, and it is the relative powerlessness of these groups which may provide a principal reason for their high viewing. In other words, choosing to watch television may, for some groups, reflect their relative powerlessness to engage in alternative, more satisfying activities.

Every act can be seen to be a reflection of an individual's power to act *and* powerlessness to do otherwise, but it is also much more than this, as Sève indicates. The vital link in his scheme between socially imposed activity and activity for oneself, and between sector I and sector II activity, is what Sève refers to as 'the intuitive evaluation of P/N'. P/N refers to 'the possible effects of the act and the needs to be satisfied...in short the relation between product(P) and need(N)'. The intuitive evaluation of this relation 'can be seen to be one of the most simple and universal regulators of activity'.[42] Sève stresses that the 'relation between needs and effects of activity are essentially mediated by the *laws of the social formation* in which this activity develops and *consequently by the overall structure of the personality* itself'.[43]

Both acts and needs are not only to be seen as existing in relation to each other, but within the total context of use-time.

One can see that the composition of the psychological product of an act, considered as its time cost, is closely related, in this connection alone, to the place which it occupies in a concrete use-time, and that the real P/N, and therefore the actual incentive to an activity, is not the P/N of the act considered in isolation but a P/N mediated by the overall structure of activity.[44]

This suggests, then, that television viewing, as a dominant leisure activity, can indeed be seen to be need-related within the *total* context of the satisfaction and frustration of needs derived from the individual's *total* actual use-time. To this we can add that the satisfaction of needs is, in the case of many needs, dependent on the actions of others, as well as on the individual's power to act.

Sève quite rightly points out that

To ensure the dominance of a use-time of general P/N as high as the objective conditions make possible appears to be the most decisive psychological function of life. On the other hand, chronic oscillation of use-time and constant ambiguity of acts seem characteristic of a personality which at least partially gives up under the excessively contradictory pressures of circumstances.[45]

It can be argued that the 'total objective conditions' of a majority do not allow a use-time of general P/N which is high. Increasingly, it would seem, people are becoming 'adapted' to a leisure-time use of relatively low satisfactions. Television viewing is one manifestation of this state of affairs. The total circumstances in which the individual is located, as we have seen, are for the most part a product of forces beyond the control of the vast majority of individuals. The economic system determines the realm of necessity, the power or lack of it to act, and thus the ability to meet needs. In saying this, we are beginning to point toward an explanation of social reproduction which is based primarily on an understanding of how economic compulsion works. The question arises as to whether or not the psychological and social consequences of economic compulsion enable us to become adapted to structures of domination, in ways which consolidate our pragmatic acquiescence to the demands of economic necessity. A number of possible answers to this question have already been touched upon in our brief encounter with Sève. There is the possibility that the underdevelopment of capacities which ensues from a low P/N takes its toll on 'human-beingness-over-time'. It may be the case that human beings today have 'developed' in ways which enable them more readily to adapt to their total life circumstances. While historical comparisons are somewhat speculative, we can assess the social and psychological consequences of trends in total use-time against the 'historical possibilities' which, prior to the modern period, indicated a future in which leisure-time use would reflect and expand human emancipation. It is in assessing these possibilities, too, that we will be in a position to extend our considerations of the social and psychological significance of television's colonisation of leisure-time.

The emancipatory potential of leisure-time

Earlier it was suggested that media theory has approached the question of the social significance of increased television viewing primarily through considering 'displacement effects' (see pp. 130–1). Such discussions have been insufficiently historical and, partly because of this, there has been a failure to grasp fully the idea that television's social significance is to a large extent rooted in the potential significance of leisure-time as a resource for the development of an emancipatory cultural and political sphere.

Time freed from necessity is a basic requirement for all those activities involved in the development of public opinion, and to its materialisation in practices addressed to improving the social conditions of life. During Marx's lifetime the need for radical improvements in working and living conditions was obviously apparent. But Marx envisaged far more than this. There was more to human existence, he supposed, than a total preoccupation with meeting survival needs. The satisfaction of the basic material needs for food, clothing and shelter, are the prerequisites for the development of the individual, which also requires time freed from the compulsion of labour. Beyond the realm of necessity, Marx wrote,

begins the development of human energy which is an end in itself, the true realm of freedom, which, however, can blossom forth only with this realm of necessity as its basis. The shortening of the working-day is its basic prerequisite.[46]

Modern societies are the beneficiaries of the long (and continuing) struggle for the reduction of the working day, in that leisure-time is significantly more plentiful today than in Marx's day. However, in the light of the discussion in this chapter, it must be highly questionable that our use of leisure-time matches the kinds of visions held by Marx. It can be agreed, with Marx, that 'time is the room of human development',[47] but it is doubtful that our primary leisure activities make significant contributions to the development of our 'vital capacities'. In short, the reduction of the working day has not brought with it the rich development of cultural activities through which individuals might develop their potential. The latter, by and large, can only occur through the 'self-management of time', as Gorz puts it, which is geared toward the expansion of autonomy.

Self-determined activity...is not principally concerned with the exchange of quantities of time. It is its own end, whether it takes the form of aesthetic activity (like games, including love) or artistic creation. When self-determined activity is one of production, it is concerned with the creation of objects destined not for sale, but to be consumed or used by the producers themselves or by their friends or relatives.[48]

Expanding the sphere of autonomy, Gorz argues, 'encourages people to become extremely critical and demanding of the nature and finality of socially necessary labour'.[49] It alters the balance, too, between dominant groups and the subordinated—structures of domination involve power-relations which are 'relations of autonomy and dependence'.[50] Similarly, the social theorists associated with the Frankfurt School believed that the development of autonomy in individuals not only promoted resistance to forms of domination, but facilitated the expansion of needs which could only be met through the establishment of a libertarian socialist society. To them the realm of culture offered arenas in which autonomy could be exercised, and in which protest against oppression could be registered and expressed. As Adorno wrote, 'culture, in the true sense, did not simply accommodate itself to human beings; but it always simultaneously raised a protest against petrified relations under which they lived'.[51]

With increased leisure-time, opportunities for involvement in 'culture, in the true sense' opened up. In other words, increased leisure-time enabled a more active participation in modes of cultural production and consumption which draw on and develop the individual's capacities for autonomy. In so far as 'true' cultural products encourage a mode of active reception characterised by a critically-reflective, attentative engagement, the Frankfurt School saw parallels between the 'function' of 'true' culture in society and their own critical social theory. Of the latter, Giddens suggests that 'if there is a single dominating element in critical theory, it is the defence of Reason (*Vernunft*) understood...as the critical faculty which reconciles knowledge with the transformation of the world so as to further human fulfilment and freedom'.[52]

It is understandable, then, that the Frankfurt School should have devoted considerable attention to the subversion of the emancipatory potential of true culture. This subversion came in the form of the emergence of the culture industry. Time freed from labour has become the target of the culture and leisure industries, which collectively have achieved a near monopoly of this time. The commercialisation of cultural production, Adorno and Horkheimer argued, not only depletes the quality of cultural goods available in society, but through processes of standardisation (imposed as a consequence of commercial interest), cultural variety is narrowed and, importantly, modes of reception demanding little effort and no critically-reflective response are encouraged. Today television is the major producer of cultural products and the principal medium of cultural consumption.

It would seem that the Frankfurt School have provided us with the means of formulating an alternative thesis with respect to television's power in Western capitalist societies. Time spent viewing hardly constitutes time devoted to the expansion of autonomy, and thus to the development of capacities which facilitate resistance to forms of domination, and which advance the 'emancipatory interest'. As such, time spent viewing television can be seen to be serving the interests of dominant groups. Human energies which could be mobilised to oppose forms of domination are soaked up by television. Has television become an instrument of domination?

The Frankfurt School's answer to this question is a complex one which media theorists, in their media- and ideology-centredness, have generally failed to grasp. The key to understanding the power of the culture industry for the Frankfurt School resides in their sensitivity to the ways in which human needs are vulnerable to manipulation over time. It is this, too, which is the key to their historicised discussions of social reproduction. 'In this society', Marcuse argues, 'the productive apparatus tends to become totalitarian to the extent to which it determines not only the socially needed occupations, skills, and attitudes, but also individual needs and aspirations'.[53]

Adorno and Horkheimer are quite clear that the power of the culture industry is rooted in the 'irrationalism of totalitarian capitalism whose way of satisfying needs has an objectified form determined by domination which makes the satisfaction of needs impossible...'[54] The 'objectified form', as we saw earlier, is work through which we earn the means to meet our survival needs. But, in industrial societies, 'the individual who is thoroughly weary must use his weariness as energy for his surrender to the collective power which wears him out'.[55] Thus while the work of the labouring classes enables them to meet survival needs, it also *generates* the need for rest, relaxation, diversions, amusements, and so on. It is worth quoting Adorno and Horkheimer at some length on this.

It is quite correct that the power of the culture industry resides in its identification with a manufactured need...Amusement under late capitalism is the prolongation of work. It is sought after as an escape from the mechanized work process, and to recruit strength in order to be able to cope with it again. But at the same time mechanization has such power over a man's leisure and happiness, and so profoundly determines the manufacture of amusement goods, that his experiences are inevitably after images of the work processes itself.[56]

Thus, in bearing the mark of what we must necessarily do in order to survive, our leisure activities have fallen prey to the very economic forces which structure the realm of necessity. But more than this, we can recall, there is insufficient uninterrupted time to satisfy our 'beyond-survival needs'. As Adorno expresses it, 'Sunday fails to satisfy, not because it is a day off work, but because its own promise is felt directly as unfulfilled...every Sunday is too little Sunday'.[57]

In this context television viewing ministers to needs which have been generated by the realm of necessity. Television invades lives already weary from work and understandably already inclined toward effortless leisure. In this sense, television becomes an extension of the economic system which has created the needs which viewing 'satisfies'. Leisure-time, instead of being used to meet 'vital needs' necessary for the development of autonomy, becomes the arena in which individuals settle for the instantaneous, insubstantial pleasures served up by the culture industry. As this state of affairs persists, Adorno and Horkheimer argued, the culture industry is afforded an opportunity to develop amongst its consumers a 'taste for substitute pleasures'. In these manipulated tastes programmers find ample justification for their claims that 'the public are given what they want'.

Adorno and Horkheimer were convinced that the products of the culture industry are fundamentally irrelevant to the satisfaction of vital needs. This view was informed by the experience of the hard-earned satisfactions derived from self-motivated productive activity, and from the reception of cultural products which 'require' a total engagement from the critically-reflective consumer. They contrasted the achievement of genuine satisfactions with the 'pseudo-gratifications' of 'effortless pleasure'. Thus they noted that 'pleasure hardens into boredom because, if it is to remain pleasure, it must not demand any effort...'.[58] As individuals settle for the substitute pleasures of the culture industry, allowing their consumption of mass produced entertainment to become a habitual routine of leisure-time use, they become adapted, it was argued, to a life in which 'pseudo-activity holds sway'.[59] This adaptation effectively replaces the development of autonomous activity. Similarly, Gorz writes that 'it will not help to enlarge the sphere of individual autonomy if the resulting free time remains empty 'leisure time', filled for better or worse by the programmed distractions of the mass media and the oblivion merchants...'.[60]

The Frankfurt School, however, believed that as individuals become adapted to alienating labour, and to a leisure-time use divorced from the fulfilment of vital needs, there was the real possibility that in time 'human-beingness' itself would be transformed. Informing this view was Marx's historical understanding of the relation between needs and 'human nature'. Geras observes that

From one work to another and often, Marx speaks of modification or development of human needs and of the emergence of new needs in the course of history. Correspondingly, he speaks also of a transformation of the nature of man.[61]

What emerges from Frankfurt social theory is a very strong concern that the manipulation of needs, which is motored by the realm of necessity, may have generated a leisure-time use which not only subverts its emancipatory potential, but contributes to the depletion of human resources necessary for resisting forms of domination. Leisure-time, instead of being used to resist the necessity of adaptation to socially imposed labour, or for the development of 'human-beingness' which sharpens the contradictions between itself and its pale 'non-human' form in labour, is used instead in a way which reinforces the individual's adaptation to the total social system.

Frankfurt social theory, as I have attempted to show above, does provide a means whereby we can understand how subordinate groups are *materially* incorporated into structures of domination. Furthermore, we can identify a clear role for television in this process. Critical media theory has made little of the Frankfurt approach to fomulating television's power. With some exceptions from the political economy of the media perspective, critical media theorists have tended to squeeze the Frankfurt School's writings into a dominant ideology thesis. But in so doing, critical media theory has failed to grasp the significance of how television participates in the manipulation of needs. For the Frankfurt School the power of ideology in social reproduction was always secondary to material forces. In criticising Lukács's emphasis on the 'false consciousness' of the working class in his attempt to account for the lack of revolutionary consciousness, Adorno wrote:

The trouble is with the conditions that condemn mankind to impotence and apathy and would yet be changeable by human action; it is not primarily with people and with the way conditions *appear* to people. Considering the possibility of total disaster, reification is an epiphenomenon, and even more so is the alienation coupled with reification, the subjective state of consciousness that corresponds to it.[62]

'The masses are', according to Adorno and Horkheimer, 'too sharp to identify with the millionaire on the screen'.[63] In several places throughout their writings, Adorno and Horkheimer warned against privileging the culture industry's ideological power—'everyone knows that he is now helpless in the system, and ideology has to take this into account'.[64]

It is true that the Frankfurt School had much to say about the ideological aspects of the mass media. But in this respect they focused more on the absence of oppositional consciousness (level four of ideological operations, see pp. 64, 81, 92), than on ideological incorporation. In a critique of Huxley's *Brave New World*, for example, Adorno complains that 'no room is left for a concept of mankind that would resist absorption into the collective coercion of the system, and reduction to the status of contingent individuals'.[65]

It is important to bear these points in mind in order to appreciate that whatever ideological effects the Frankfurt School attributed to television and the mass media, these were not only understood as having a basis in the manipulation of needs, but the latter was understood as a product of the social totality, of which the culture industry is one part. In response 'to the objection that we overrate greatly the indoctrinating power of the "media", and that by themselves the people would feel and satisfy the needs which are now imposed upon them', Marcuse wrote:

The objection misses the point. The preconditioning does not start with the mass production of radio and television and with the centralisation of their control. The people enter this stage as preconditioned receptacles of long standing; the decisive difference is in the flattening out of the contrast (or conflict) between the given and the possible, between the satisfied and the unsatisfied needs.[66]

The distinction between being and consciousness, and thus between 'material effects' and 'ideological effects' which arises from social practices, including the practice of watching television, is not always an easy one to make. This is particularly so in the case of television's role in the socialisation process. Both material and ideological effects are intertwined in the production of adults as 'preconditioned receptacles of long standing'.

Television and socialisation

Media theory, as I have already noted (see pp. 131), has tended to treat television's power in the socialisation of children primarily as an ideological power. Programmes intended for adult viewing do attract younger viewers, and this is a continuing source of concern amongst television's critics, especially so in view of the widespread belief that children are more vulnerable to influence than adults. It is this belief which has also prompted a considerable number of analyses of children's television fare. Not all children's programmes fit a one-way ideological thrust. Often within the same programmes, for example, the co-operative ethic sits uneasily amidst the idealisation of competition, and 'cost nothing' do-it-yourself projects are interrupted by 'hard sell' advertising promoting expensive toys. Perhaps more than in adult programmes, children are presented with a 'psychomorphic view of society' (see p. 48) which feeds 'the illusion of the autonomous ego'. But, more ominously, especially in programmes for younger viewers, there is a steady diet of sexism, and of adult ideals which are not merely confined to traditional gender-related roles, but which also express a close connection between being middle class and 'being good', and the latter with 'being successful'. In the case of gender-related myths, children's television supplies images which may serve to 'naturalise' sexist practices in the family, which in turn are further confirmed and naturalised in the 'more real' adult fare, which in turn reflect gender relations in the wider society.

One is left to speculate on the kind of self-images high viewing black and working-class children are encouraged to develop, given the relative absence from the screen of 'positive' black and working-class subject positions inviting realistic identification, and the relative abundance of positive models with which realistic identification is unlikely. Television's power is obviously not isolated in this respect. It works in conjunction with a social reality in which real-life black and working-class persons, male and female, occupy social positions hardly supportive of positive self-images. In the case of white children having no direct social contact with black people, television, it can be argued, may have a more direct bearing on the development of racial attitudes.

There is, then, a rather strong case to be made that television exerts a powerful ideological influence on the young. Be that as it may, I shall argue that television's participation in the socialisation of young children involves far more than the potential ideological manipulation which has been noted. It can be suggested that television as a material power (the practice of viewing) contributes to those material forces involved in the formation of personalities less resistant than they might otherwise be to forms of domination. This view is based on the common observation that television viewing has historically displaced more autonomous forms of activity in early childhood, and that it has also displaced the role of inter-generational communication in child-rearing practices. The significance of both forms of displacement for the development, or more precisely for the underdevelopment, of autonomy, can be understood in the context of social changes which have influenced changes in the patterns of family life.

'Above all', Gorz maintains, it is 'family background...which makes some individuals more autonomous than others'.[67] One line of argument available in the writings of the Frankfurt School, and in the early work of Fromm[68] and Reich,[69] focuses on the material force of repressive practices as being fundamentally involved in producing submissive character types which are psychically prepared for a future of obedience and conformity to the demands of dominant groups. The repetitive onslaught of repression, it was argued, operates against the development of autonomy in individuals. The material force of repression is most effective in the early years when the child is relatively powerless to resist parental power. However, the Frankfurt School believed that although the family had always been a principal arena for repressive practices, it also provided the means whereby the individual could develop its 'inner resistances' to domination. Two factors were important here. First, the 'authority of the father', and second the 'protective function of the mother'.

The economic independence of the father, derived from his position as head of the economically productive household, provided him with a substantial basis for his authority in the family. The 'authoritarian father' was seen as a contradictory character—the agent of repression, on the one hand, and a model of independence and autonomy with which his children could identify, on the other. Additionally, the family, however repressive, did provide, mainly through the mother, protection for children against the harsher realities of the outside world. In this sense the family constituted a social space for a relatively 'safe' and 'secure' passage through childhood, a prerequisite for the development of 'ontological security', which, Laing argues, is an important basis for the exercise and growth of autonomy.[70]

With the development of capitalism, however, the economic independence of the father has been seriously undermined, and the family as a potential haven from the real world has been invaded by that world. The father no longer presents himself as a model of independence and autonomy, yet often continues to be a repressive force. Of the withering away of the structure of the traditional family, Adorno wrote:

With the family there passes away...not only the most effective agency of the bourgeoisie, but also the resistance which, through repressing the individual, also strengthened, perhaps even produced him. The end of the family paralyses the forces of opposition. The rising collectivist order is a mockery of a classless one: together with the bourgeois it liquidates the Utopia that once drew sustenance from motherly love.[71]

These changes were well under way prior to the invention of television. Even though the underlying historical trend pointed toward a decline in the presence of autonomous individuals, the Frankfurt School noted that 'resistant' individuals had not entirely disappeared. Drawing 'sustenance from motherly love' and preferably 'parental love' in conjunction with an 'incomplete' or deviant socialisation would seem to be facilitative of the development of autonomy. Thus Gorz states that

On the whole, autonomous individuals, particularly 'creators', artists, intellectuals and so on, most often come from families where parental authority is absent or inadequate...

In short, autonomous individuals are those whose socialisation has been defective, incomplete—where the non-socialised part of their lives prevails over the socialised part.[72]

Before television's 'capturing' of their time, working-class boys, at least, developed some autonomy outside of the family sphere, though no doubt with the security of the family behind them. Lack of space and material resources often meant that boys were 'encouraged' to 'go out', being left to their own devices to create their own fun in spaces well distanced from the heavy hand of authority, and beyond the socialising influence of adults.

All this was to change with the coming of television. The cramped spaces of working-class homes, while repressive for mobile infants, are irrelevant for sedentary viewers of television. With the growth of daytime broadcasting, children were brought 'back inside' into the safety of the home. Now withdrawn from those adult-free spaces, which are vital for the development of autonomy, young children are undergoing a television-dominated childhood. The experience of watching television is far removed from the experience of self-motivated activity through which autonomy develops. Not practised in the exercise of autonomous agency, today's young children emerge as teenagers (teenagers have always been one of the lowest television viewing groups), well prepared for a period of drifting from one media-orchestrated sub-culture to another. Of course, not all youth sub-cultures are manufactured by media conglomerates, and not all children go through a television dominated socialisation—but it would seem to be the underlying historical trend. As Horkheimer noted, 'the stereotyped rejection of television...which was still customary a few years ago in German families which considered themselves educated, highlights with special clarity the impossibility of turning the clock back'.[73] He continues:

Yet the absence of a set from his parents' home only leads to the child being looked down on by his companions in school, to feelings of inferiority and worse. The flight into the past is no help to the freedom that is being threatened.[74]

It would seem, then, that television has intervened rather powerfully in the socialisation process. In attempting to assess how powerful this intervention has been, it is necessary to bear in mind that the family was already being displaced by 'the rising collectivist order' into which children were being inserted prior to the age of television. During this age Horkheimer argued that

From the day of his birth, the individual is made to feel that there is only one way of getting along in this world—that of giving up his hope of ultimate self-realization. This he can achieve solely by imitation. He continuously responds to what he perceives about him...emulating the traits and attitudes represented by all the collectivities that enmesh him—his play group, his classmates, his athletic team, and all the other groups that...enforce a more strict surrender through complete assimilation, than any father or teacher in the nineteenth century could impose.[75]

Individuals, Horkheimer proposed, were being over-socialised. Opportunities for the development of autonomy were dwindling, and the individual was more effectively socialised 'by adapting himself to all the powerful groups to which he eventually belongs'.[76]

Since then, of course, television has intervened—children are born into families already equipped with a television set. This has led to speculations about what has been observed as a relative lack of concern amongst today's youth (the television generation) for resisting threats to their own autonomy. If the latter is underdeveloped then supposedly threats to it are not experienced as such. Horkheimer made a related observation, widely echoed amongst academics in their perceptions of today's students.

It may indeed be true that when a child acquires its first knowledge of the world not through interaction with his father but through the screen and its images, not through spontaneous stimuli but through immediate reaction to signs, the end result is intellectual passivity.[77]

To this we can add that 'interaction with the *mother*' may have always been more important, and it is this which has been displaced in contemporary patterns of socialisation. As I noted earlier, the experience of ontological security, albeit in conjunction with opportunities for the exercise of autonomous agency, would seem to be essential for the production of autonomous individuals. In modern societies the period during which such security was once attainable (or potentially attainable) through parental love, has decreased. Anonymous agencies, including television, have taken over a crucial period in the child's formative years, replacing the intimate parent–child relationship.

More than this, it would seem that the basis of the parent–child relationship is undergoing a transformation, and with it, the child's expectations of the parent. Parental commitment, which was once expressed in terms of 'providing for the children' within the context of giving them both time and love, tends now to revolve much more around material provision. It is too easy to condemn parents and television for these trends, and for fuelling a consumerist orientation in children. Rather, it must be understood that trends in the changing patterns of family life have arisen within the context of far-reaching economic and political changes. I shall discuss some of these changes in the next chapter. But it can be noted here, for example, that changes in the occupational structure alone, in which permanent 'meaningful' careers are decreasingly available, have begun to uncouple the normative connections between school and the future. The society for which children were prepared by family and school no longer exists. Or, to put it another way, traditional patterns of socialisation have become increasingly irrelevant in contemporary society. Whereas, in the early days of television, it seemed that family, school *and* television were in concert with each other, preparing children for 'the collectivist order', today this is no longer so—not least, because it is no longer clear that society has a discernible order. It is difficult to see what kind of 'moral guidance', let alone 'career guidance', might best prepare children for an uncertain future.

It is in this context that television has become aligned with the modern agencies of socialisation, and indeed is central to them. Socialisation through television, play groups, pop-culture and youth sub-cultures, would seem to be preparing the young for a leisure-time use which at one and the same time is an extension of their socialisation into adulthood, and reproduces the dominant patterns of leisure-time use currently in evidence. The manufactured experiences of contemporary childhood bypass those needs which must be satisfied if the individual is to develop a sense of autonomy. In this respect tomorrow's adults are, as Marcuse put it, 'pre-conditioned receptacles of long standing'.

The underdevelopment of autonomous agency

While the dominance of television in leisure-time can be understood as a product of the stranglehold which necessity exercises over subordinate groups, the effects of this dominance, as we have seen, can be identified in the changing relationship between experience and need. The amount of time television consumes is 'experienced time', but it is a form of experience which, for the most part, is irrelevant to the satisfaction of basic existential needs, for example the need for ontological security, and to the satisfaction of 'vital needs' associated with self-realization. As we become adapted to this state of affairs, it has been argued, there is the possibility that individuals will become reconciled to a life in which their capacity for autonomy will remain underdeveloped. Television, it would seem, is involved in creating what Schatz and Winter refer to as 'the anthropological problem'.

Before the contemporary leap into the realm of free time, work had increasingly become the realm of necessity. With leisure, a new chance for realizing men's eternal longing, the possibility of a non-alienated creative being has appeared. However, for far too many the result has been the alienation of leisure time...in a consumer, entertainment, and welfare society, alienated leisure time, analogous to alienated labour, becomes the anthropological problem.[78]

But, as I have been at pains to stress, forces much greater than television have generated a social context in which television participates in the production of lives, which Fritzhand claims are 'one-sided, partial' and 'limited'.[79] For the more affluent, 'the use-value of freedom', Marcuse argued, has been reduced; 'there is no reason to insist on self-determination if the administered life is comfortable and even the "good" life'.[80] For the most subordinated, 'the realm of freedom has lost its classical content, its qualitative difference from the realm of necessity'. [81] To this we can add that television is centrally involved in socialising children for a future of 'organised relaxation'. To the extent that this socialisation is effective, *one* important resource for resistance to domination—the individual's capacity for autonomy—will remain underdeveloped.

Since television may be seen to participate in the production of personalities which are more prepared to acquiesce to the demands of the total social system, we can say that television's capturing of time does serve the interests of dominant groups. Whether or not this power is *necessary* for social reproduction, however, is highly debatable. Much hinges on the relative significance attributed to the force of economic necessity on the one hand, and the absence of oppositional forces of change on the other, in promoting pragmatic acquiescence to forms of domination. We have already seen that the control of time alone, by employers or parents, for example, effectively determines the total range of action available to an individual. The control of time alone makes 'free time' fragmented, which severely restricts its usability. The latter is already determined by the availability of resources for use in time, and these resources, for non-capitalists, are obtainable through employment which is determined by capitalists, or through some other relationship of forced dependency. The force of economic necessity is a formidable one, and for the most part a sufficient one for the reproduction of capitalist societies. Should it come under serious threat from working-class opposition, its force is invariably restored by the consequences of another force—the State.

In this view of social reproduction, economic necessity and State coercion would not seem to require the psychological consequences which may ensue from their practices, even though the manipulation of needs does reinforce the control over people exerted by economic necessity. The power of television within this perspective is a secondary one, since it is basically involved in extending the psychological consequences already produced by the workings of economic necessity.

On the other hand, there is the view which emphasises the absence of effective opposition to forms of domination as necessary for their reproduction. If we accept that forms of domination will continue to be reproduced until such time as they are overcome by forces of progressive social change, arising from participatory forms of collective self-determination, then it is difficult to see how such forces of change could take-off without the widespread existence of autonomous individuals. In this respect, television's power can be viewed as more central to social reproduction, in that it poses obstacles to social change. It would be far too media-centred, however, to accept this proposition without considering forces other than television which are involved in the under-development of the capacity for autonomous agency, and it would be far too psychologistic to explain the absence of effective opposition to prevailing forms of domination, primarily in terms of the individual's lack of autonomy.

Notes

1. John Urry, *The Anatomy of Capitalist Societies*, London, Macmillan, 1981, p. 45.
2. Shaun Moores, 'Review of Len Masterman, editor, *Television Mythologies:*

Stars, Shows and Signs (London: Comedia/MK Media Press, 1984)', *Media,*
Culture and Society, vol. 7, 1985, p. 391.

3. See A. Szalai *et al.*, *The Use of Time*, The Hague, Mouton, 1972.

4. Pam Mills, 'An international audience?', *Media, Culture and Society*, vol. 7, 1985, p. 498.

5. Ibid., p. 497.

6. H. Sahin and J.P. Robinson, 'Beyond the realm of necessity: television and the colonization of leisure', *Media, Culture and Society*, vol. 3, 1980, p. 91.

7. Ibid., p. 90.

8. James Curran and Jeremy Tunstall, 'Mass media and leisure' in Michael A. Smith, Stanley Parker and Cyril S. Smith, eds, *Leisure and Society in Britain*, London, Allen Lane, 1973, p. 201.

9. Pam Mills, op. cit. , p. 499.

10. Ibid.

11. From *British Labour Statistics*, London, HMSO, 1953–86, Table 185.

12. See Jeremy Tunstall, *The Media in Britain*, London, Constable, 1983, p. 135.

13. Curran and Tunstall, op. cit., p. 205.

14. See, for example, R. McCron, 'Changing Perspectives in the Study of Mass Media and Socialization' in J. Halloran, ed., *Mass Media and Socialization*, Leicester, IAMCR, 1976, pp. 13–44.

15. Denis McQuail, *Mass Communication Theory*, London, Sage, 1983, pp. 82–3.

16. Ibid., p. 163.

17. Jay G. Blumler, 'The Role of Theory in Uses and Gratifications Studies' in G. Cleveland Wilhoit and Harold de Bock, eds, *Mass Communication Review Yearbook, Vol. 1, 1980*, London, Sage, 1980, p. 214.

18. Ibid., p. 215.

19. Mills, op. cit., pp. 495–6.

20. Sahin and Robinson, op. cit., p. 94. This idea was formulated in detail by Raymond Williams, *Television: Technology and Cultural Form*, London, Fontana, 1974.

21. Mills, op. cit., p. 496.

22. Sahin and Robinson, op. cit., p. 93.

23. McQuail, op. cit., p. 162.

24. Curran and Tunstall, op. cit., p. 205.

25. Ibid., p. 206.

26. Ibid., pp. 205–6.

27. Ibid., p. 206.

28. Sahin and Robinson, op. cit., p. 93.

29. Anthony Giddens, *Central Problems in Social Theory*, London, Macmillan, 1979, p. 210.

30. Sahin and Robinson, op. cit., p. 93.
31. Theodor Adorno, *Minima Moralia*, London, Verso, 1978, p. 175.
32. Lucien Sève, *Man in Marxist Theory and the Psychology of Personality*, Hassocks, Harvester, 1978, p. 335.
33. Ibid., p. 308.
34. Ibid., p. 311.
35. Ibid., p. 336.
36. Ibid., p. 339.
37. Ibid., p. 343.
38. André Gorz, *Farewell to the Working Class*, London, Pluto, 1982, p. 71.
39. Sève, op. cit., p. 338.
40. Ibid., p. 340.
41. Giddens, op. cit., p. 91.
42. Sève, op. cit., p. 321.
43. Ibid., p. 319.
44. Ibid., p. 340.
45. Ibid., p. 346.
46. Karl Marx, *Capital, Volume III*, London, Lawrence and Wishart, 1959, p. 820.
47. Karl Marx and Frederick Engels, *Selected Works*, London, Lawrence and Wishart, 1968, p. 219.
48. Gorz, op. cit., p. 2.
49. Ibid., p. 97.
50. Giddens, op. cit., p. 93.
51. Adorno, 'Culture industry reconsidered', *New German Critique*, vol. 6, 1975, cited in David Held, *Introduction to Critical Theory*, London, Hutchinson, 1980, p. 81.
52. Anthony Giddens, *Studies in Social and Political Theory*, London, Hutchinson, 1977, p. 65.
53. Herbert Marcuse, *One Dimensional Man*, London, Abacus, 1972, p. 13.
54. Theodor Adorno and Max Horkheimer, *Dialectic of Enlightenment*, London, Verso, 1979, p. 55.
55. Ibid., pp. 152–3.
56. Ibid., p. 137.
57. Adorno, *Minima Moralia*, p. 175.
58. Adorno and Horkheimer, op. cit., p. 137.
59. Adorno, *Minima Moralia*, p. 131.
60. Gorz, op. cit., p. 87.
61. Norman Geras, *Marx and Human Nature: Refutation of a Legend*, London, Verso, 1983, pp. 89–90.
62. Theodor Adorno, *Negative Dialectics*, New York, Continuum, 1973, p. 190.
63. Adorno and Horkheimer, op. cit., p. 145.

64. Ibid., p. 151.
65. Theodor Adorno, *Prisms*, Cambridge, MA, MIT Press, 1981, p. 114.
66. Marcuse, op. cit., p. 21.
67. André Gorz, *Paths to Paradise: On the Liberation from Work*, London, Pluto, 1985, p. 65.
68. See, for example, Erich Fromm, *Escape from Freedom*, New York, Avon, 1965.
69. See, for example, Wilhelm Reich, *Mass Psychology of Fascism*, Harmondsworth, Pelican, 1975.
70. R.D. Laing, *The Divided Self*, Harmondsworth, Penguin, 1959.
71. Adorno, *Minima Moralia*, p. 23.
72. Gorz, *Paths to Paradise*, p. 66.
73. Max Horkheimer, *Critique of Instrumental Reason*, New York, Continuum, 1974, p. 140.
74. Ibid.
75. Max Horkheimer, *Eclipse of Reason*, New York, Continuum, 1974, p. 141. (NB: This was originally written in 1946).
76. Ibid.
77. Horkheimer, *Critique of Instrumental Reason*, p. 140.
78. Oskar Schatz and Ernst Winter, 'Alienation, Marxism, and Humanism' in Erich Fromm, ed., *Socialist Humanism*, New York, Anchor, 1966, p. 329.
79. Marek Fritzhand, 'Marx's Ideal of Man' in Fromm, op. cit., p. 174.
80. Marcuse, op. cit., p. 52.
81. Herbert Marcuse, 'Socialist Humanism?' in Fromm, op. cit., p. 115.

6 Television and Social Fragmentation

'Most sociologists would agree that the principle of continuous *structural differentiation* both underlies the development of modern societies and constitutes the essence of their "modernity"...'.[1] By 'structural differentiation', Offe is referring to the 'separation of formerly integrated patterns of life', for example, the domestic household from economic production, and the separation of 'manual and mental labour, labour and capital, state and society, law and morality, and state and church'.[2] For some social commentators, structural differentiation leads to a 'post-industrial society', which in its most advanced examples provides individuals with 'diversity, choice, freedom, change' and 'the opportunity for personal development'.[3] Such a society is considered to be a decentralised one, and thus, as Schiller notes, 'it is to be expected that whatever changes do occur will be effected through individualistic and private organizational means'.[4]

An alternative interpretation of modern societies suggests that 'social fragmentation' rather than decentralisation is a more appropriate characterisation. It is agreed that in Western societies there is an increasing 'domestication of living functions' and 'privatization of social life',[5] but it is questionable that this signals a newly achieved freedom. What it does signal, however, is the subject of much debate. Of particular interest here is the contribution of media theory to contemporary debates on the nature of post-industrial society, and the role of television therein.

Interestingly, both pluralists and critical media theorists, in articulating the role of television, either in a decentralised society for pluralists, or in a fragmented society for critical media theorists, emphasise the integrative and unifying functions of television. Basically it is assumed that a society, to qualify as such, must 'cohere', and it is the coherence of a society which provides it with its stability. A highly fragmented society or a highly decentralised one requires some powerful 'cohering agent'. For pluralists the cohering agent is a value consensus reflecting the commitment of the vast majority to individualism, freedom, democracy, and so on. To critical media theorists this value consensus is an ideological one, and it is ideology which is the social cement binding together a socially fragmented totality.

There is no need to dwell on television's power to unify society by means of effecting a value consensus, ideological or otherwise. The arguments presented in Chapters 3 and 4 lead us to a rejection of such views. If societies do cohere, then the key to such coherence is not to be found in what individuals think and believe, but rather in what they do. To say this is not to deny a powerful influence to television. Some possible effects of the activity of viewing television were discussed in the previous chapter. We can extend that discussion by way of considering how the colonization of leisure-time in private space is not only descriptive of one aspect of social fragmentation, but also how it is connected to social stability.

Television and social isolationism.

Our use of time is always a use of time in space. 'In all societies', Giddens notes, 'the vast bulk of daily activity consists of habitual practices, in which individuals move through definite "stations" in time–space'.[6] The habitual routine of television viewing confines individuals to domestic/private space, and is severely restrictive of face-to-face social interaction whether in the home or outside it. As an activity, it can be said that television has 'a physically isolating effect'. As Laywood has pointed out, there is nothing contentious about positing 'social isolationism' as an effect of television viewing, since it is 'descriptive of aspects of the social context of mass media reception, and of the mass media audience'.[7]

What Sartre writes of the radio listener is even more relevant of the television viewer.

the important point is not whether a particular radio listener possesses his own transmitter and can make contact as an individual, *later* with some other listener...the mere fact of *listening to the radio*, that is to say, of listening to a particular broadcast at a particular time, establishes a serial relation of *absence* between the different listeners.[8]

'By concentrating activities within the home', Elliott observed, 'the broadcast media of radio and television set up a type of human group which has no other connection with each other than their common use of the same service'.[9]

The socially isolated viewer does not overcome the isolation by spending increasing amounts of time viewing, but may take comfort in the knowledge that millions of others are involved in the same activity. The 'concrete unity' of reciprocal face-to-face interaction, which television viewing can never be, is in a sense replaced by an abstract unity. Thus, as Negt and Kluge argue, 'collectives come into being, but without self-regulating interpersonal relationships; there are satisfactions, but these are passive. What they are becomes organized, but minus their spontaneity. But even better: the appearance of this spontaneity is then added separately'.[10]

Both Negt and Kluge and Sartre reiterated some important observations which the Frankfurt School made with respect to the mass media's effect on social relationships. Social isolationism, reflecting the 'privatization of social relations' and their abstraction, constituted, in the view of the Frankfurt School, a tremendous obstacle to progressive forms of social change. As Elliott put it, 'this process of privatization deprives people of the possibility of answering back because it deprives them of the opportunities of association in which common needs might be recognized and demands formulated'.[11] What this suggests is that heightened social fragmentation, which is characterised by privatised social relations, is itself a barrier to participatory forms of social change, and it is this which enables capitalist societies to maintain their stability, while at the same time reproducing forms of domination.

Some critical media theorists, working within a perspective of the political economy of the media, have developed a view of television's power which utilises the idea that social isolationism prevents social change. Progressive forms of social change are understood as involving the mobilisation of public opinion. As a source of information, television is a key resource for the formation of public opinion, but in the context of privatised reception and the amount of time given over to viewing, the information remains underprocessed socially. On the one hand, television encourages the search for individual solutions to problems rather than collective or political solutions. This is compatible with 'the shift away from involving people in society as political citizens of nation states towards involving them as consumption units in a corporate world'. Elliott argued that 'the consequence of this for the culture is a continuation of the erosion of what Habermas called the public sphere or C.

Wright Mills the community of publics'.[12] As Habermas himself has put it:

> The ever more densely strung communications network of the electronic mass media today is organized in such a manner that it controls the loyalty of a depoliticized population, rather than serving to make the social and state controls in turn subject to a decentralized and uninhibited discursive formation of the public will.[13]

While it is inappropriate to view the subordinated as being 'loyal' to the system which dominates them, the idea of a 'depoliticized population' does express an understanding of social reproduction as accountable in terms of the lack of effective opposition to structures of domination. Further, the increasing social isolationism of a television-viewing public alone, can account for a substantial element of depoliticisation.

It is within this context, on the other hand, that media theorists have focused on television's power, not so much in terms of social isolationism, but more in terms of the nature and quality of the information provided by television. It will be useful to consider very briefly how television contributes to the depoliticisation process through the kind of information it disseminates. I shall want to point out that the perspective of the political economy of the media offers a number of pertinent and fundamentally correct observations which are informed by a clear understanding of recent developments in capitalism. However, the direction of analysis pursued in this perspective leads to a media-centred view of television's power, which is compatible with the ideology-centredness of perspectives considered in earlier chapters. The direction of analysis tends to exclude a consideration of how the forces of economy and State bear rather directly on what people do, irrespective of any power wielded by the media. Consequently, the perspective of the political economy of the media does not provide an adequate basis for assessing television's power—the latter, as we began to see in the previous chapter, can only be found in a 'social-totality' perspective.

Television, information and public opinion.

Both Logan and Simonds, from a social-totality perspective, and Elliott, from a perspective of the political economy of the media, compare the resource value for the formation of opinion of information provided by television, on the one hand, and by print, on the other. Logan suggests that 'the printed text demands more mental activity of the reader...the reader controls the rate of absorption and comprehension of the written text'.[14] By contrast, Simonds argues, information via television is 'sender paced', 'up-to-the-minute', fragmented in 'short-units', tends to be 'simple', 'concrete' and affective, and elicits a 'passive' response.[15] More cautiously, Logan comments that 'this is not to suggest that all receivers of television news are passive, non-critical and non-reflective, but...that the very *nature* of television news reduces the probability of reflection, debate and also action'.[16]

Consistent with these views are the comments Elliott made on the press.

The growth of the press was based on two processes, the provision of useful information, mainly commercial and financial intelligence to interested parties, and political controversy. Print was the medium which underpinned the concept of the public sphere by providing an arena for public debate. Over time, both these functions have been transformed. From its original base in elite information, the commercial function has expanded beyond all recognition and with the transformation of news into a commodity, the political function has been eclipsed.[17]

Elliott acknowledged that television, for the most part, provides an ideological service for dominant groups, but he maintained that it nevertheless performs a useful public-service function, especially through some high-quality documentaries and current affairs programmes. This liberalising influence on public opinion, he believed, is under threat. The threat comes from 'developments in electronics, data systems and the new distributive media', which, in the hands of international companies seeking profits in international markets, is likely radically to reduce the availability of information relevant for political debate.

The new information producers are commercial corporations who have a primary interest in keeping information secret to protect their commercial secrets. Their secondary interest is to produce a commodity for sale in the market...Information which was once available to the public as of right will, in the future, be available at a price...Information for which there is not a market will not be produced.[18]

These are all valid points which constituted a major part of Elliott's critique of those who claim that the development of post-industrial society will 'involve changes in the power relations within the mode of production'. In particular, Elliott argued against the view that 'those who control the information, intellectuals in one form or another, will have control of one of the means of production and so have a base for class power'. Elliott quite rightly pointed out that post-industrial society is still capitalist society, and as such cannot signal the removal of class domination. In fact he reasoned that, if anything, with the internationalisation of capital, and the inability of nation-states to halt its progress, the post-industrial society consolidates capitalist class domination. 'The point', Elliott argued, 'is not who is allowed to contribute to the process of production but who extracts the surplus value from it and so has the resources to control the course of its development'.[19]

What lies ahead is not so much '*false* belief but the *absence* of belief'. As Simonds goes on to point out, 'passivity, resignation, bewilderment and confusion, disorientation and marginalisation have all been more consequential elements of effective systems of social domination than false consciousness...'[20] Whereas Elliott's analysis connects this to the political economy of information, Simonds and Logan incorporate the fruits of Elliott's discussion within a much broader framework. Elliott's position could very easily be used to support the view that television and its future developments will be largely responsible for the erosion of the public sphere, in which public opinion can be formulated, and further that this is accountable in terms of changing patterns of ownership and control in the media industries.

There is no need to deny that media industries have *some* responsibility in creating obstacles for the formation of public opinion. The question is, how much responsibility? It is this kind of question which is of the utmost importance if we are seriously going to assess the power of television in the total order of things. To answer this question, it is necessary to consider *all* forces responsible for the erosion of the public sphere. This point is not restricted to the particular issue at hand here, but applies equally to all claims about television's power. Unless this is done, there is the distinct possibility, as we saw in Chapters 3 and 4 with respect to claims advanced about television's ideological power, that media theory will continue to overestimate and misconstrue television's power.

Thus with respect to the debilitating effects of television and the new distributive media on the formation of public opinion, Simonds sees these as an extension of more primary forces. He argues that 'the conditions that produce and reproduce such incapacity are largely publicly identifiable features of the social environment'.[21] The absence of belief, or political indifference, arise out of the conditions which generate powerlessness, and it is powerlessness which accounts for 'an erosion of optimism of the public will'. As Simonds comments, 'the predictable consequence...is not ignorance or moral subordination but cynicism, resignation, political withdrawal, and the eclipse of civic virtue'.[22] Further, following an extensive review of public opinion research, Simonds recognises that there is an absence of mass commitment to progressive social policies. But this is to be seen not so much as a consequence of an underinformed citizenry, as an undermotivated one. Lack of interest in political debate, furthermore, is more likely to reflect low levels of political motivation among the public, than the volume and quality of information available. The political economy of information, it can be argued, is irrelevant to an understanding of how many of the most subordinate have come to develop patterns of motivation reflecting an indifference to political matters.

There are two additional points to be made with respect to television's informational power. First, there is little point in having an informed public unless public opinion finds expression in material practices intent on transforming relations of domination and subordination. Before the age of television, Lazarsfeld and Merton argued that exposure to a 'flood of information may serve to narcotize rather than energize the average reader or listener'.

The individual reads accounts of issues and problems and may even discuss alternative lines of action. But this rather intellectualized, rather remote connection with organized social action is not activated. The interested and informed citizen can congratulate himself on his lofty state of interest and information and neglect to see that he has abstained from decision and action. In short, he takes his secondary contact with the world of political reality, his reading and listening and thinking, as a vicarious performance. He comes to mistake *knowing* about problems of the day for *doing* something about them...[23]

Hence the suggestion that 'mass communications may be included among the most respectable and efficient of social narcotics'. Interestingly, Lazarsfeld and Merton go on to draw a conclusion, more or less identical to the argument made in the previous chapter, with respect to television's contribution to the underdevelopment of autonomous agency. They note that 'that the mass media have lifted the level of information of large populations is evident. Yet...increasing dosages of mass communications may be inadvertently transforming the energies of men from active participation into passive knowledge'.[24]

The possibility that informed opinion does not necessarily lead to political action leads directly to the second point I want to make. Even for the most informed who do not mistake 'knowing for action', the existing channels for political action may be unattractive, and this perception may support a low level of political motivation. Such individuals are not so much 'narcotized' by an abundance of information, but by the failure of oppositional politics to offer any hope in transforming relations of domination and subordination.

It can be argued, then, that the connection between the output of information on television and the formation of public opinion is not a straightforward one. The context in which information is received, the motivations of the audience, and the opportunities available in the social environment for effective political action would all seem to be important determinants of the formation of public opinion, and, as I shall argue, of political action. It is to the latter that we shall now turn.

Television viewing and political inactivity

We have encountered two major arguments with respect to the power of television viewing as an activity. First, it was argued in the previous chapter that both in early socialisation, and in later life, television viewing contributes to the underdevelopment of autonomous agency. Second, it was noted earlier in this chapter that, to the extent that progressive forms of social change require the participation of individuals in collective practices, television viewing, as a decollectivised activity, poses an obstacle to such participation.

Both arguments can be used to support the more general proposition that television viewing promotes political inactivity. The relative absence of activity oppositional to forms of domination accounts, in part, for the reproduction of relations of domination and subordination. The question arises of how much political inactivity we are to attribute to the influence of television viewing. In order to answer this question, and in keeping with earlier remarks (see p. 164), it is necessary to step outside the narrow confines of media theory. Television's contribution to promoting political inactivity can be assessed after due consideration has been given to major forces, other than television, which play some part in preventing progressive forms of social change.

It is beyond the scope of this book to deal with the major obstacles to social change in the kind of detail they deserve, but we can nevertheless consider some of the principal arguments which have been formulated. We have already touched upon the force of economic necessity as a barrier to social change. I shall offer some further comments, later, on the role of economic compulsion and State coercion in securing the pragmatic acquiescence of the subordinated to forms of domination. Related to this, I shall consider how modern living conditions in urban environments pose additional obstacles to social change. We have noted the failure of political representatives effectively to challenge structures of domination—this will be discussed in the context of the 'erosion of the public sphere'. In what follows, we will continue to develop the perspective introduced in the previous chapter, in which human action and intransigence are closely bound up with the availability of resources for action, and with the manipulation of needs. Through this focus, we will be able to understand how major obstacles to progressive social change have supported the development of motivational patterns which, on the one hand, lead to political inactivity, and, on the other hand, 'steer' people towards private spaces in which television viewing occurs.

The erosion of the public sphere

When the House of Commons was debating the 'right to vote' for working men, in 1866, Robert Lowe, as a defender of privilege, feared 'the worst'.

the working men of England, finding themselves in a full majority of the whole constituency, will awake to a full sense of their power. They will say, 'We can do better for ourselves. We have objects to serve as well as our neighbours, and let us unite to carry those objects. We have machinery; we have our trades unions; we have our leaders all ready. We have the power of combination, as we have shown over and over again; and when we have a prize to fight for we will bring it to bear with tenfold more force than ever before.'[25]

The failure of the subordinated to grasp the democratic possibility of controlling the State has never been realised in most Western democracies, and as time goes on such a possibility seems more remote.

There is an absence of a sufficient commitment to a socialist programme among a majority of the populations in Western societies. This can be understood, in part, in terms of the way in which the political party system has evolved, and in terms of the increasing bureaucratisation of State power. As Habermas observes:

> The depoliticization of the mass of the population and the decline of the public realm as a political institution are components of a system of domination that tends to exclude practical questions from public discussion. The bureaucratized exercise of power has its counterpart in a public realm confined to spectacles and acclamation.[26]

Elsewhere, Habermas notes that 'the opposition to the system which emerged in the labour movement has been defused by regulated competition between political parties'.[27] Originally much of this opposition was represented by social-democratic parties advocating radical social reforms. Considerable gains were made with respect to improving the social conditions of existence. The need to maintain and protect these improved conditions led to the development of an elaborate State bureaucracy. This alone, both Marcuse and Habermas argue, has made a considerable contribution to the erosion of the public sphere in which 'the arrangement of formal democratic institutions and procedures permits administrative decisions to be made largely independently of specific motives of the citizens'.[28] The erosion of the public sphere, in this respect, refers to how political ('practical') problems, which ought to be the subject of public debate and decision, become translated into technical problems, how this justifies the close relationship between government and technical-scientific research, the making of political decisions without public consultation, and how the growth of these processes underpins a form of reasoning—'technical rationality'—which permeates the consciousness of policy-makers, including leaders of political parties. The latter have become an elite, and at times a ruling one.

Basically, the only form of political participation 'requested' from the public, by the political system, is that of vote-casting at elections. Almond and Verba thus argue that:

> If elites are to be powerful and make authoritative decisions, then the involvement, activity, and influence of the ordinary man must be limited. The ordinary citizen must turn power over to elites and let them rule. The need for

elite power requires that the ordinary citizen be relatively passive, uninvolved and deferential to elites.[29]

Additionally, it must be said that social-democratic parties have always been parties of reform, oriented to 'managing capitalism', rather than to transforming relations of domination and subordination in any fundamental way. The 'successful' management of capitalism would seem to have provided sufficient affluence amongst a majority who are reluctant to support political programmes which in the short term may jeopardise minor material gains. Electoral contests, as I have argued earlier (see pp. 76–9), have been increasingly conducted for that majority. One consequence of this is the emergence of 'catchall' political parties, which has left the most subordinated without political representation. In the contemporary arena of party politics, not only is active participation on the part of the public not encouraged, but the most marginalised groups have nothing to bargain with, and thus no pressure to exert, other than physical and illegal protest. Their lack of financial resources effectively bars them from creating their own political party. 'A striking feature of the political system', Miliband argues, 'is its very effective insulation against people outside the mainstream of political thinking, as defined by the party leaderships'.[30]

It is ironic that those claiming to represent the most subordinated should frequently blame television and the mass media for electoral defeats. Not only has the public sphere developed into a form which hardly encourages hope for change or a political interest amongst the public, but the actual use of television by parties of social reform tends to promote in the public both the lack of hope and political indifference.

Economic compulsion, State coercion and pragmatic acquiescence

In the previous chapter, I argued that our potential and actual range of action is governed first and foremost by the specific character of our forced dependence on the realm of necessity. In a capitalist society the realm of necessity is ultimately determined by economic practices. Given our need to survive, as *individuals* we have little choice other than to acquiesce to the demands of employers. Effective resistance and opposition to employers, as the history of the class struggle testifies, requires *collective* action. Even though the relatively powerless have, through the power of combination, achieved a reduction in work hours, and an increase in financial rewards for their labour, they have not been able to win control of the means of production, and hence over the means of their own survival. Indeed, the labour movement has not been unified around the purpose of seeking control of the means of production. It would seem that much collective action is over issues of jobs (opposing their reduction) and wages, which invariably confines the opposition within the structural relation between capital and labour.

Throughout the history of capitalism the collective power of employees has been under a gradually increasing threat. The forces of opposition have been fragmented by an increasing division of labour—the division of subordinates into managers and managed, and the latter into further divisions reflecting their relative value to employers. Managers have aligned themselves with employers, and, as Armstrong *et al*. point out, 'the central problem for management has always been how to make workers work hard enough'.[31] 'The increased division of labour', Abercrombie *et al*. note, 'gives management greater control by lessening opportunities for resistance'.[32]

In recent times, with the increasing internationalisation of capital and the technologicalisation of work processes, workers 'rightly believe that opposition may lead to redundancies or closure, and that it may be impossible to get another job'.[33] Armstrong *et al*. discuss the effects of a number of State policies designed to re-establish the 'conditions for profitable production and sustained accumulation'. The most obvious consequence has been that of increasing unemployment. This in conjunction with cutbacks in welfare provision, which 'make it more imperative for people to hold down a job', increased taxes on the poor, 'privatization and deregulation...in which firms can seek profits at the expense of workers and consumers', and the weakening of trade unions through legislation, to 'reinforce the central discipline which capitalism imposes on workers—the need to work for their employer on their terms in order to obtain a living'.[34] Would-be strikers today know that a prolonged strike is not only increasingly difficult to maintain in a context of eroded welfare provision, but that, in addition to this obstacle, they are likely to be met by the forces of State violence. More significantly in today's circumstances, support from other workers is very likely to be non-existent.

The manipulation of the realm of necessity has thus been a major force in fragmenting potential opposition to the prevailing structure of class domination, and increases the dependence of subordinates on the capitalist class. Recognition of this dependence fuels the justified feelings of powerlessness, which are by no means confined to the work sphere.

Whatever influence we may want to attribute to television viewing as a force promoting political inactivity, it must be judged to be a relatively trivial force in comparison with the manipulation of the realm of necessity by capitalist enterprises in conjunction with repressive State practices. Our need to survive translates into our need for employment, which, as I shall argue below, in contemporary urban living conditions generates further needs which reinforce our dependence on employer and state, and which drive people increasingly toward that private space in which television viewing is situated.

Urbanism

In most capitalist societies, at least until the early 1960s, the development of communities and the work opportunities available tended to be reciprocally related. Houses were built close to work, and the need for labour brought new firms and businesses to where the people lived. Community life was possible, given the existence of relatively stable populations in fixed locations.

All this was to change. Investment capital exploited new technological developments, replacing inefficient machinery in older industries, and creating new industries manufacturing new consumer goods. Many of these developments brought about a geographical relocation of work. The labour requirements of the new industrial developments were met from a variety of sources: more women entered the paid labour force, immigrant workers were recruited, and farm mechanisation had reduced the labour requirements of agriculture, releasing a pool of labour which drifted into the cities. The cities expanded via urban sprawl, and some new towns were developed.

Full employment and increases in household incomes enabled families to look beyond day-to-day survival. Ironically, time saved in domestic labour by the purchase of labour-saving devices was more than swallowed up by time lost in paid employment. But the most significant item which higher earning families were able to purchase was the car. The story of how the car became transformed from a luxury item into a 'functional necessity', or as Offe puts it, 'a structurally imposed need',[35] is, in microcosm, the story of the transformation of traditional lifestyles, of the increasing pace of modern living, of our increasing dependence on the economic system, of the transformation of communities into dehumanised space, of the marginalisation of the poor, and of the general decollectivisation of social life.

In the context of the relocation of work and urban sprawl, in a period of full employment, ownership of a car offered a time-saving convenience. With the growth in car ownership and the consequent reduced dependence on public transport, the total social demand for the latter decreased. Demand declined further, initially as a consequence of increased fares—a response to reduced demand!—and then by the privatisation of public transport which reduces the public service to profitable routes.

Government policies have reflected a keen eye for profit-making in the car industry. Railways have been heavily pruned, while taxpayers' money has funded the necessary infrastructure of roads. Town-planning departments have bureaucratised what should in fact be a public decision-making process. As the private ownership of cars has increased, along with the spreading network of roads, retail businesses have been concentrated in city centres, on the one hand, and new outlets located on sites accessible only to car owners.

During the early period of these changes extensive rehousing onto suburban estates took place, fuelling the need for private transport, or increasing estate dwellers' dependence on a dwindling and more expensive public transport service. Alternatively, those without a car can remain 'functional' within Western societies by living in the inner city. For the poor this is not so much a choice but a socially created confinement either to 'battery-hen' living conditions of tower-blocks, or to the squalor of sub-standard flats and bedsits, often administered by exploitative landlords.

Offe argues that 'a large number of needs for consumer goods which consumers express on the market are directly linked with their *living conditions* which, in turn, may not be in accordance with the needs of the consumers'.[36] In addition to the car, as a structurally imposed need, Offe cites the example of 'medicaments individuals require in order to ward off illness which would otherwise result from the poor environmental conditions at their place of work or residence'. He elaborates:

the fact that individuals live and work under conditions detrimental to their health can only be interpreted as being in accordance with their needs if they had the objective possibility of living and working elsewhere. Where this is not the case, it can be said that the choices made by consumers within the market-place are not always actions for the satisfaction of their 'own' needs, but are in fact responses to a situation where certain needs are 'structurally imposed'.[37]

It can be acknowledged that some consumer goods enable the user to exercise autonomy but, as in the case of the car, for example, it is an autonomy which can only be sustained so long as the user has the financial resources to fill it with petrol, to maintain and repair it, to tax and insure it, and so on. It is thus an autonomy which at one and the same time increases the user's dependence on the system which imposed the need for a car.

Generally, however, modern urban living conditions involve people in empty routines, which are functional to the manufactured habitat, and irrelevant to the individual's own vital needs and to the exercise of meaningful autonomy. The modern city dweller has become progressively distanced, both from natural resources and from human resources supportive of meaningful autonomy, which were once available in close-knit communities. Instead the individual has become increasingly dependent on the depersonalised services of massive, heavily bureaucratised organisations. The technocratic structuration of all public policy, public institutions and many professional services understandably promotes a disinterested instrumentalism amongst public, social and consumer service workers, which is often transferred onto the public for whom the 'service' exists. Horkheimer has written about the decline in 'the service orientation' in today's supermarkets and megastores.[38] A similar decline in public, welfare and social services tends to be experienced as the imposition of anonymity, that is, the experience of one's own irrelevance and impotence in the total order of things. In many respects the empty routines of urban living parallel the experience of work-routines in deskilled, monotonous work, where more often than not 'autonomy is constrained strictly within the straight-jacket of management work norms and targets'.[39]

The significance of the experience of meaningless work, and of the meaningless routines of urban living for eroding opposition to the total social order, resides in the consequences of this experience for the individual. The major consequence is that so much of what we must do to survive, and to remain 'minimally functional' in today's society fails not only to meet vital needs, but, as I shall argue later, fails to meet basic existential needs. Our capacity for autonomous agency, rather than being given a political expression, is turned instead towards attempting to satisfy unmet needs in spaces in which we can exercise some control. 'The most seemingly "powerless" individuals', Giddens argues, 'are able to mobilise resources whereby they carve out 'spaces of control' in respect of their day-to-day lives and in respect of the activities of the more powerful'.[40]

These spaces of control are areas in which individuals are able to retain some sense of their own autonomy, and in which they are able to exercise some autonomous agency. But, these spaces are 'power-bound' in the sense that the consequences of autonomous agency within power-bound spaces have very little impact, if any at all, on structures of domination. The more private the spaces in which we exercise agency, the more distanced we are from those realms in which the resources for effective opposition to structures of domination can be developed. Television viewing occupies such a power-bound space. However, it would be a mistake to equate the privatistic nature of television viewing with the power of television to lure people away from the public spaces in which oppositional political activity takes place. Before television, Horkheimer wrote:

There are still some forces of resistance left within man...despite the continuous assault of collective patterns, the spirit of humanity is still alive, if not in the individual as a member of social groups, at least in the individual as far as he is left alone. But the impact of the existing conditions upon the average man's life is such that the submissive type...has become overwhelmingly predominant.[41]

I am not convinced that 'the submissive type has become overwhelmingly predominant', but I am convinced that privatism, in one form or another, has become an overwhelmingly predominant response of the vast majority to those conditions, in which, as Giddens observes 'there are no longer any guaranteed normative connections between the distinct time-encapsulated sphere of work and the remainder of social life, which itself becomes substantially disembedded from traditionally established practices.'[42] Furthermore, the powerlessness which the individual experiences in these conditions appears to be of little concern to traditional social-democratic politics. The latter, it would seem, has become split off from the lived experience of the vast majority, which, in part, accounts for its perceived irrelevance.

However much television viewing as an activity can be said to 'involve' people in politically ineffective activity, or however much it promotes the underdevelopment of autonomous agency, we can begin to appreciate that far greater forces than television have created this state of affairs. It is these forces, too, rather than television, which tend to propel people towards privatism.

Privatism

The non-public character of our dominant leisure-time activity is of relevance for the reproduction of structures of domination, since it is only through public and collective practices that the latter can be effectively opposed. However, the relevance of privatism for social reproduction and social transformation is much broader than its non-public manifestations. Again, I shall want to show that television viewing is more a consequence of privatism than a determinant.

Essentially, privatism denotes a self-orientation which permeates all that we do, including our participation in the more public aspects of social life. Not everybody is privatistic, but as Schiller notes, 'privatism in every sphere of life is considered normal', and it 'reflects an exclusively self-centered outlook'.[43]

In its successful periods, as in times of full employment, capitalism promotes forms of self-seeking orientations, or patterns of motivation which bind, at least those most heavily rewarded, to the total system. This is achieved by virtue of the ability of the system to support notions of self-improvement which are identified with career advancement and the acquisition of material goods which supply beyond-survival needs. This corresponds to a pattern of motivation which Habermas identifies as 'family-vocational privatism'. This 'consists in a family orientation with developed interests in consumption and leisure on the one hand, and in a career orientation suitable to status competition on the other'.[44] Family-vocational privatism, according to Habermas, is complemented by 'civic privatism', which reflects a self-seeking interest in the operation of the political system. As a form of 'political abstinence', civic privatism is a passive, non-participatory and depoliticised orientation towards the public sphere.

Habermas believes that these two syndromes of privatism were important in securing the stability of capitalist societies. But, in the light of the kinds of changes in contemporary society, which I have outlined in relation to the division of labour and urbanism, he argues that these patterns of motivation have been eroded. As he puts it, 'the *market* +

administration cannot satisfy a whole series of collective needs'.[45] The self-seeking orientations of 'possessive individualism', and 'status-achievement' are 'now losing their basis as a result of social change'.[46]

Habermas argues that when the social system no longer supports the self-seeking privatism which it has promoted, a motivation crisis arises with repercussions for the maintenance of ego and social identities, producing an identity crisis. Drawing upon Keniston's analysis of identity crisis in adolescence, Habermas posits two possible outcomes of identity crisis:

(1) withdrawal as a reaction to an overloading of personality resources (a behavioural syndrome that Keniston has observed and examined in the 'alienated') and (2) protest as a result of an autonomous ego organization that cannot be stabilized under the given conditions (a behavioural syndrome that Keniston has described in his 'young radicals').[47]

If we acknowledge that the system still 'produces the goods' for some (in other words that self-seeking privatism is not totally eroded), then, we are left with a picture of motivational patterns in contemporary society, in which privatism is still dominant. Those inclined toward protest remain a small minority, and the vast majority appear to be caught up in either a self-seeking privatism, or a privatism of withdrawal, which I shall refer to as 'self-maintaining privatism'. The growth of the latter, connected as it is to the lack of resources for autonomous activity, that is, powerlessness, in part explains an increase in television viewing, in addition to the experienced relative meaninglessness of this activity. While empirical studies relevant to this claim were cited in the previous chapter, no such studies are available for a related claim, namely that those who experience more satisfaction in viewing television, including the high video users, are likely to be those more steeped in self-seeking privatism. Reasons for this claim will be made apparent below.

Self-seeking privatism

What Habermas saw as the erosion of family-vocational privatism has turned out to be a decline in the identity-building potential of work, on the one hand, and (opposite to what Habermas predicted) a heightened focus on financial rewards which enable higher earners to construct and maintain identities in the realm of consumption. The latter includes the consumption of television's products.

Habermas quite correctly notes that

fragmented and monotonous work processes are making increasing inroads even into sectors in which previously a personal identity could be formed by way of the occupational role. An 'inner-directed' motivation for achievement is less and less supported by the structure of the work process in areas of work which are dependent on market considerations; an instrumental attitude to work is spreading in the traditionally middle-class occupations...[48]

However, higher earners are still offered an 'effective identity', through what Williams refers to as 'a relatively new condition', which he terms 'mobile privatization'. His observations on mobile privatisation capture the ingredients of self-seeking privatism in its contemporary form.

...the identity that is really offered to us is a new kind of freedom in that area of our lives that we have staked out inside these wider determinations and constraints. It is private. It involves, in its immediate definition, a good deal of evident consumption. Much of it is centred on the home itself...Much of it...enlists many of the most productive, imaginative impulses and activities of people—moreover sanely so, as against the competing demands of orthodox politics. Because what you put in, in effort...you usually get to live with and have its value.[49]

Williams is obviously not referring to the poor, since this self-seeking privatism 'is not a retreating privatisation, of a deprived kind, because what it especially confers is an unexampled mobility'.[50]

Williams discusses mobile privatisation in the context of the decline of traditional community life, which at one time provided an identity-building potential, in that each person 'had a place' in the community. Television, it is commonly suggested, is responsible for the disappearance of a whole range of community-based participatory cultural activities, supportive of positive identity formation. But, as we have already seen, it was largely economic forces which were responsible for breaking up old communities.

Williams suggests that mobile privatisation is 'offered as a primary identity, as your real life'. Further, the benefits derived from this orientation reinforce privatism and distance the individual from more universal concerns. In other words it reinforces 'civic privatism'.

...most people underwrite it as their real life, against which those big things, in whatever colour of politics they appear to come, are interpreted as mere generalities, mere abstractions, as at best rather boring interferences with this real life and at worst destructive interventions in it.[51]

Those caught up in this self-seeking privatism are not merely politically apathetic, but very likely to be hostile to political activists and militant trade unionists intent on disturbing the status quo. For although Williams has described mobile privatisation as a relatively new condition, it does arise, in his view, from the kinds of expectations developed in times of 'full employment, easy cheap credit', and 'easy cheap petrol'. Thus he notes with respect to those who are self-seekingly privatistic, that 'the consciousness that was formed inside them was hostile, in some cases understandably hostile, to anything from outside that was going to interfere with this freely-chosen mobility and consumption'.[52]

Self-seeking privatism, while addressing identity needs, not through sustained autonomous activity, but through consumer and leisure activities, does so in ways which are unlikely to promote the development of autonomous agency. The individual, however, is able to maintain a minimal level of personal security and significance so long as earnings are high enough to support the self-seeking lifestyle. By contrast, self-maintaining privatism has its immediate source in the frustration of basic identity needs.

Self-maintaining privatism

I have already referred to self-maintaining privatism as a privatism of withdrawal, and I have identified powerlessness as one of its major sources. To this we can add that it is a form of privatism which is 'negatively' promoted by unemployment, monotonous, deskilled work, the empty routines of urban living, loss of community, changes in the structure of family life, and the experienced meaninglessness of many popular leisure pursuits, including the watching of television. Self-maintaining privatism is a far more complex phenomenon than self-seeking privatism, not confined to any particular group, and is ambiguous with respect to political affiliation, but is unlikely to be an orientation amongst political activists.

The notion of self-maintaining privatism trades on observations of what happens to human beings in enduring conditions in which basic existential needs are frustrated. These conditions are those which I have referred to above, as 'negatively promoting' self-maintaining privatism. They are the conditions of contemporary society which have replaced, for an increasing number of people, those conditions which at one time offered support for the traditional patterns of privatistic motivation posited by Habermas. The support for family-vocational privatism was such that individuals could maintain some sense of 'place', of 'belonging', of 'being part of a social nexus', which provided a sense of security. More than this, it provided the means whereby individuals could achieve some sense of personal significance. The removal of this support creates a 'critical situation', as Giddens puts it, in which basic existential or identity needs are exposed. The need for 'ontological security' (see pp. 152–3), and the need for a sense of personal significance are essential to the development and maintenance of identities. They are basic to the requirements of an autonomous personality. It is the lack of ontological security, and the lack of a sense of significance, which motivate individuals experiencing these lacks to become preoccupied with self-needs. Since support for these needs within wider social networks is increasingly unavailable, individuals generally respond to this state of affairs by placing themselves in situations which are perceived to be more supportive, or potentially supportive of the self's requirements. Correspondingly they tend to seek to avoid situations in which they know that basic identity needs are unlikely to be met.

This would seem to imply that self-maintaining privatism is not indicative of the individual's total submission to the social forces which have generated widespread feelings of powerlessness, but reflects the individual's 'last line of resistance'. The underlying historical trend, as I argued in the previous chapter, is one in which the social conditions which are basic for the development of ontological security have so altered that we may be producing individuals less resistant to threats to their own autonomy. Beyond the effects of early socialisation, Giddens argues that 'in the everyday life of capitalist society ontological security is relatively fragile as a result of the routinisation of many day-to-day activities'.[53] However, it would be an error to equate the underdevelopment of autonomous agency with its eradication. Thus Giddens quite rightly argues that

we should not conceive of the structures of domination built into social institutions as in some way grinding out 'docile bodies' who behave like the automata suggested by objectivist social science...all forms of dependence offer some resources whereby those who are subordinate can influence the activities of their superiors.[54]

Thus, the 'submissive type', or as Giddens puts it, the 'most dependent actor or party in a relationship', 'retains some autonomy'.[55] Indeed, this is one important aspect of what Giddens refers to as 'the dialectic of control'—the other aspect being that 'even the most autonomous agent is in some degree dependent'.[56] For Giddens, the dialectic of control 'operates even in highly repressive forms of collectivity or organisation', and it 'is built into the very nature of agency'. He emphasises that '*an agent who does not participate in the dialectic of control, in a minimal fashion, ceases to be an agent.*'[57]

When Held reasons that self-maintaining privatism 'is both a product of, and adaptive mechanism to, contemporary society',[58] he is indicating that our capacity for autonomous agency, in self-maintaining privatism, is being exercised against the historical trend. Because this response is privatistic, however, it is an exercise of autonomy in the context of more intimate social relations in which one might hope to find support for basic identity needs. Ironically, the privatistic response, which is intelligible in terms of protecting the self from the undermining experiences of the more public social world, increases the individual's dependence on a limited circle of others, which in turn may be an additional threat to the achievement of ontological security, and this in turn reinforces the historical trend.

While, as Logan argues, ontological insecurity is by no means gender-specific, the conditions out of which it arises tend to be the normal conditions of women's experience.[59] Further, the socialisation of girls, more than boys, is generally a socialisation into dependence, which is clearly antithetical to the development of security and autonomy. It is a preparation for placing one's own life into the hands of others, which means that one's own security is dependent on others, both during the formative years and in later life. The knowledge of this alone, Logan suggests, may be anxiety provoking, and related to that kind of response in which the individuals seek 'guaranteed assurances' from those on whom they are dependent.[60] Leonard spells out some of the consequences of this response.

Self-blame, guilt and ultimately depression are the frequent results of the experience of a certain kind of subordinacy where the subordinate status is perceived not only as existing, but as necessary and even desirable. Where can the anger at an intolerable social reality go, except inwards?[61]

Self-maintaining privatism is, as Held observes, 'a pre-occupation with one's own "lot in life"', and 'with the fulfilment of one's own needs',[62] precisely because the basic requirements of an 'autonomous ego-identity' are under more or less continuous threat. But even amongst those who manage to experience ontological security, contemporary society, as we have seen, provides diminishing opportunities for developing a sense of personal significance, and thus for achieving a positive identity. Here again the social system would seem to be exhibiting an underlying historical trend which can be described as one in which the individual is increasingly undervalued.

In 1972 May wrote:

I cannot recall a time during the last four decades when there was so *much* talk about the individual's capacities and potentialities and so *little* actual confidence on the part of the individual about his power to make a difference psychologically or politically.[63]

Today there is much less talk of the individual's potentialities and even less confidence about the individual's power to make a difference in his or her world. Indeed such talk, in the context of the erosion of career structures, meaningless work and the prospects of a future lacking in opportunities in which the individual can make 'a difference', seems decidedly irrelevant. The importance of a sense of personal significance is stated clearly by Laing.

Every human being, whether child or adult, seems to require *significance*, that is, *place in another person's world*. Adults and children seek 'position' in the eyes of others, a position that offers room to move. It is difficult to imagine many who would choose unlimited freedom within a nexus of personal relations, if anything they did had no significance for anyone else...It seems to be a universal desire to wish to occupy a place in the world of at least one other.[64]

In these observations, Laing is anticipating today's privatism. While there are still available social positions which give individuals opportunities for achieving a sense of significance, by virtue of performing socially useful and appreciated services, these positions are in limited supply.

It could be argued that everybody has the opportunity to achieve 'a place in the world of at least one other'. The main difficulty here, however, is that with people increasingly seeking a sense of significance through intimate personal relationships, the latter have become overloaded with expectations. As Giddens notes,

personal relations in the domestic sphere may indeed appear as a refuge from a 'heartless world'. But, in the absence of quite profound transformations in the broader society, the family is likely to remain riven by opposing tensions—liberation and oppression, hope and despair.[65]

This is one of the ironies of self-maintaining privatism: the inability of the social system to support needs for significance and security steers individuals towards the domestic realm, which is itself, especially for children and women, a primary agency in undermining existential needs. Yet experience outside of the family is such that many still see in the family the 'best bet' there is for meeting needs. In view of this, we can understand rising divorce *and* remarriage rates as a consequence of 'an increased determination to make of these rewarding and satisfying relationships'.[66]

May has argued that experiencing a sense of significance is directly connected to the resources available to an individual, that is, to the individual's relative power and powerlessness. Powerlessness throws the individual onto an excessive reliance on the capacity of autonomy, and this may produce psychological consequences which reproduce and reinforce self-maintaining privatism.

The experience of emptiness...generally comes from people's feeling that they are *powerless* to do anything effective about their lives or the world they live in. Inner vacuousness is the long-term, accumulated result of a person's particular conviction towards himself, namely his conviction that he cannot act as an entity in directing his own life, or change other people's attitudes toward himself, or effectually influence the world around him. Thus he gets the deep sense of despair and futility which so many in our day have. And soon, since what he wants and what he feels can make no real difference, he gives up wanting and feeling.[67]

The long-term effects of unmet identity needs can lead, Logan argues, to the individual's being caught up in 'a spiral of hopelessness and despair'.[68] The possibility arises that, for such individuals, the fantasy world projected by television becomes the only world in which a sense of autonomy can be maintained. As such, however, it is an autonomy confined to the workings of the imagination, cut off from the real world.

In the sub-cultures of poverty found in most Western societies, there tends to be strong social disapproval for public displays of self-concern. In this context television viewing offers a socially acceptable means of 'turning off' from direct social relations, a rest and a diversion from self-preoccupations, and perhaps an opportunity to 'turn off' from the set, while in its presence, in order to escape into an inner world without making this escape publicly obvious. Whether or not this corresponds to the experience of at least some who are trapped in self-maintaining privatism must remain at the level of conjecture.

The potential psychological consequences of advanced forms of self-maintaining privatism do not necessarily fetch up in states which some might consider to be pathological, but we can nevertheless appreciate how trends in the emerging conditions of existence in Western societies generate escalating levels of mental illness. Self-maintaining privatism, already a form of political impotence, can, in so far as it extends into self-blame, serve the interests of dominant groups far more effectively than any form of ideological manipulation. The whole range of psychological services, which are increasingly available in Western societies, Smail argues, 'threaten...to mesh with...the interests of a fundamentally repressive political order which seeks to promote a view of, in particular, economic failure, and the distress it gives rise to, as personal inadequacy'.[69]

In less advanced forms of self-maintaining privatism, Giddens observes that, 'particularly in times of severe social or economic dislocation, large segments of the population are potential recruits for demagogic leaders or authoritarian political movements'.[70] The ontologically insecure, as a number of famous historical events have demonstrated, are particularly vulnerable to manipulation from the Right. However, the frustration of basic identity needs, can stimulate a critique of the conditions responsible for this frustration. Feminism is an example of such a critique. Feminism can be too readily dismissed as a bourgeois concern, 'a family dispute within the middle classes', or a politics of subjectivity which reinforces self-maintaining privatism. Even though the class composition of feminist activists may constitute an obstacle to wider active participation in the feminist movement, their impact on consciousness cannot be denied. The experience of socialisation into dependence, in conjunction with low-status employment and an undervalued position in the family, let alone being subjected to surplus and unnecessary forms of male oppression, ensures that women, more than men, are likely to experience a frustration of basic identity-needs. Feminism is able to articulate this experience in ways which stave off self-blame, on the one hand, and encourage the development of critical-oppositional consciousness, on the other.

This suggests that, while self-maintaining privatism is a form of political *inactivity*, it does not necessarily denote a politically indifferent consciousness. A preoccupation with unmet self-needs can coexist with a critical-oppositional consciousness. As Marcuse has noted,

people see the power structure behind the alleged technocracy and its blessings. Outside the small radical minorities, this awareness is still unpolitical, spontaneous; repressed time and again; 'ideological'—but it also finds expression at the very base of society.[71]

Thus, although self-maintaining privatism and self-seeking privatism produce identical consequences as far as political activity is concerned, they are potentially 'radical opposites' at the level of consciousness. For those for whom this is true, there can be no question of exchanging any hope of meaningful autonomy for the pseudo-gratifications of self-seeking privatism. The material rewards of the latter are real enough, but not universally meaningful. As I argued in the previous chapter, genuine satisfactions and personal fulfilment tend not to be easily acquired, but tend rather to derive from a more or less continuous engagement in activities making demands on the individual's capacities. For those seeking genuine and meaningful satisfaction of basic identity needs, the easily acquired, fleeting and instantaneous pleasures made available through mass-produced leisure and consumption, including television, tend to produce and reproduce feelings of insignificance, and are nowhere near substantial enough to begin to address security needs.

Television and social reproduction

Much of the discussion in this chapter has been *necessarily* distanced from the traditional concerns of media theory. I emphasise that this should necessarily be so, because it is only through a consideration of the relation between the social totality and the individual that we can come to understand the 'ground' on which television may or may not exert its influence. Against those views of social reproduction, which stress the socially integrative force of ideology in conjunction with the practices of our major institutions, the stability of capitalist societies, it has been argued, is based on 'the lack of consistent commitment and the propagation of social divisions'.[72] Further, this is to be understood as 'the outcome of a complex web of interdependencies between political, economic and social institutions and activities...which create multiple pressures to comply...'.[73]

'The multiple pressures to comply' is a reference to the ways in which economic and political forces impinge rather directly on what we do, and indeed must do in order to survive. These forces effectively determine our range of possible actions as individuals. While we can expect that our pragmatic acquiescence to necessity, and the habitual routines in which we are ensnared, exert an influence on consciousness, it is not necessarily the case that our consciousness falls under the same constraints as our actions. The arguments of this and the previous chapter are based in an understanding of human action as primarily the product of its range being limited by the availability of resources, and thus by the manipulation of needs, rather than the manipulation of consciousness. Consequently, an explanation of social reproduction, which does not require an account of the ideological manipulation of consciousness, is made available. This enables an avoidance of one of the most glaring weaknesses in all forms of media theory, namely the failure to acknowledge the complexities of human consciousness. These complexities, or 'subtleties of "superficial psychology"' as Timpanaro refers to them, do not allow any kind of straightforward relationship between television and the viewer. Within consciousness there coexist long- and short-term interests, self- and universal concerns, the capability of foregrounding specific concerns, while retaining all thoughts once thought in the background, and most importantly an endless capacity to shift amongst these intersecting dualities. The major determinant of what is foregrounded and backgrounded in consciousness is the experienced needs of the individual.

Given the complexities of consciousness, we can understand the lack of opposition to the prevailing social order, *not primarily* as a consequence of the absence of oppositional consciousness. Far more important as an obstacle to social change, and thus as a force in social reproduction, is the privatisation of social life. Although there is a sense in which it can be said that 'television sets up a human group' or a type of human group which is characterised by an absence of direct interpersonal interaction, the most important 'setting up' has already been accomplished by forces other than television. Privatisation in terms of social isolationism arises from the failures of the public world to meet the basic identity needs and the vital needs of individuals. Both sets of needs are indispensable for the maintenance and development of individual autonomy. The exercise of meaningful autonomy, for many, occurs in private spaces because relevant opportunities in public spaces have been closed off.

Heightened social fragmentation is also the physical separation and fragmentation of potential opposition to structures of domination. But the forces which have privatised social life have also, through the frustration of needs, given rise to patterns of privatistic motivation, which consolidate the obstacles to progressive forms of social change.

As a socially isolated, privatised and decollectivised activity, television viewing can be seen as an obstacle to the reconstitution of the public sphere, through which effective oppositional practices can be organised. But the arguments of this chapter strongly suggest that television is a relatively trivial obstacle to participatory forms of social change. To blame television for the general misfortunes of the potential forces of change is to divert attention away from a more comprehensive understanding of contemporary societies, and away from the failures within the organisations of change.

In view of my remarks above on consciousness, the challenge for social democratic parties, for trade unions and for the new social movements is not primarily one of fuelling an awareness amongst the public of alternatives to the present system, but of articulating these alternatives in ways which address the experienced needs of individuals. Additionally, there is the somewhat lesser challenge of transforming the agencies and organisations of change so as to make participation in them a more attractive prospect than television viewing.

Notes

1. Claus Offe, *Contradictions of the Welfare State*, ed. John Keane, London, Huchinson, 1984, p. 220.
2. Ibid.
3. Denis McQuail, *Mass Communication Theory*, London, Sage, 1983, p. 217.
4. Herbert I. Schiller, *The Mind Managers*, Boston, Beacon Press, 1973, p. 10.
5. Philip Elliott, 'Intellectuals, the "information society" and the disappearance of the public sphere', *Media, Culture and Society*, vol. 4, 1982, p. 245.
6. Anthony Giddens, *A Contemporary Critique of Historical Materialism*, Lon-

don, Macmillan, 1981, p. 38.

7. Cressida Laywood, 'The Effects of Television on Social Interaction', *Reflections*, no. 53, April 1985, p. 4.
8. Jean-Paul Sartre, *Critique of Dialectical Reason*, London, Verso, 1982, p. 271.
9. Elliott, op. cit., p. 245.
10. Oskar Negt and Alexander Kluge, 'The context of life as object of production of the media conglomorate', *Media, Culture and Society*, vol 5, 1983, p. 69.
11. Elliott, op. cit., p. 245.
12. Ibid., p. 244.
13. Jürgen Habermas, *Theory and Practice*, London, Heinemann, 1974, p. 4.
14. Josephine Logan, 'Powerlessness, Misinformation and Democracy', *Reflections*, no. 46, October 1984, p. 4.
15. A.P. Simonds, 'On Being Informed', *Theory and Society*, vol. 11, 1982, p. 608.
16. Logan, op. cit., pp. 4–5.
17. Elliott, op. cit., p. 246.
18. Ibid., p. 245.
19. Ibid., p. 247.
20. Simonds, op. cit., pp. 593–4.
21. Ibid., p. 594.
22. Ibid., p. 599.
23. Paul F. Lazarsfeld and Robert K. Merton, 'Mass Communication, Popular Taste and Organized Social Action' in Wilbur Schramm, ed., *Mass Communications*, Urbana, University of Illinois Press, 1960, p. 502.
24. Ibid.
25. Cited in Simonds, op. cit., pp. 587–8.
26. Jürgen Habermas, *Toward a Rational Society: Student Protest, Science, and Politics*, London, Heinemann, 1971, pp. 75–6.
27. Jürgen Habermas, *Communication and the Evolution of Society*, London, Heinemann, 1979, p. 194.
28. Jürgen Habermas, *Legitimation Crisis*, London, Heinemann, 1976, p. 36.
29. G.A. Almond and S. Verba, *The Civic Culture*, Boston, Beacon Press, 1965, cited in Habermas, *Legitimation Crisis*, p. 77.
30. Ralph Miliband, *Capitalist Democracy in Britain*, Oxford, Oxford University Press, 1984, p. 46.
31. Philip Armstrong, Andrew Glyn and John Harrison, *Capitalism since World War II: The making and breakup of the great boom*, London, Fontana, 1984, p. 396.
32. Nicholas Abercrombie, Stephen Hill and Bryan S. Turner, *The Dominant Ideology Thesis*, London, Allen & Unwin, 1980, pp. 160–1.
33. Armstrong *et al.*, op. cit., p. 408.

34. Ibid., p. 412.
35. Offe, op. cit., pp. 224–7.
36. Ibid,. p. 224.
37. Ibid., p. 225.
38. Max Horkheimer, *Critique of Instrumental Reason*, New York, Continuum, 1974, pp. 124–35.
39. Armstrong *et al.*, op. cit., p. 399.
40. Anthony Giddens, *Profiles and Critiques in Social Theory*, London, Macmillan, 1982, pp. 197–8.
41. Max Horkheimer, *Eclipse of Reason*, New York, Continuum, 1974, p. 141.
42. Giddens, *Historical Materialism*, p. 153.
43. Schiller, op. cit., p. 10.
44. Habermas, *Legitimation Crisis*, p. 75.
45. Cited in David Held, 'Critical theory and political transformation', *Media, Culture and Society*, vol. 4, 1982, p. 159. Habermas is quoted here, in an interview for *Rinascita*, the weekly journal of the Italian Communist Party, a translation of which appears in *New Left Review*, vol. 115, 1979.
46. Jürgen Habermas, 'Problems of Legitimation in Late Capitalism' in Paul Connerton, ed., *Critical Sociology*, Harmondsworth, Penguin, 1976, p. 381.
47. Habermas, *Legitimation Crisis*, p. 92.
48. Habermas, 'Problems of Legitimation', p. 382.
49. Raymond Williams, 'Problems of the Coming Period', *New Left Review*, vol. 140, 1983, p. 16.
50. Ibid.
51. Ibid.
52. Ibid.
53. Giddens, *Historical Materialism*, p. 154.
54. Anthony Giddens, *The Constitution of Society: Outline of the Theory of Structuration*, Cambridge, Polity Press, 1984, p. 16.
55. Anthony Giddens, *Central Problems in Social Theory: Action, Structure and Contradiction in Social Analysis*, London, Macmillan, 1979, p. 93.
56. Ibid.
57. Ibid., p. 149.
58. Held, op. cit., p. 158.
59. Josephine Logan, 'Ontological Insecurity in Women', *Reflections*, no. 52, March 1985, pp. 1–41.
60. Josephine Logan, 'The Privatized Individual in Contemporary Society: the Problem of Existential Needs', *Reflections*, no. 54, June 1985, pp. 1–50.
61. Peter Leonard, *Personality and Ideology: Towards a Materialist Understanding of the Individual*, London, Macmillan, 1984, pp. 155–6.
62. Held, op. cit., p. 158.
63. Rollo May, *Power and Innocence*, London, Fontana, 1976, p. 21.

64. R.D. Laing, *Self and Others*, Harmondsworth, Penguin, 1969, p. 136.
65. Anthony Giddens, *Sociology: A Brief but Critical Introduction*, London, Macmillan, 1982, p. 139.
66. Ibid.
67. Rollo May, *Man's Search for Himself*, New York, Signet Books, 1953, p. 22.
68. Logan, 'The Privatized Individual', pp. 22–32.
69. David Smail, 'Psychotherapy and "Change": Some Ethical Considerations' in G. and S. Fairbairn, eds., *Ethical Problems in Professional Helping* (Forthcoming).
70. Giddens, *Historical Materialism*, p. 154.
71. Herbert Marcuse, *Counterrevolution and Revolt*, Boston, Beacon Press, 1972, p. 21.
72. John B. Thompson, 'Ideology and the Social Imaginary: An Appraisal of Castoriadis and Lefort', *Theory and Society*, vol. 11, 1982, p. 672.
73. David Held and John Keane, 'Reflections on the welfare state and the future of socialism: An interview', with Claus Offe, in Offe, op. cit., p. 267.

7 Critical Social Theory and the Study of Television

In assessing the various claims which have been advanced with respect to television's power, periodic reference has been made either to the general failure of media theory and research adequately to consider television's power 'in *the total order of things*', or, in the case of critical media theory, the failure adequately to consider the role of ideology 'in *the total order of things*'. Both failures, it has been argued, reflect the media-centredness of media theory and research. Critical media theory, in addition, reflects an ideology-centredness. The general consequence of media-centredness and ideology-centredness is that television's power has been exaggerated. The two major sources of this view are 'empirical evidence', on the one hand, and a perspective on the *societal totality* which is at odds with the various perspectives informing media theory, on the other. Placing television's power in the total order of things involves three interrelated considerations:

1. A consideration of the social totality, understood in terms of the social structure and the most significant practices producing and reproducing this structure.
2. A consideration of the impact or power-effectiveness of the practices sustaining the social totality in the lived experience of members of society. (It is here that 'empirical evidence' is crucial.)
3. A consideration of the role of television in the light of (1) and (2) above.

In pursuing this scheme in the two previous chapters, television's 'capturing of time–space' was seen to be something other than it first appears. Our time–space is already 'captured' as a consequence of economic and state practices in a context which has been heavily shaped by these practices. Further, the impact of society's most power-effective practices in the lived experience of individuals, it was argued, can be best understood in terms of the resources available for individuals to meet basic and existential needs. The individual's consciousness of 'where she or he stands' in relation to needs to be satisfied and the resources available (power/powerlessness) for their satisfaction, is the key to the individual's total motivational pattern, and the latter holds the key to understanding the particular acts undertaken by individuals, within the total range of action which is potentially available. 'Doing what it takes' to survive, that is to meet basic needs, within a capitalist society, involves almost everybody in a relation of dependency on an employer, or on the state, a parent or spouse. This alone already limits our potential range of action.

This view connects with an understanding of social reproduction in which the consequences of economic and state practices, through the manipulation of needs, secure the pragmatic acquiescence of individuals to structures of domination in a socially fragmented universe, which in itself constitutes a serious obstacle to the emergence of collective practices intent on opposing the prevailing relations of domination and subordination. Our understanding of social reproduction is a major determinant in formulating the social significance of television's power. The major difference between the 'social totality' perspective adopted here, and the various critical media theory perspectives, hinges on the relative importance of ideology in social reproduction. The implications of this difference for how we are to approach the study of television's power can be most clearly pinpointed by discussing the divergences between critical media theory and the social totality perspective.

Power, social totality and the individual

First, it must be said that both the social totality perspective and critical media theory stand in opposition to those who characterise the social totality of Western societies as 'industrial', and more recently as 'post-industrial', rather than 'capitalist' or 'late capitalist'. The terms 'industrial society' and 'capitalist society', are, as Giddens notes, 'not innocent labels, but call attention to two contrasting ways in which social thinkers have tried to understand the nature of the changes that have transformed the modern world'.[1] Basically, proponents of the theory of industrial society place a greater emphasis on the impact of industrialisation in shaping Western societies than on the fact that industrialisation has been and still is under the control of a capitalist class. While there is an acknowledgement of the existence of class divisions in Western societies, these divisions are assumed to have been progressively eroded as people have come to receive the benefits of industrialisation. These benefits, it is argued, have been made possible by the development of the liberal-democratic State with its system of parliamentary democracy, which has developed hand-in-hand with industrialisation. Contemporary societies are generally believed to offer increasing 'equality of opportunities', such that any substantial inequalities are attributable, in the main, to the assumed inherited capacities of individuals. In summarising this aspect of the theory of industrial society, Giddens states that it is believed that 'individuals will find social positions commensurate with their talents, helped along by the guiding hand of a friendly state'.[2]

The industrial/post-industrial society theorists celebrate the 'spectacle of affluence and private experience', as Brittan puts it, and see in this 'a confirmation of the promise of capitalism'.[3] That promise is construed in terms which emphasise the increasing freedoms available to individuals in Western societies. From a Marxist viewpoint (and from critical social theory) the theory of industrial/post-industrial society is quite unacceptable. It is generally conceded that there have been changes in patterns of class, although the fundamental contradiction, between those who own the means of survival and those who do not, remains. It is also acknowledged that the State, under sustained pressure of the labour movement, does make welfare provision, but 'the guiding hand of the State' pales into insignificance alongside its 'repressive hand'. While Marxists will not deny that there have been substantial gains in the material circumstances of everyday life in capitalist societies, they are most reluctant to equate these gains with the expansion of freedom. The alleged freedoms available in the 'mobile privatization' described by Williams, or in what Jacoby refers to as 'a rampant narcissism', which both he and Lasch detect as increasingly characteristic of the self-indulgent lifestyles adopted by many of the more affluent middle classes,[4] do not match Marx's vision of human emancipation embodied in the notion of the 'progressive development of the individual's capacities'. Besides, these alleged freedoms are not equally available to all members of Western societies, and their availability is dependent on the continuing exploitation of labour, both in Western societies and increasingly in the Third World.

When theorists of the post-industrial society celebrate 'freedom' and 'diversity of opportunity', they are, from a Marxist perspective, depicting an affluent-centred view of the social totality, which overlooks social inequalities, the power of international capital and the repressive power of the State. In short, theorists of the post-industrial society embrace a flawed conception of power which enables them to misconstrue the relation between the social totality and the individual. In the West, Gorz argues,

A society based on mass unemployment is coming into being before our eyes. It consists of a growing mass of the permanently unemployed on one hand, an aristocracy of tenured workers on the other, and, between them, a proletariat of temporary workers carrying out the least skilled and most unpleasant types of work.[5]

This is directly related to the fact that multinational companies 'fly under flags of convenience', as Williams has aptly put it,[6] setting-up 'shop' increasingly in the Third World, where raw materials are cheap, where labour is relatively disorganised and also very cheap, and where governments, in desparate need of foreign currency, compete with each other in showering multinational companies with inducements that can be ill afforded. The stable social conditions which are required by capitalist enterprises for continuous production are invariably achieved by the repressive forces of the State. High military expenditure in the development of these forces expands the coffers of the First World suppliers, depletes the resources of those already steeped in poverty, and deters organised opposition.

The dual power blocs of economy and State, and the relation between them, in controlling the major resources constitutive of Western capitalist societies, renders the vast majority relatively powerless. Although the State has its own sphere of influence, in capitalist societies this sphere is essentially one already marked out by the consequences of capitalist-class practices. Giddens summarises the State's realm of jurisdiction as follows:

The nation-state, which exists in a complex of other nation-states, is a set of institutional forms of governance maintaining an administrative monopoly over a territory with demarcated boundaries, its rule being sanctioned by law and direct control of the means of internal and external violence.[7]

Governments vary in their commitment to providing capitalism with a 'human face'. But in today's world of international capitalism, the State has very little control over capitalist enterprises. The taxation of profits in order to fund programmes of social reform can easily deter international companies from producing goods in reform conscious societies.

Most Marxists would agree that it is the economic power of the capitalist class which exerts the dominant influence in determining the structure of capitalist societies. In recent times most of the debates within Marxism have revolved around the power-effectivenss of economic practices in the structuration of the totality. These debates have been highly influential in the development of critical media theory. In their critique of culturalist media theory, launched from a perspective of the political-economy of the media, Golding and Murdock argue that culturalists have given insufficient attention to the 'cardinal principle of Marxism', namely economic determinations.

On the one hand sociologists of communications working from within a Marxist framework are obliged to evoke economic determination, since this is what distinguishes their position from others. At the same time, the fact that they fail to investigate how these determinants operate in practice severely weakens both the power and distinctiveness of their analysis. Determination becomes a kind of ritual incantation rather than a necessary starting point for concrete analysis.[8]

Golding and Murdock go on to suggest that one source of the failings of Marxist cultural media theory is to be found in the underlying Marxist theory which informs it. In particular they identify the influence of Althusser and Gramsci in leading culturalist media theory astray. Under this influence, they argue, the ideological analysis of media products has been cut loose from the underlying economic determinants. They acknowledge the need for Marxism to rid itself of crude forms of mechanical materialism in which ideology is portrayed as being automatically determined by the economic infrastructure. In their view, however, culturalist media theory has gone too far along this route in its adoption of the idea that 'ideology is a relatively autonomous set of practices'. Yet those espousing Althusserian and Gramscian Marxism argue that they are attempting to overcome weaknesses which are inherent in orthodox Marxist treatments of ideology.

From the social totality perspective the debate between culturalist and political economy media theorists is a relatively trivial one. Their argument is essentially concerned with the *sources* of ideology. While their dispute holds implications for how the ideological analysis of television is to proceed, both perspectives assume that television is ideologically effective, and both perspectives attribute a similar significance to ideology in the total order of things. The role attributed to ideology in social reproduction is such that both perspectives in fact underplay the power-effectiveness of the material practices of the economy and State. There is no need here to repeat the arguments presented in Chapters 3 and 4. It can be noted, however, that in critical media theory the ultimate target of ideology is the subordinated. Quite correctly, it is assumed that society reproduces itself through the practices of *all* groups. The subordinated are thus implicated in reproducing structures of domination. The actions of the subordinated, at least in culturalist and political economy of the media perspectives, if not in structuralist media theory, are quite correctly assumed to be 'conscious actions'. However, and this is the problem, it is then assumed that the ideological contents of the consciousness of the subordinated explain their compliance to the system which dominates them. The ideological effectiveness of television resides in its impact on the consciousness of the subordinated.

In opposition to these views, the social totality perspective emphasises that the ideological contents of the consciousness of the subordinated are, for the most part, irrelevant in explaining the actions of the subordinated. The social totality perspective embraces an entirely different view of the relation between action and consciousness. What we *do* is in the first place to be explained in terms of what we are able to do, and what determines the latter, again in the first instance, is the availability of resources. In other words human action is to be explained primarily in terms of the individual's relative power and powerlessness. (One of the main reasons for doing 'this' is the unavailability of resources which are necessary for doing 'that'.) This is consistent with Marx's statement that

In direct contrast to German philosophy, which descends from heaven to earth, here one ascends from earth to heaven. In other words, to arrive at man in the flesh, one does not set out from what men say, imagine, or conceive, nor from man as he is described, thought about, imagined, or conceived. Rather one sets out from real, active men and their actual life-process...[9]

As far as consciousness is concerned, there is no question here of invoking a 'mechanical materialism'. Larrain, in summarising Labriola's position, puts it as follows: 'The economic structure determines in the first place and directly the practical activities of men and women, but only secondarily and indirectly the objects of imagination and thought'.[10]

Some of the most radical oppositional sentiments are expressed by those who are most impoverished by, or within, the capitalist system. This is not to say that these sentiments are expressed in the theoretical language of Marxism or feminism, but they do reveal that there is no justification in assuming that the individual's pragmatic acquiescence to the system in which she or he is subordinated reflects a consciousness whose ideological contents somehow explain the individual's pragmatic acquiescence.

Relevant here is a comment made by Harrington about the way in which a lecture he delivered in Mexico was received by Latin American trade unionists. In the lecture, Harrington 'explained how the poor nations of Latin America were transferring wealth to the United States'.

...my theories, which most Americans would probably find strained and far-fetched, struck them as the merest common sense. These people were, for the most part, not intellectuals; they were veterans for the struggle for daily bread. That, however, was the point. My analysis, complex and abstract from the perspective of the American innocence, was reportage as far as they were concerned.[11]

This, in fact, constitutes a form of 'empirical evidence' which, together with other forms of evidence, supports the view that the most subordinated, at least, possess a considerable awareness (consciousness) of their own relative powerlessness (lack of resources). It is this awareness or knowledge which is more or less continuously present as 'a basic content of consciousness', and which is involved in what Giddens refers to as 'the reflexive monitoring of conduct',[12] or, in what Sève refers to as 'the intuitive evaluation of...the relation between *the possible effects of the act* and *the needs to be satisfied*'.[13] The experiencing of needs, it has been argued, is a primary influence in determining the contents of consciousness which are foregrounded and backgrounded.

But if the social totality perspective emphasises that consciousness is far more complex and wide-ranging than its reduction to ideological contents suggests, its interest in consciousness diverges in other ways from the central concerns of critical media theory. The latter looks to the ideological contents of consciousness as *properties* of consciousness which explain action. In the social totality perspective, by contrast, the contents of consciousness provide one kind of evidence which is potentially useful in the explanation of action. The explanation of action, however, is not to be found in the contents of consciousness as properties of consciousness, but as *referents* to the individual's lived experience. In other words, the consciousness of the individual tells us something about how that individual experiences daily life, and it is this experience which provides the key for explaining the shape of particular acts.

The relation between consciousness and action, if we are to respect the accounts of the subordinated with respect to their lived experience, can be best understood, not in terms of the ideological contents of consciousness, but in terms of the individual's relative power/powerlessness. As Giddens notes, that

large areas of routine social reproduction are in a specific sense 'unmotivated', and in many other contexts social actors have 'calculative' attitudes towards normative sanctions, since they are indifferent or hostile to the commitments entailed by them...bear directly upon the significance of power in social relations.[14]

This observation, in conjunction with Mann's distinction between 'pragmatic acceptance' and 'normative acceptance' (see pp. 84–6), and in conjunction with the arguments of Chapters 3 and 4, suggests that the specific relevance of television's content, ideological or otherwise, for human action, has to be understood in relation to the positions of power occupied by individuals in social relations. The ideological analysis of television, and its relation to television's ideological effectiveness, is crucial in helping us understand the conduct of those who occupy positions in social relations which enable them to enact the ideologies. Men, for example, by virtue of their material power position in relation to women, are able to enact myths about gender. Ideology, then, may figure more centrally in the explanation of the actions of dominant, rather than subordinated groups. Thus, whereas critical media theory focuses on the impact of television's ideological content on subordinate groups, the social totality perspective turns its attention to the ideological expressions of dominant groups, and to the resource value of ideologies in legitimating the actions of the dominant.

The implications of this difference between critical media theory and the social totality perspective for the study of television's power can be illustrated by a brief consideration of some of the claims which have been formulated with respect to the impact of Western media in the Third World.

Power and ideology: the case of 'media imperialism'

One of the strengths of the perspective of the political-economy of the media is that it focuses much of its analysis on the value of the mass media, and of information technologies, for the capitalist class. In the hands of some authors, however, as Fejes has argued, this analysis is too closely aligned with problematic assumptions concerning the impact of the mass media, including television, on the subordinated.[15]

With respect to the power of the Western media, their dominance over the Third World media and the value of this dominance for international capitalism is well charted. Third World countries are largely dependent on Western news agencies, and this, in conjunction with the importation of Western entertainment (importing soap operas, films, and so on, is cheaper than producing their own) 'advertising' Western lifestyles, constitutes a form of cultural imperialism serving the interests of multinational capitalist enterprises. The expansionist policies of the latter are also served by the development of the latest information technologies.

As in the First World, it is a relatively simple matter to make direct connections between the ideologies which loom large in the media and the *practices* of dominant groups. As in the First World, too, it is not difficult to see the influence of dominant ideologies in shaping the aspirations of high-ranking subordinates. In both of these senses one can locate the ideological impact of media imperialism. But, as I noted above, some who operate within a framework of the political economy of the media are not content to let matters rest here—the ideological impact of the media is assumed to extend to the most subordinated. In formulating such an extensive ideological influence, we are led to believe that the mass media are instrumental in subordinating Third World populations. The evidence of political unrest and revolution suggests otherwise.

The media- and ideology-centredness of some accounts of media imperialism can produce some incredible distortions, underplaying as it does the realities of poverty and military repression in governing the *actions* of the most impoverished in the Third World. It is the consequences of the material enactment of ideologies, that is, the *material* consequences of the practices of multinational capitalism, and the *material* consequences of the practices of military/police repression, which constitute the *material* oppression of Third World populations. The *experience* of this oppression is hardly likely to endear the oppressed to the ideologies which are enacted by their oppressors, and which are used to legitimate oppression.

While Marxist media theory generally tends to overestimate the significance of the media's ideological impact on the subordinated, it must be said that this impact is rarely seen as a uniform one. Theorists within the perspective of the political economy of the media, and within the culturalist perspective, do acknowledge that the subordinated possess capacities to resist ideological manipulation, and that there are those amongst the subordinated who embrace alternative or even oppositional ideologies. This recognition, however, does not go far enough in that it still reduces the relation between experience and consciousness to ideological considerations. Such a reduction not only bypasses what is significant in the lived experience of the subordinated, but it also reflects, at the same time, a theoretical interest in consciousness which is underinformed empirically.

Empirical realities

In the above comments, and implicit in the principal arguments of this book, much has been made of the need for critical media theory to be 'tuned-in' to the lived experience of those it theorises about. The general failure of Marxist media theory, and the Marxist social theory informing it, to be 'in touch with' the lived experience of the subordinated is directly related to inflated views of television's power. There are essentially two problems here. First, the failure to 'trace through' the power-effectiveness of economic and State practices in structuring the experiences of the subordinated has led to an underestimation of the material force of economic necessity and State coercion, and allows space for overestimating the power of ideology, and thus the power of television. Since I have discussed this problem at length there is no need to dwell on it further.

The second problem, which is closely related to the first, is that the manipulation of consciousness by television which critical media theory assumes, can be entertained only if we ignore a whole range of factors, which are rooted in the individual's lived experience, and which exert a strong influence on *what* the individual thinks about, as well as on *how* the individual thinks.

My sporadic remarks about the need for television's power to be formulated in ways which are sensitive to the lived experience of the subordinated, allude to the need for media theory to be better informed than it currently is by 'empirical evidence'. Given the arguments of

Chapter 1, in which the 'empirical evidence' of positivist social science was seen to be seriously deficient, my call for 'empirical evidence', here, cannot be equated with a call for the adoption of scientific methods inappropriate for the study of human affairs. What is required is a practical commitment to allow the evidence of the lived experience of the subordinated to enter into theorising, whether in media theory or social theory.

The types of evidence which I have in mind include ethnographic studies ranging from the more purposive, disciplined approaches of which the studies by Laing and Esterson,[16] and Willis,[17] for example, are excellent models, to observations based on more casual encounters, such as everyday conversations. An example of the latter are the observations made by Harrington (see p. 196). Within this range, I would include autobiographical accounts.[18] These types of evidence which tap into the empirical realities of individuals need to be used in conjunction with what Brittan refers to as 'the evidence of the situation'.

...in everyday life, exploitation is not a mystery, but is experienced and understood without the benefit of a philosophical or theoretical gloss. No doubt, there are countless millions of people who are not able to verbalise their exploited state—very few Blacks in South Africa describe their everyday lives in terms of alienation, or false consciousness. There is no need for them to do so—the evidence of their situation is all around them. Their everyday routines are bounded and shaped by law-enforcement agencies, by Apartheid legislation, by police action, by the crude exploitation in mines and factories, by the constant reminder of their deprived and subjected status.[19]

Of course, a number of objections can be raised against my proposal that theory should be informed by empirical evidence of the kind which I have suggested. It can be argued, for example, that there are intractable problems inherent in attempting to 'know' the experience of others. All experience is 'interpreted experience', and our frameworks of meaning with which we interpret experience are so thoroughly enmeshed in what and how we experience, that we are unable to disentangle 'actual experience' from accounts of experience. In fact, accounts of experience are all we have to go on. Since all accounts of experience are formed through the meaning systems available to individuals, and since these systems reflect the dominant ideologies in society, then accounts of experience are shot through with ideology. Such thinking can readily justify the refusal to treat accounts of experience seriously. As I argued in

Chapter 4, structuralist media theory has found in the Althusserian notion of the 'ideologically constituted subject' a convenient justification for engaging in what Foucault has adroitly called 'the indignity of speaking for others'.[20] What enables this kind of practice is the reduction of experience to ideology. This is also true in the case of those essentially non-Marxist perspectives in the social sciences, in which the focus of study is language, rhetoric, narrative, and so on. As Brittan notes:

Everybody is now concerned with language, communication, grammars, deep and surface structures—and from a different set of premises, structuralists place language at the heart of their account of the naturalness of human conduct. Levi-Strauss's programmatic slogan 'Whoever says "Man" says "Language", and whoever says "Language" says "Society"' sums up the current commitments of hundreds of practitioners in the social and human sciences.[21]

'If we take this position to its logical ending point', Brittan argues, 'then not only does the study of sociology become the study of language in use, but the problem of the self becomes a problem of word play'.[22] More importantly, the self's accounts of lived experience are treated not as evidence of the self's experience, but as samples of word play. When priority is placed on 'the stories people tell themselves', the 'facts' or 'realities' of experience are undervalued and even ignored.

There is no need to deny the methodological problems involved in attempting to understand what goes on in the lived experience of the subordinated, but far too much can be made of these difficulties. We are not, after all, seeking to develop a scientific knowledge of experience, and we are not seeking to replace theory with a form of non-theoretical empiricism. We are merely saying that the least one can do is to consult those about whom one theorises, and that this consultation should be conducted in a manner which respects what people have to say about their lived experience. The evidence obtained is a tremendous resource for both social theory and media theory. Without it, theory can easily run away with itself and further distance itself from the concerns of ordinary people.

No doubt the stories people tell themselves are of immense psychological interest, but a degree of moral bankruptcy is involved when social scientists concentrate their attention on the stories as stories, and neglect the underlying experience. The rape victim, for example, may have a fine story to tell, but in the total order of things the story is fundamentally irrelevant compared with the actual experience of rape.

Throughout this book I have drawn upon what evidence there is in order to test the claims about television's power, against the lived experience of those who are alleged to be 'victims' of that power. Although the evidence is patchy, there is enough of it about to suggest that critical media theory has become so divorced from what is most relevant in the lives of the subordinated that its value for a critical social theory is in many respects problematic.

Critical social theory, critical media theory and social transformation

There is little value, apart from an academic one, in attempting to understand how structures of exploitative domination are reproduced unless this understanding is put to use in practices intent on removing the prevailing forms of domination. The ultimate purpose of theorising, at least as far as critical social theory is concerned, is to change the world such that conditions exist in which the development of human potential can flourish. While the particular forms of this development cannot be specified, and while the conditions necessary for the advancement of the emancipatory interest are to be established through practices of collective self-determination, we can, at least, identify the major obstacles which need to be removed if the freedom of everybody to develop their potential is to be maximised.

Both critical social theory and critical media theory are steeped in the emancipatory interest, and both have identified the prevailing forms of exploitative domination—imperialist, class, gender and race—as the major obstacles in the way of the creation of a truly egalitarian and just world, which are the conditions necessary for the 'free development of the individual's capacities'. Exploitative forms of domination are inherently oppressive, unjust and inegalitarian, and while they exist a role for critical theory is guaranteed.

Although both critical social theory and critical media theory are joined in opposition to forms of exploitative domination, their theoretical tasks are quite different. Critical social theory addresses the whole range of practices, including the mass media and television, in which exploitative forms of domination are produced and reproduced. Critical media theory is primarily concerned with specifying the role of the media in reproducing structures of domination. As we saw in Chapter 2, one of the major accomplishments of critical media theory is that it has detailed the ways in which the mass media and television provide an ideological service for dominant groups.

Critical social theory and critical media theory are both concerned about the consequences of exploitive forms of domination for the prospects of progressive forms of social change. It is here that the particular tasks of critical social theory, on the one hand, and critical media theory, on the other, have generated divergent views. Within critical media theory, the consequences of exploitative forms of domination have been almost exclusively understood in terms of ideological manipulation. In this view, the transformation of capitalist society into socialism is dependent on the mobilisation of oppositional ideologies. Whether progressive forms of social change are to be instituted as a consequence of mass participation in oppositional movements, or initially in a more passive mass support for a socialist programme, it is difficult to deny the central importance of 'ideological struggle'. On this, critical social theory and critical media theory are in agreement. Radical differences, however, arise with respect to how the ideological struggle ought to be conducted, and these differences stem from a crucial divergence between critical social theory and critical media theory in their understanding of social reproduction.

For critical social theory, at least that variety of it represented in this book, the ideological incorporation of the subordinated into the capitalist system is not necessary for the reproduction of relations of domination and subordination. There is a problem with consciousness in so far as there is very little mass support for oppositional viewpoints (and television exacerbates this problem), but this problem does not necessarily mean that the subordinated masses are ideologically duped in some way. It is assumed that the subordinated are relatively knowledgeable about the immediate life's circumstances in which they are subordinated, that they possess a fair degree of 'ideological penetration', as Giddens puts it, and, above all, that they possess the capacity to develop a critically-reflective, oppositional consciousness. Within this framework, ideological struggle takes the form of articulating the lived experience of the subordinated with a socialist critique of the conditions in which individuals are confined to power-bound spaces, in addition to the consideration of socialist alternatives. Of course, this is easier said than done. As we saw in the previous chapter, ideological struggle, let alone mass oppositional movements, encounter the obstacles of privatistic patterns of motivation. At least some of those caught up in self-maintaining privatism have, it would seem, given up hope of a political solution to the kinds of problem they face. This, in part, is due to the failure of those who claim to represent the subordinated to inspire confidence or credibility. Further, experiencing frustrated needs, which is an immediate source of self-maintaining privatism, tends to promote a 'present-orientation' antithetical to the development of 'future-consciousness'. As Spencer has argued, the lack of a developed future-consciousness is an obstacle, though not an unbridgeable one, to the willingness or otherwise to become involved in emancipatory political practices.[23]

There are many other obstacles to progressive forms of social change. Perhaps the major problem facing critical social theory is the absence of mass oppositional movements in Western capitalist societies. Whereas feminist theory stands in a recognisable relation to the women's movement, theory and practice vitalising each other, critical social theory is for the most part addressed to individuals, in the hope of fuelling the development of oppositional consciousness.

Whatever difficulties arise in critical social theory's relation to practice, as a theory it is at least relevant to the experiences of the subordinated, and, again in theory, keeps alive the emancipatory interest.

In failing to trace through the impact of economic necessity and State coercion in the lived experience of individuals, and in being underinformed by the latter, critical media theory has been able to embrace a distorted view of social reproduction, in which the power of ideology is central, and with it the mass media as agencies of ideological transmission. From this position, the ideological critique of the mass media becomes, in and of itself, a significant practice in ideological struggle. Such a position is self-consciously adopted by many working within the perspectives of culturalist and structuralist media theory. Structuralists go so far as to refer to their own ideological analyses of media products as 'political'. Tomlinson correctly observes that

There is plenty of talk of the 'struggle in ideology' or the 'politics of the signifier', but none of this refers directly to political interaction between individuals or collectivities. Its site is *within* the subject, rather than *between* subjects, conceived as coherent moral-political agents.[24]

Even though culturalist and political economy of the media theorists avoid the over indulgent theoretical excesses of structuralism, it is difficult to see how, from within these perspectives, ideological struggle in a non-elitist and a non-patronising form can proceed. With the subordinated being ideologically duped, their consciousness stands in need of correction by those who have avoided ideological contamination by dint of their intelligence.

As I have argued throughout this book, critical media theory has arrived at this unfortunate position by underplaying the power of material forces in the lives of the subordinated, and in overestimating the power and relevance of ideology. In exaggerating television's social significance and its ideological effectiveness, critical media theory offers 'a way of interpreting general change through a displaced and abstracted cause', and as such, Williams argues, is 'part of the study of television's effects' which 'has then to be seen as an ideology'.[25]

It is difficult to see how this judgment can be avoided, unless critical media theory submits its claims about the power of television to the wider court provided by critical social theory's more comprehensive understanding of the relation between the social totality and the lived experience of individuals.

Notes

1. Anthony Giddens, *Sociology: A Brief but Critical Introduction*, London, Macmillan, 1982, p. 30.
2. Ibid., p. 42.
3. Arthur Brittan, *The Privatized World*, London, Routledge and Kegan Paul, 1977, p. 40.
4. Russell Jacoby, *Social Amnesia: A Critique of Conformist Psychology from Adler to Laing*, Hassocks, Harvester, 1975, p. 116. See also Christopher Lasch, *The Minimal Self: Psychic Survival in Troubled Times*, London, Pan, 1985.
5. André Gorz, *Farewell to the Working Class: An Essay on Post-Industrial Socialism*, London, Pluto, 1982, p. 3.
6. Raymond Williams, 'Mining the Meaning: Key Words in the Miners' Strike', *New Socialist*, March 1985, no. 25, p. 7.
7. Anthony Giddens, *A Contemporary Critique of Historical Materialism*, London, Macmillan, 1981, p. 190.
8. Peter Golding and Graham Murdock, 'Ideology and the Mass Media: The Question of Determination' in Michèle Barrett, Philip Corrigan, Annette Kuhn and Janet Wolff, *Ideology and Cultural Production*, London, Croom Helm, 1979, p. 201.
9. Karl Marx, 'The German Ideology' in Loyd D. Easton and Kurt H.

Guddat, eds., *Writings of the Young Marx on Philosophy and Society*, New York, Anchor, 1967, pp. 414–15.

10. Jorge Larrain, *Marxism and Ideology*, London, Macmillan, 1983, p. 59. Larrain is referring to A. Labriola, *Essais sur la conception matérialiste de l'histoire*, Paris, Gordon and Breach, 1970.

11. Michael Harrington, *The Vast Majority: A Journey to the World's Poor*, London, Simon and Schuster, 1979, p. 202.

12. Anthony Giddens, *Central Problems in Social Theory: Action, Structure and Contradiction in Social Analysis*, London, Macmillan, 1979, pp. 56–9.

13. Lucien Sève, *Man in Marxist Theory and the Psychology of Personality*, Hassocks, Harvester, 1978, p. 321.

14. Giddens, *Historical Materialism*, p. 56.

15. Fred Fejes, 'Media imperialism: an assessment', *Media, Culture and Society*, vol. 3, 1981, pp. 281–9.

16. See, for example, R.D. Laing and A. Esterson, *Sanity, Madness and the Family*, Harmondsworth, Penguin, 1964.

17. Paul Willis, *Learning to Labour*, Farnborough, Saxon House, 1977.

18. As in written autobiographies, and 'stories' told and written down by others, for example, *Harry: The story of Harry White as related to Uinseann MacEoin*, Dublin, Argenta, 1985.

19. Brittan, op. cit., p. 23.

20. Alan Sheridan, *Michel Foucault: The Will to Truth*, London, Tavistock, 1980, p. 114.

21. Brittan, op. cit., pp. 14–15.

22. Ibid., p. 11.

23. Martin E. Spencer, 'Social Science and the Consciousness of the Future', *Theory and Society*, vol. 11, no. 2, 1982, pp. 683–712.

24. John Tomlinson, 'Habermas and Discourse' in *Trent Papers in Communication*, vol. 1, *Power and Communication*, Nottingham: Trent Polytechnic, 1983, p. 90.

25. Raymond Williams, *Television: Technology and Cultural Form*, London, Fontana, 1974, p. 129.

Index

Abercrombie, N. 70–92, 95, 96, 97, 99, 101, 109, 124, 170, 187.
action/agency and
  choice 138
  consciousness 122–3, 184–6, 195–7
  necessity 135–7
  needs 137–42, 185
  resources (power) 136, 139–41, 185, 195–7
Adair, J. 12, 33
Adorno, T. 121, 127, 135–7, 143–4, 147, 150, 157, 158
advertising and
  racism 62–3
  sexism 62–3
  soap operas 40–1
  TV production 32, 133
  women 40–2, 104
agenda setting 55–61, 63–4, 86–92
Almond, G. 168–9, 187
Althusser, L. 25, 28, 71, 113, 127, 194, 201
  on ideology, 99–103, 105–6, 119–24
American Broadcasting Company 39
apartheid 200
Archard, D. 115–16, 126
Armstrong, P. 170–3, 187, 188
audience
  active or passive 31, 92–5, 131–4
  concept of 92–5
  ideological manipulation of 68–9, 89, 99–124
  motivations of 166

  research on 68–9, 93–5, 131–4
authoritarian populism 86–92
authoritarian statism 88–9
autobiographical accounts 200–2
autonomous agency 135–7, 142–55, 169–74, 178–83
autonomous ego 120–1, 148

Baggaley, J. 43, 65
Barrett, M. 36, 67, 125, 126, 205
Barthes, R. 25, 28
Bechofer, F. 81, 97
Beharrell, P. 40, 64
behavioural effects of TV 6–20, 29–30
behaviourism and media research 6–20, 29–33, 68
being and consciousness 148–50
beliefs of working class 71–86
Belsey, C. 103, 124, 125
Bennett, A. 34, 66, 96, 105, 107, 125
Berger, A. 4, 109, 126
bias in TV news and current affairs 43–64
  sources of 43–5
Blumler, J. 20, 22, 34, 35, 36, 93–5, 98, 132–5, 156
Bonnett, K. 35, 97
Bottomore, T. 69, 95
British Broadcasting Corporation 46
Brittan, A. 192, 200–1, 205, 206
broadcasters and the state 60–1
Bromley, S. 35, 97
Brooks, K. 113, 126
Brown, P. 126

Brunsdon, C. 36, 40, 65
bureaucracy and the state 168

capitalism and
  dominant groups 86–92
  economic necessity 135–7, 142–6,
    154–5
  ideological incorporation of
    working class 68–79, 84–6
  ideology 43–64; Althusser on
    100–3
  industrial disputes 54–61
  manipulation of needs 137–42,
    144–8, 171–84
  social reproduction 79–84, 121–4,
    154–5, 169–71, 184–6, 191–7
  social transformation 202–5
  the state 50–4, 167–71, 193
  theory of post-industrial society
    163–4
  the Third World 198–9
censorship 39–40
Chamberlain, C. 72, 81, 95, 97
children and TV 148–53
class domination and
  economic power 135–42, 169–75,
    191–7
  ideology 50–64, 68–79
  social reproduction 79–84, 121–4,
    154–5, 169–71, 184–6, 191–7
codes 51–2
Cohen, S. 43, 53, 65, 67
Collins, R. 43, 44, 65
common-sense and ideology 51, 63
community, decline of 173, 177
Connell, L. 50, 66
consciousness
  and action 122–3, 184–6, 195–7
  and being 148–50
  false 147
  future 204
  and lived experience 195–7
  and motivation 191

and needs 137–48, 185
oppositional 147, 184
and powerlessness 196
and privatism 183–6
and social reproduction 122–4,
  191–7
and the unconscious 111–16
working class 70–9, 84–6, 144–8
consent/consensus 68–79, 84–6,
  159–60
content analysis 30
Coronation Street 40
Corrigan, P. 36, 125, 126, 205
critical media theory
  audience, concept of 93–5
  culturalist perspective 24–5,
    28–33, 50–4, 86–92, 110–1,
    194–5
  and Frankfurt School 143–8
  ideological analysis in 37–61,
    86–92, 103–11
  ideology-centredness of 79, 85,
    93–4, 123, 130, 134, 144, 162,
    190–8
  media-centredness of 2–3, 32–3,
    70, 79, 92–4, 123, 134, 144,
    155, 162, 190–8
  political economy perspective 25–7,
    28–33, 161–6, 194–5, 197–9
  structuralist perspective 27–8,
    28–33, 100–21
critical social theory 190–205
Crossroads 40
cultural imperialism 198–9
culturalist media theory *see* critical
  media theory
culture industry 143–8
Curran, J. 20, 23, 24–5, 34, 35, 36,
  95, 96, 124, 125, 131
current affairs presentations
  ideological aspects of 48–64
  and news values 48–50
Curti, L. 50, 66

Davis, H. 40, 64
de Bock, H. 34, 35, 95, 156
deconstructionism 28, 99–124
  as elitist 117
  open and closed 117–24
democracy and ideology 52–3
  and public opinion 162–9
dialectic of control 180
Dichter, E. 108, 125
discourse
  alternative 38–40
  and dominant groups 86–92
  and dominant ideology 38–61,
    86–92
  materiality of 28, 118–20
  and middle class subordinates
    86–92
  official/established 38–40, 57–61,
    86–92
  oppositional 38–40, 57–61
  power of 28, 86–92, 103–5, 111–20
  and social practices 90–2, 102–3
  and subject positions 102–11,
    120–1
  and the unconscious 105–10
dissensus 73, 81–3
dominant class/groups
  access to TV 54–5
  consciousness of 86–92
  fractions of 71–3
  interests of 54, 83
  see also capitalist class,
    domination
dominant ideology
  ambiguity of 38–42, 89
  and common sense 51, 63
  in current affairs presentations
    43–64
  elements of 51–4, 70–84
  in entertainment 42–3
  and middle class subordinates
    86–92
  shifts in 51, 86–92

and soap operas 40–1
and social reproduction 68–86,
  121–4, 143–8
and socio-centralism 56
The Dominant Ideology Thesis
  68–95, 147; critique of 70–95;
  critique of critique of 79–84
in TV news 43–64
and women 40–2, 79–81
domination
  gender 79–81, 121–4
  and ideology 37–42, 61–4, 68–70,
    121–4, 184–6
  imperialism 196, 197, 198–200
  race 79–81
  see also class domination,
    capitalism
Douglas J. 10, 33, 95
Duck, S. 43, 65
Dyer G. 107, 117, 125, 127
Dyer, R. 64

Easton, L. 67, 206
economic determinism 194
economic necessity 135–7, 142–6,
  154–5, 169, 199
economic practices and social
  totality 191–7
economics of media production 133
  see also political economy of
    media
editorial policies 43–4, 56
effects of television
  behavioural 6–20, 29–30
  behaviourist research on 6–20
  ideological 29–30, 68–95, 99–124,
    128
  material 91–2
  on social relationships 160–2
  on the unconscious 105–10,
    111–16
  and violence 7–20
elections *see* general elections

elites *see* dominant groups
Elliott, P. 38–41, 43, 45, 64, 65,
    160–4, 186, 187
emancipatory potential of leisure
    142–8
empirical evidence
    on audience 68–9, 93–5, 131–4
    behaviourist 6–20
    and dominant ideology 70–86
    election results as 74–7
    ethnographic 71, 75, 94, 199–200
    situational 199–202
employment and leisure time 129,
    135–7
entertainment
    and ideology 42–3
    and racism 62
    and sexism 62
Esterson, A. 200, 206
ethnographic research 71, 75, 94,
    199–200
existential needs 142–8, 173–84
experiments in psychology 9–13
exposure time and media
    impartiality 56–7
Eysenck, H. 6–20, 22, 33, 34

family
    changing structure of 150–5
    contradictions in 182–4
    and familialism 62
    interaction and TV 149–50
Fejes, F. 5, 20, 33, 34, 93, 95, 98,
    198, 206
feminism 184, 196, 204
Feuer, J. 38, 64
Fiske, J. 104, 125
Flitterman, S. 40, 65
Foucault, M. 28, 118, 127, 201
Frankfurt School 26, 27, 142–55, 161
    see also Adorno, T.;
        Horkheimer, M.; and
        Marcuse, H.

Freud, S. 111–12, 113–15
Freudian theory 28, 42 105–16 *see
    also* Lacan, J.
Fritzhand, M. 154, 158
Fromm, E. 149, 158

Galtung, J. 46–50, 65
Garnham, N. 27, 36
Gauld, A. 33
general elections 50, 168–9
    and media impartiality 56
    results as empirical evidence 74–7
    TV campaigns 78
    voter turn-out 77
Geraghty, C. 64
Geras, N. 146, 157
Gerbner, G. 98
Giddens, A. 45, 60, 61–3, 65, 67,
    84, 86, 97, 135, 140, 143,
    156, 157, 160, 174, 179–80,
    182–3, 187, 188, 189, 191–3,
    196–7, 203–4, 205, 206
Glasgow University Media Group
    43, 54, 65, 67
Glyn, A. 170–3, 187, 188
Goban-Klas, T. 49, 66
Golding, P. 24, 25–7, 35, 36, 43,
    45, 48, 58, 65, 66, 67, 69, 95,
    110, 126, 194, 205
Goldthorpe, J. 81, 97
Gorz, A. 139–40, 143, 146, 149–50,
    157, 158, 193
Gramsci, A. 25, 53, 71, 87, 194
Guddat, K. 67, 206
Gurevitch, M. 20, 34, 35, 36, 66,
    93, 96, 98, 124

Habermas, J. 161–2, 168–9, 175–7,
    187, 188
Hall, S. 21, 24–5, 31, 35, 48, 50–4,
    58, 65, 66, 67, 73–4, 76–8,
    81, 86–90, 92, 95, 96, 97, 101,
    110–11, 119, 124, 126, 127

Halloran, J. 66, 156
Harrington, M. 196, 200, 206
Harris, K. 67
Harrison, J. 170–3, 187, 188
Hawkes, T. 36, 120, 127
Heath, S. 103, 125
Heck, M. 107, 125, 127
hegemony 51, 77, 89
Heim, A. 17, 34
Held, D. 97, 157, 180–1, 188, 189
Henderson, P. 15, 34
Hewitt, J. 40, 64
Hill, S. 70–92, 95, 96, 97, 99, 101, 109, 124, 170, 187
Hobson, D. 65, 95, 125
Holzer, H. 35
Horkheimer, M. 135, 144–7, 151–2, 157, 158, 173–4, 188

ideology
    Althusser on 99–103, 105–6, 119–24
    analysis of in TV 37–64, 99–124
    and culture industry 143–8
    and discourse/language 103–21
    effects of TV 2, 23–8, 29–30, 68–95, 100–24, 128, 149, 198–9
    forms of 61–4
    and identity 120–1
    and Lacan 106–10
    levels of 61–4, 81, 83, 92, 147
    and motivation 69, 79, 85, 183
    necessity of 121–4, 198–9, 202–5
    and news values 45–50
    penetration of 92, 147, 199, 203
    shifts in 86–92
    and significant absences 48–50, 58
    and socialisation 148–9
    and social reproduction 99, 121–4, 128, 137, 143–8, 191–7, 198–9, 202–5
    in TV news and current affairs 43–64
        in TV presentation of industrial disputes 54–61
    and the unconscious 31, 105–16
    see also dominant ideology
identity
    crisis of 176
    and ideology 120–1
    and needs 178–81
    and sense of significance 181
imperialism 198–9
individual and social totality 184, 191–7
industrial disputes, TV presentation of 54–61
industrial society, theory of 191–3
inference in psychological research 19–20
information
    and political debate 163–4
    political economy of 165–6
    technologies 198
    and TV 161–6
intellectuals 164
interdiscursive spaces 110
interests of dominant groups 44, 54, 83
interpellation 102–5
    and subjection 120–1
Ireland 39–40, 46
Irish Republican Army 40, 46

Jacoby, R. 113, 121, 126, 127, 192, 205
Jessop, R. 35, 89, 97
Joynson, R. 19, 33, 34

Katz, E. 35, 66, 95
Keane, J. 96, 186, 189
Keywords 53
Klapper, J. 29, 36
Kluge, A. 35–6, 161, 187
Kuhn, A. 36, 125, 126, 205

Labriola, A. 195, 206
Lacan, J. 23, 28, 125, 127
 and theory of unconscious 105–10
Laclau, E. 27, 28, 36
Laing, R.D. 33, 112, 113, 126, 150,
  158, 181, 189, 200, 206
Lang, G. 43, 65
Lang, K. 43, 65
language *see* discourse
Larrain, J. 35, 195, 206
Lasch, C. 192, 205
Laywood, C. 160, 187
Lazarsfeld, P. 165–6, 187
leisure time
 decline of 129–30
 emancipatory potential of 142–8
 and employment 129, 131–7
 as fragmented 137–40
 and manipulation of needs 137–55
 and TV 128–55
 use of 131–5
 and women 129–30
Leonard, P. 127, 180–1, 188
Lesser, S. 109, 126
Levi-Strauss, C. 201
Libya 52
Ling, T. 35, 89, 97
lived experience 123, 174, 191–7,
  199–202
Lockwood, D. 81, 97
Logan, J. 113, 126, 127, 162–4,
  180–2, 187, 188, 189
Lovell, T. 40, 64
Lowe, A. 65, 95, 125
Lowe, R. 167

MacCabe, C. 103, 125
male domination 79–81, 92, 121–4
Mann, M. 82–3, 85–6, 96, 97, 197
Marcuse, H. 86, 97, 144–8, 153–4,
  157, 158, 168, 184, 189
Marx, K. 25, 59, 67, 138–42, 157,
  192, 195, 206

May, R. 181–2, 189
McQuail, D. 5, 20–1, 33, 35, 74,
  96, 131–4, 156, 186
media amplification 53–4, 76–7,
  85–92
media-centredness 2–3, 20, 32–3,
  70, 79, 92–4, 123, 130, 134,
  144, 155, 162, 190–8
media imperialism 198–9
media research
 effects of TV 6–30, 68–95, 99–124
 uses and gratifications approach
  22, 131–4, 137
 on violence 7–20
media theory
 pluralism 20–2, 92–5, 118
 theoretical perspectives in 20–8
 see also critical media theory
Merton, R. 165–6, 187
metaphor 106–7
metonymy 106–7
Miliband, R. 96, 168–9, 187
military/police repression 198–9
modernity 159
money as resource 135–7
Moores, S. 124, 127, 128, 156
Moorhouse, H. 72, 81, 95, 97
Morley, D. 36, 110–11, 117, 126
motivation
 of audience 166
 and consciousness 191
 crisis of 175–80
 and ideology 69, 79, 85, 123, 183
 and needs 137–42, 178–84
 privatistic patterns of 175–86
Mouffe, C. 27, 28, 36
Murdock, G. 25–7, 35, 36, 38–9,
  64, 69, 95, 110, 126, 194, 205

narcissism 192
*National Commission on the Causes
  and Prevention of Violence* 7

necessity
and action 135–7, 191–7
and autonomy 143, 153–5
and power/powerlessness 135–42,
184–6, 191–7
and pragmatic acquiescence
169–71, 185
psychological consequences of
138–42, 178–84
and social change 166
and structuration of time
135–7
necessity of ideology 102, 105,
121–4, 184–6, 198–9, 202–5
needs
and action 137–42, 199
and autonomy 143, 153–5
basic 135–7, 137–42, 173
and consciousness 137–48,
185
existential 142–8, 154, 173–84
and experience 154
and human nature 145–6
manipulation of 137–42, 144–8,
171–84
and politics 186
and power/powerlessness 135–42,
184–6, 191–7
and social reproduction 144–5,
184–6, 191–7
and TV viewing 131–4, 147
vital 142–8, 153–5
Negt, O. 35, 161, 187
news
agencies 45
ideological analysis of 43–64
production of 43–4
significant absences in 48–50, 58
values 45–50
Nias, D. 6–20, 22, 33, 34
Nigerian Broadcasting Corporation
45
normative acceptance 85, 197

Offe, C. 77–8, 96, 159, 171–2, 186,
188, 189
ontological security 150–5, 179–80,
182–4
oppositional consciousness 57, 92,
147, 179, 199
oppositional politics 166, 170

Panorama 50
patriarchal domination 122
phenomenology 25
Philo, G. 40, 64
Pilger Report 39
Platt, J. 81, 97
pluralist media theory 20–2, 68,
92–5, 118, 159
political economy of information
162–7
political economy of media theory
25–7, 28–33, 161–6, 194–5,
197–9
political inactivity and TV viewing
166–7
political indifference 165–7
political party system 50, 76–9, 87,
92, 168–9, 174
politics
and information 162–7
and needs 186
oppositional 166, 170
pornography 8
positivism 29
post-industrial society, theory of
159–60, 191–3
critique of 163–4
Poulantzas, N. 25, 58, 88, 90
power
and action 136, 139–41, 185,
195–7
of economy 135–7, 142–6, 154–5,
169, 191–202
of discourse/language 28, 86–92,
103–5, 111–20

power (*cont*)
  of ideology 68–79, 84–92, 92–5,
      102, 103–5, 110–11, 116–24,
      184–6, 198–9, 202–5
  of information 161–6
  and needs 135–42, 184–6, 191–7
  and social reproduction 138–41,
      169–71, 184–6, 191–7
  and social totality 191–7
  of state 61, 84–92, 154–5, 167–72,
      193–7
Power, M. 67
privatism 175–84
  and agency 174
  civic 175, 177–8
  and consciousness 183–6
  and identity crisis 176
  mobile privatisation 177–8
  and motivation crisis 175–80
  as normal 175
  and powerlessness 176, 179
  and public sphere 175
  self-maintaining 176, 178–84
  self-seeking 175, 176–8
  and social change 186
  and social reproduction 175,
      184–6
  and TV viewing 174, 176
psychoanalysis 105–16
psychological experiments 9–13
psychological measurement 13–18
psychologism in TV and media
      theory 48, 137–8, 148
public opinion
  and action 165
  and social change 161
  and TV 162–6
publis sphere
  erosion of 161–9
  and privatism 175

Qadhafi, Col. 52

racism, 62, 74, 79, 149
  in advertisements 62–3
  in entertainment 62–3
  and reification 62
realism and subjectivity in film
      103–10
Reich, W. 149, 158
reification 61–3, 147
repression
  and autonomy 149
  and desire 115
  military/police 198
resources
  and action 136, 140
  money as 136
  time as 135–42
Reuters 45
Robins, K. 36, 126
Robinson, J. 133–5, 156
routines, 136–7, 173
Ruge, M. 46–50, 65

Sahin, H. 133–5, 156
Sartre, J-P. 112, 126, 160–1, 187
Scargill, A. 67
Schatz, O. 154, 158
Schiller, H. 159, 175, 186, 188
Schlesinger, P. 38, 43, 64, 65
scientific psychology 6–20
self-images and TV 149
self-maintaining privatism 178–84
self-seeking privatism 175, 176–8
semiotics 23–5, 27–8, 37–43,
      103–11, 116–24
Sennett, R. 48, 66
Sève, L. 137–42, 157, 196, 206
sexism 40–2, 62, 74, 79, 148
Sex, Violence and the Media 6–20
Sheridan, A. 206
Shotter, J. 33
significant absences in TV news and
      current affairs 48–50, 58,
      92

signification spiral 53–4, 76–7, 85–92
Simonds, A. 162–6, 187
situational evidence 199–202
Slaughter, C. 36
Smail, D. 183, 189
soap operas 40–2
social change
  and critical social theory 202–5
  and economic necessity 166
  and ideological struggle 203
  and privatism 184–6
  and public opinion 161
  TV viewing as obstacle 155, 166–7
social fragmentation 159–86
  and economic compulsion, state
    coercion and acquiescence
    169–71
  and erosion of public sphere
    167–9
  and information and public
    opinion 162–6
  and political inactivity 166–7
  and privatism 175–184
  and social isolationism and TV
    160–2
  and social reproduction 184–6
  and urbanism 171–5
socialisation
  and TV viewing 131, 148–53; of
    girls 180
social isolationism and TV viewing
  160–2
social relationships
  effects of TV on 161–2
  privatisation of 161–2, 175–84
social reproduction
  of capitalist societies 79–84,
    121–4, 154–5, 169–71, 184–6,
    191–7
  and consciousness 122–4, 191–7
  and dominant ideology 68–86
  and economic necessity 121–4,
    135–42, 169–71, 191–7

and needs 144–6, 184–6, 191–7
and power/powerlessness 123,
  138–41, 169–71, 184–6,
  191–7
and privatism 161–2, 175, 184–6
and social fragmentation 161,
  184–6
and the state 61, 84–92, 154–5,
  167–72, 193–7
and TV viewing 121–4, 153–5,
  160–2, 166–7, 184–6
and the unconscious 109
social totality 32–3, 147, 162,
  191–7
socio-centralism 56
South Africa 200
Spencer, M. 204–6
state
  and broadcasters 60–1
  and bureaucracy 168–9
  coercion of 169–71, 192, 199–205
  and economy 50–4, 61, 167–71,
    193
  neutrality of 50
  and social reproduction 61, 84–92,
    154–5, 167–72, 193–7
  violence 170, 191–3
structural anthropology 25
structuration of time 135–7
structuralist media theory 23, 27–8,
  37–42, 99–124
  culturalist objections to 110–11
  effects of TV in 99–124
  and feminism 27
  and ideological struggle 204
structural linguistics 28
structurally imposed needs 171–3
subject
  concept of in Althusser 102–3,
    120–1
  social 110–11
  of text 110–11
subjectivity and realism 102–10

Surgeon General's Scientific Advisory Committee on Television and Social Behavior 7
Szecskö, T. 35, 66 95

taken-for-grantedness and ideology 51, 53, 62
technical rationality 168–9
television
  and advertising 32, 40–2, 62–3, 104, 133
  analysis of messages 30, 37–64, 99–124
  attractiveness of viewing 131–4
  audience maximisation 32, 133
  and audience response 107, 131
  and autonomy 153–5, 182–4
  behavioural effects of 6–20, 29–30
  changing perspectives on power of 28–33
  and children 148–55
  and critical social theory 190–205
  as diversionary 132, 142–8
  effects research 6–20
  entertainment 32, 42–3, 62, 142–8
  and family interaction 149, 152–3
  and fragmented leisure time 135–7, 140
  ideological analysis of 37–64, 99–124
  ideological effects of 29–30, 68–95, 99–124, 128, 195
  and ideological shifts 86–92
  industrial disputes on 54–61
  and intellectual passivity 152
  and leisure time 128–55
  and lived experience 199
  and manipulation of needs 137–48
  material effects of 91–2, 149
  news on 43–64
  and party politics 169–171
  plays on 39

  and political inactivity 166–7, 174
  and the poor 136
  and powerlessness 140
  primary, secondary, and tertiary viewing 130–1
  and privatism 161, 174, 175–84
  psychoanalytic readings of 105–16
  as public service 163
  and the reluctant voter 78–9
  as routine 134
  set ownership 129
  and social change 155, 161
  and socialisation 131, 148–53
  and social isolationism 160–2
  and social relationships 161–2
  and social reproduction 121–4, 153–5, 160–2, 166–7, 184–6
  as source of information 161, 162–6
  and subject positions 110–11, 121
  and temporal structure of daily life 133, 135–7
  uses and gratifications 130–4
  viewing hours 129–30
  and violence 6–20
  and work 135, 142–8
temporal structure of daily life and TV viewing 134, 135–7
textual deconstruction *see* deconstructionism
Third World
  media in 198–9
  poverty in 49, 192–3
time
  and autonomy 143, 147
  and media impartiality 56–7
  as resource 135–6
  and structuration of 135–7
  see also leisure time
Timpanaro, S. 113–5, 126, 185
To Die for Ireland 39
Tomlinson, J. 126, 204–5, 206
totality *see* social totality

trade unions 54–61, 169–71
Tunstall, J. 65, 131, 156
Turner, B. 70–92, 95, 96, 97, 99,
    101, 109, 124, 170, 187

unconscious
    and consciousness 111–16
    and discourse/language 105–10,
        116–21
    Freud's theory of 111–16
    Lacan's theory of 105–11
    and metaphor 106
    and metonymy 106
    and mystification of experience
        112
    and slips of the tongue 114
    and social reproduction 109,
        121–4
    theory of, and elitisms 116
unemployment 170, 193
urbanism 171–5
Urry, J. 128, 155
uses and gratifications research 22,
    131–4, 137
U.S. imperialism 39

Van Den Berg, J. 126
Verba, S. 168–9, 187
Veron, E. 118, 127
violence
    effects of TV portrayals of 7–20
    of state 170, 191–3

Westergaard, J. 49, 66
western bias in news agencies 45

western media in relation to Third
    World, 198–9
Wilden, A. 116, 127
Wilhoit, G. 34, 35, 156
Williams, R. 24, 51–3, 66, 67, 117,
    127, 156, 176–8, 188, 192–3,
    205, 206
Williamson, J. 104, 125
Willis, P. 65, 95, 125, 206
Winship, J. 42, 65, 104, 125
Winter, E. 154, 158
Wolff, J. 36, 125, 126, 205
Woollacott, J. 24, 34, 35, 66, 96,
    124, 125
women and
    advertising 40–2, 104
    autonomous ego 121
    feminism 204
    leisure time 130–2
    ontological insecurity 180–4
    soap operas 40–2
work
    and autonomy 173
    de-skilling of 173
    routinisation of 136–7
    and TV viewing 135, 142–8
working class
    beliefs of 71–86
    consciousness 70–9, 84–6, 144–8
    expectations 83
    self-images of 121, 149
Wren-Lewis, J. 94, 98
Wybrow, R. 96

Young, J. 43, 65